Rushes

Other Books by the author:

The Complete Guide to Low-Budget Feature Filmmaking (2006)

Going Hollywood (forthcoming)

Films by the author:

Thou Shalt Not Kill... Except (1987)
Lunatics: A Love Story (1992)
Hercules in the Maze of the Minotaur (1994, TV)
Running Time (1997)
If I Had a Hammer (2001)
Alien Apocalypse (2005, TV)
Harpies (2007, TV)

JOSH BECKER has written and directed four independent feature films, *Thou Shalt Not Kill . . . Except, Lunatics: A Love Story, Running Time* and *If I Had a Hammer.* He has also directed nine episodes of "Xena: Warrior Princess," as well as the pilot TV movie for the series, "Hercules: The Legendary Journeys." His TV movie made for the Sci-Fi Network, *Alien Apocalypse* (2005), which he both wrote and directed, was Sci-Fi's highest-rated original movie ever. Mr. Becker resides in Bloomfield Hills, Michigan.

Rushes

by

Josh Becker

POINTBLANK

To Rick

*"Just because a man loves a thing,
nothing says it has to love him back."*

James Jones, From Here to Eternity

Set in Sabon

POINT*BLANK* is an imprint of Wildside Press
www.pointblankpress.com
www.wildsidepress.com

Edited by J.T. Lindroos

For more information contact Wildside Press

ISBN: 0-8095-7300-8

Table of Contents

Josh Becker, Steve "The Dart" Frankell, Sam Raimi, during the shooting of *Evil Dead* in 1980.

Rushes: Introduction

These essays, when taken all together, equal a reasonably large hunk of my life. Specifically, my life in regard to filmmaking, which happens to be a great deal of it, since most of my life has been dedicated to making movies: coming up with ideas, writing scripts, raising money, shooting film in many different places (from Michigan to L.A. to New Zealand to Bulgaria), as well as my many encounters with the other folks who make movies: producers, actors, DPs, ADs, composers, FX guys, etc.

I have been obsessed by films and filmmaking my entire life, from my very earliest memories. I began shooting movies with stories when I was thirteen, in 1971. Thirty-six years later I'm still doing exactly the same thing, and it still completely fascinates me. I love the way shots go together to form scenes, the way images play against music, the way an actor's performance effects the viewer, the way light falls on someone's face, or how something that's legitimately funny seems to be funny to people in other countries, too. Movies can speak a universal language, if they're good enough.

I've also been making movies with the same guys my entire life: Bruce Campbell, Sam Raimi, Scott Spiegel, Joe LoDuca, Gary Jones and Kurt Rauf, among others. Sam and I grew up around the block from each other and have known each other since he was eight, I was nine, and we were at the same bus stop. I've known Bruce and Scott since we were all eleven and in 7th grade together. I've known Rob, Joe, Gary, and Kurt since I was about twenty. Now we're all nearing fifty (Rob and Joe have already zipped past), so that's 30-40 years working with the same people. That's pretty unique, I think.

While we were shooting *Evil Dead* in Tennessee in 1979, after a long, grueling, freezing cold night shoot, the FX supervisor, Tom Sullivan, and I were eating breakfast and enthusiastically talking movies. One of the actresses, Betsy Baker, stood there listening for a minute, then shook her head in exasperation and asked:

"How on earth can you stay up all night working on a movie, then come home and keep right on talking about movies, too?"

Tom answered without even turning around. "It's the only endless topic," he said, then went right back to describing some scene from some movie.

The subject of movies is in fact finite, but it's so much bigger than any one person's knowledge that it may as well be infinite. There are far more movies extant than any one person could possibly see in their lifetime, with more coming out all the time. I've tried to see as many movies as I possibly could throughout much of my life, and I keep a list of every movie I've ever sat all the way through.

But I'm anything but a cheerleader for *all* movies. Many of the movies I don't like, I really and truly despise. And I'm severely displeased with the state of contemporary movies. I seriously believe that movies have devolved into a lesser, sillier, dumber form than they were previously. Most Hollywood movies now are too big and too stupid. Most indie films now are pointless and inconsequential shot hand-held with no visual scheme or style, no script, no point, and are often ugly, particularly when shot on digital video. I believe these are the porno versions of what indie movies used to be, with no reason for their existence other than the filmmaker's desire to see their name on the big screen, with unrealistic expectations of wealth and fame. The old expression in the film business is, "It's hard to make a good movie and it's hard to make a bad movie," meaning it's just hard to make movies. When making movies becomes easy, the movies become worthless. If the filmmaker isn't knocking themselves out working overtime and nearly killing themselves trying to make their movies as well-written, intelligently-directed, and as beautifully shot and acted as humanly possible, they're not trying hard enough.

These essays are about me trying as hard as I possibly can making my own personal movies. It's also about me working on other peoples' movies. Clawing my way forward, inexorably, inch by inch, in this hellish, glorious madness called the film business.

I am neither a success nor a failure, by my own estimation, and probably in the world's view of me, as well. My movies are in the film books, and most get reasonably good reviews. But beyond that, I'm just passionately obsessed by the subject. Movies utterly fascinate me. I've persevered in the movie business my entire life, even if the business has never embraced me. It's often said, "If you persevere, you'll succeed." That's a lie. The truth is, "If you don't persevere, you absolutely won't succeed," and that's the only assurance you get.

The ultimate truth in my opinion is that perseverance in and of itself is success. If you're in the game, then you're playing.

Josh Becker
Bloomfield Hills, MI
August 2, 2007

Bruce Campbell in 1979 while shooting *Holding It*.

Making Short Films

I made my first short film in 1971 when I was thirteen years old. The film was entitled *Public Enemy Revisited* and was shot in Super-8, plus I recorded sound on a cassette tape recorder that I was subsequently never able to synchronize with the picture. It is the story of a fellow, played by me, who has just finished watching James Cagney's movie *Public Enemy*, and now feels inspired to call a girl and make a date, which he does. So he calls another girl and makes a date for the next night, then the next, and the next. Everything looks great until the girls all call back and one by one they all reschedule for that same night. Now he has one date at 7:00, one at 8:00, one at 9:00, etc. The resolution was seeing me going into various houses, then coming out, supposedly an hour later, each time wearier and wearier, ostensibly from having had sex with all of these girls. I finally collapse, crawl to the camera and say, just like James Cagney riddled with bullets at the end of *Public Enemy*, "I ain't so tough," then die. Since I never got the sound synched up, though, I always had to narrate the film and attempt to verbally synch up the dialog whenever I could. The best aspects of this film are: 1. I made it; 2. I caught a few minutes of a pretty day 35 years ago on Kodachrome 40 film, a terrific film stock with gorgeous colors; and 3. I get to see myself at thirteen years old.

In an 8th grade English class the teacher suggested that if anyone had any Super-8 movies to bring them in and we'd all watch them. The teacher showed some of his home movies, then I showed *Public Enemy Revisited*, lacking its soundtrack and needing to be narrated, and received a rather tepid response. Next, Scott Spiegel, a goofy guy I didn't know very well, got up and showed several of his Super-8 films. They were all remakes of Three Stooges shorts, with Scott as Moe, and two of his friends as Curly and Larry. Scott had the actual soundtracks of the Stooges shorts on cassette tape and was miraculously able to synch up his remade picture with the original soundtrack. Every time he got it to synch up to a face-slap or an eye-poke he got a *big* laugh. I looked around in astonishment at the enthralled audience, eagerly awaiting the next synchronous sound moment so they could laugh. Clearly, something was going right here that had previously been going wrong during my films. Scott's films also contained several clever cinematic devices that I thought were pretty cool, like shooting at the edge of a wall with people talking on phones mounted on both sides of the wall so it looked like it was shot in split-screen. I felt slightly humiliated by the whole experience, even though Scott now acted rather friendly toward me having realized that we both made movies.

The next year in ninth grade two English classes joined together for a special project on ancient Greece. Everybody had to choose their own final project, that would be for your whole grade for this special event. I made a film version of *Oedipus Rex*. My clever plan this time was to write out hunks of text from the play on the blackboard and photograph them as title cards between the action, just like an old silent movie. I cast a bunch of my friends in the various parts, the requirement being—bring a sheet to wear as a toga. Bruce Campbell, who was cast in the pivotal role of King Creon, actually arrived in a real purple toga with gold trim, borrowed from the local theater group he belonged to. I was totally impressed, and thought to myself, "Now *that's* my idea of an actor!" I cast myself in the lead, and I cast the girl I'd always had a crush on, Ann Debenham, as Queen Jocasta. Ann burst out laughing in every single shot she's in, a feat I still find remarkable. Bruce's good buddy Mike Ditz photographed the film. The highlight of the film was Oedipus turning his back on the camera and tearing his eyes out. It then cut 180-degrees to reveal my hands and face covered with fake blood. When I was about to show the film to the two combined classes, I had a moment of panic when I realized that the reel I had put the film on would not fit onto the projector. The two teachers and two entire classes sat and watched me as I panicked. I finally put a pencil through the reel and held it as it un-spooled. Then, to my complete horror, you couldn't read *any* of the titles on the blackboard because the writing was too small and the focus was soft. My teacher, Miss Cutler, blithely suggested, "Just tell us what it says," but I couldn't read it either, and I certainly hadn't memorized the play, so I was stuck. I stood there holding a pencil with the spinning reel of film on it, blushing with shame, and I thought, "Next time I'll be more prepared." My classmate Jane Gordon baked baklava for her project and got an A. I made a motion picture and got a C. Admittedly, though, Jane's baklava was delicious, although I'm still not convinced they even had such a thing in ancient Greece.

Oedipus Rex, 1972, Lori Davis, Bruce Campbell, Josh Becker, Ann Debenham, Al Barnett.

At the end of ninth grade, in preparation for the big step up to high school, they allowed us to have elective classes for the last six weeks of school. Just what those electives would be was opened up to everybody in the auditorium. Some boy immediately raised his hand and hollered "Sports," and a teacher stepped up and said, "Sports are good, I'll teach that." Not wanting to get stuck in nothing but stupid classes, I said, "Movies," and Mr. Buck the social studies teacher stepped up and said, "I'll teach that." Mr. Buck was also the high school football coach and was a big barrel-chested guy who, as it turned out, was also a crazy movie fan, and a lifelong member of The Sons of the Desert, the official Laurel and Hardy fan club. Mr. Buck wore a red fez to this film class every day. He then proceeded to show us his entire collection of 16mm Laurel and Hardy shorts, which took several class periods.

After that, however, Mr. Buck had seemingly run out of ideas as to what more he might teach us about movies. Once you've seen ten Laurel and Hardy shorts, what else is there? I raised my hand and suggested, "Why don't we make a film." Mr. Buck looked relieved and happily agreed. He brought in his own Kodak Super-8 camera and simply let me take over. I came up with a concept and shot it and everyone just went along with me. It was really a wonderful situation now that I think about it. The film was called *Super Student*, and was completely based on the gag of making things disappear by shooting, stopping the camera, removing something from frame, then shooting again. Super Student, played by my friend Kevin Corcoran, could point at anything and make it disappear. First it was other students, then teachers, then the principal, and finally the school itself.

Mr. Buck cut the film together and set up a screening in front of the whole school. Each person the Super Student made disappear brought louder laughter and applause. When it got to the principal, whom we first see scolding the Super Student, who then looked at the lens, winked, then made the principal disappear, it brought the house down. That the Super Student then went outside and made the entire school disappear was simply more than they could have possibly dreamed, and the audience went wild. At the audience's loud demand they had to immediately show the film again, and the second time it got an even bigger response. This screening had a profound effect on not only me, but also Bruce Campbell. Sam Raimi and Scott Spiegel were both in the audience, too. Bruce asked me later why I hadn't cast him in the film? Had he somehow failed me in his performance as King Creon in *Oedipus Rex*? I asked, "Why weren't you in the class?" Bruce replied glumly, "I took History of Sports instead." Sam, meanwhile, can be seen in the background of a hallway scene in *Super Student*, wearing his then-trademark deerstalker cap.

I took my GAF Super-8 camera to camp that summer, and shot some footage for a film, but not enough to cut anything together. At one point I was sitting on the roof of my cabin holding the camera attempting to get a wide-shot of the whole camp. As I tried to find a comfortable position on the top edge of the roof, the camera slipped out of my hand, slid down the roof, flew off the edge, hit the cement step and exploded into a hundred pieces.

Over the course of the next year I saved all my money and bought a Yashica Super-8 camera with a 12-to-1 electric zoom lens—a *very* big zoom in those days. It also had the ability to do dissolves and fades.

I attempted making a Super-8 movie the next year with a bogus double-system synch recorder I purchased from an ad in Super-8 Filmmaker Magazine that simply didn't work. The film was an adaptation of a very short science fiction story by Mack Reynolds called *The Business, As Usual*, and the footage looked terrific. It took place in the future, so I shot the whole film in front of a gold-mirrored high-rise building that beautifully reflected the clouds. But the sound was screwed and I couldn't figure out how to fix it, so I dumped the whole film. I've always been a bit sad about that, too.

The next year I made two Super-8 shorts for a college film class. The first was an adaptation of an Edgar Allan Poe story called *The Imp of the Perverse*. I finally got past my synchronized sound difficulties by shooting the film silent, then sending the edited film to Kodak and having them put a sound stripe on it. I then read Poe's story as narration. I got enough footage and it all went together. I even had a few bits of visually interesting lighting, and a couple of cool dissolves. The other film was a horror story absurdly entitled *The Magnificent Severed*, a title I thought very witty at the time. It starred my mother, who was killed, but then came back from the dead. It was shot silent, had no narration or title cards and was entirely understandable. This was a cinematic breakthrough for me.

I then tried to make my first 16mm short. This was at the local community college where they had a roomful of old 16mm film equipment. Unfortunately, I was technically overwhelmed. The film was called *The Long Walk* and it was a gangster story shot in back-and-white. The guy who had stepped forward to run the camera—a huge old Auricon with an electric motor that plugged into the wall (most cameras run on batteries)—said he knew how to run it. He walked around with a light meter, and to all appearances seemed like he knew what he was doing. All of the footage went into the lab in one batch. When it all came back with every single shot improperly exposed, I was utterly horrified, and completely screwed. It meant a total reshoot, and I had neither the money nor the time, so the film was never finished. This moviemaking thing seemed to be getting harder and harder.

The next year I planned out and entirely storyboarded a samurai revenge film, but never figured out how or when to put the production together, and I never shot anything.

I was seriously beginning to feel daunted by the whole process—filmmaking was *way* more difficult than I'd ever suspected.

Soon thereafter, I was trying to put together yet another short film, and was on my way to deliver a script to an actor, when I got hit broadside in my '68 VW bug by a big old Chevy Impala. My car was totaled. I felt that fate was trying to tell me something, so instead of making that film I took the money I'd been saving and bought a brand new single-system sound Super-8 camera—meaning the sound was recorded directly onto a little magnetic stripe on the film—made by Sankyo (the camera store joke at the time when you said Sankyo, they'd reply, "You're welcome"). It was Sankyo's cheapest model ($249), with a little 3-to-1 zoom lens, and it was built like a big black plastic tank. This camera, I'm proud to say, outlasted everybody else's more expensive sound Super-8 cameras.

I quickly wrote a short detective script, *The Case of the Topanga Pearl*, and shot it in one day at my parents' house. The film starred me as detective Victor Temple, Sam Raimi as the Peter Lorre-like bad guy (played entirely on his knees as though he were three feet tall), Ellen Sandweiss (later to star in *Evil Dead*) as the femme fatale, and Scott Spiegel (co-producer of *Hostel* and *Hostel 2*, and writer-director of *From Dusk Till Dawn 2*) as the white-bearded old man from whom the pearl is initially stolen. This was not only my first synchronized sound film, but also the first time I ever worked with Sam, Scott and Ellen.

I then promptly packed all of my stuff and moved to Hollywood. I edited *Topanga Pearl* in L.A. and, as I did, I sincerely wished that I had put a lot more time into shooting it. It was okay, but what was there was a bit sloppy. I was also missing a few shots that I could no longer get, and the film wasn't really finished without them. I had screwed up yet again. I hadn't properly completed a movie in a few years and I was starting to doubt if I actually could.

So I decided to make another one-day, very short film with the easiest production imaginable. I found a short-short story called "The Choice" by W. Hilton-Jacobs, with only two characters in one room sitting in chairs speaking (one was played by me, the other by my late friend, Rick Sandford, doing a British accent). I thought, I can handle this: it doesn't get any simpler on a production level. Nevertheless, I still managed to do a poor job wrangling the few people and items I needed to the location, then had to rush like mad to get it all shot in the time remaining. I got all the shots I'd planned to get, but again they all turned out kind of sloppy. When I got the footage back and watched it, I had somehow picked up a loud buzzing radio frequency signal in the microphone cable that distorted the sound badly enough to make it worthless. I edited it all together, but since you couldn't decipher the dialog it was a big waste of time. Lack of a sound projector kept me from dubbing it.

I became seriously distressed. So much so, in fact, that I hitchhiked to Alaska in an attempt to clear my befuddled mind. What was my big hairy problem? Why couldn't I finish a movie so that it could be shown to people? The only response I received in Alaska that summer was the constant buzzing of the bird-sized mosquitoes. The sun revolved around in a circle overhead and it never got dark. After leaving Alaska and getting back to Vancouver, I had to choose to either continue south and go back to L.A. or turn east and visit Detroit? I decided to swing by Detroit. What the hell, round-trip it was only an extra 5,500 miles. While I was there I got together with Sam and he showed me his newest Super-8 film called *Six Months to Live*, made with Scott and Bruce and their new "company," The Metropolitan Film Group (MFG). I laughed all the way through it. I may have been in Hollywood for the past year, but these guys were making better movies than me; movies you could actually show to people, and gets laughs with. I decided right there that I would move back to Detroit and make films with Sam, Bruce and Scott.

When I moved back to Detroit a few months later I had already written an eighteen-page script called *The Final Round*, a boxing comedy that I wanted Sam to star in. He was living in East Lansing going to Michigan State University at this point, and was just starting production on his first, big Super-8 film, *The Happy Valley Kid*. Sam said that he was too busy to take the lead part in my film, but he would be happy to take a smaller part, and, by the way, could I come up to East Lansing on the weekends with Bruce and Scott and help make his movie (and bring my camera)? I said sure. Sam told me to give Bruce a call, and said he'd probably be happy to give me a hand. So, I gave Bruce a call and we met up at the local hang-out, Howard Johnson's.

I hadn't seen Bruce in a couple of years, and he was now working full-time as a production assistant for a local commercial production company, which I thought was impressive. I gave him my hilarious 18-page script for the zany boxing comedy, *The Final Round*. Bruce read the entire script right there in front of me, never once cracking a smile, let alone actually laughing. When he was done he looked up and said, "Let's make it."

I was somewhat aghast. "I guess you didn't think it was funny, huh?"

Bruce finally smiled. "It'll be funny when we get out there and make it."

So, for the next several months the entire Metropolitan Film Group and I worked on *The Final Round* in our spare time during the week, then we all drove up to East Lansing and worked on *The Happy Valley Kid* on weekends.

Bruce and I had meticulously planned the whole production of *The Final Round*, and, for the first time in my life, I got all the shots I had planned to get and the movie actually cut together in a rational form. Except that it was supposed to be a comedy and it wasn't funny (I should've known when Bruce didn't laugh reading the script). There were a few laughs, but none of them were gotten by me and I played the lead character. Sam got several legitimate laughs as the former heavyweight boxing champ who appears to have some sort of brain damage. Bruce and Scott were also both quite good as the shady promoters. Other members of he MFG, John Cameron (who would later be the producer of *Fargo* and *Bad Santa*) was excellent as the announcer, and Bill Kirk was funny as the referee. I, however, stunk up the joint in the lead. I minimally learned two important lessons from this: (1) casting is crucial, (2) I am not an actor. But it all cut together and the exposures were correct, the lighting was good (with help from the other MFG member, Mike Ditz), and the titles were (just barely) readable.

Bruce's and my next cinematic endeavor was a film entitled *Acting & Reacting*, written and directed by me, starring and produced by Bruce. This was a troubled production from the outset, with those around us loudly proclaiming both before and during the shoot that we were making a stupid artsy-fartsy movie. The film subsequently went through some reshoots, photographed by my friend, Sheldon

Lettich (who would later write and direct *Lionheart* and *Double Impact*, both with Jean-Claude Van Damme). In the course of time, however, I think *Acting & Reacting* remains one of the most interesting of the Super-8 films. It's the only film of its day to attempt to capture what we all actually looked and sounded like at the time, and it succeeds to some extent, too. It's also a nice little production with several well-photographed sequences, achieved with helpful lighting assistance from Mike Ditz.

One night Scott called me up and asked if I'd like to meet him up at the nearby bar/restaurant, Hogan's (formerly Howard Johnson's), for a drink? I said sure, but I was a tad suspicious since Scott and I had never gotten together on our own before. When I got there I found not only Scott waiting for me in a booth in the bar, but also John Cameron and Mike Ditz, as well. I thought, "Okay, what's this all about?" I wasn't really friends with any of these guys, they were just part of this silly MFG thing that Sam and Bruce goofed around with (there was also the other MFG member, Bill Kirk, but he wasn't there). After a beer and some pleasantries, I was informed by John that I was officially being kicked out of the Metropolitan Film Group. I honestly didn't really feel like I had ever joined the group, even if Bruce had given me MFG business cards for my recent 20th birthday, which is what had set this all off. John, Scott and Mike demanded that I give up the business cards. Since I thought we'd all gotten along just fine on *The Final Round, Acting & Reacting*, and *The Happy Valley Kid*, I really didn't know where they were coming from. I asked, "Why?" John pointed in my face and stated, "We don't work for you!"

I was dumbfounded, "I never said that you did."

"Then why do we keep working on *your* movies?"

"We've been working on Sam's movie, too."

"Yeah, but not *our* movies!"

Now I was confused. "But you don't have any movies."

"But we could," stated John decisively, "if we weren't working on your movies all the time."

I was flabbergasted. "*All the time?* Both of my films took a couple of days each. Sam's film has taken *way* longer than both of my films put together. And I'm perfectly happy to help you with your movies in any way I can, including you can use my camera and lights."

"We don't need your stuff, and turn in your cards," commanded

John in his loud, authoritative voice.

"Oddly, I don't have them on me. I'll just throw them out when I get home, will that do?"

They all nodded. It would do.

I asked, "Since I don't see them here, what do Bruce and Sam say about all of this?"

John said, "Ask them."

I nodded and stood. "Okay, I will," and I left.

When I got home there was a message from Bruce waiting for me. He and Sam wanted to see me right away at Sam's house. I walked the one block over to the Raimi's house, just as I had done thousands of times throughout my youth, having been best friends with Sam's older brother, Ivan, for many years. But this time the short walk seemed different. First of all, Bruce and I had become very close over the course of making these movies, and I now considered him a good friend. Second, I sincerely believed that as I had helped Sam make his movie as much as I knew how, both supplying and running the camera, lighting, playing a small part, driving over an hour to Lansing on many weekends for several months, and I would happily do the same thing for Scott, John and Mike. Just as Sam had been coming in from Lansing to help Bruce and I make our movies.

But what if Bruce and Sam didn't want to work with me anymore, either? Then I'd completely blown it. Because I had honestly been as helpful and upbeat as I knew how to be, and if that wasn't good enough, then I simply didn't have it in me to work with other people, particularly the ones I most wanted to work with. I didn't really give a damn if John, Scott and Mike didn't want to work with me anymore, but if Sam and Bruce didn't, then I truly had to be an asshole. Since that seemed like a possibility, I began making vague plans for my return to L.A.

Mr. Raimi answered the door and sent me to his study where Sam and Bruce were waiting for me. They both quickly assured me that they had nothing to do with my expulsion from the MFG, and they would both be pleased to keep making movies with me, and hoped that I would keep making movies with them. I sighed the deepest, most relieved sigh of my entire 20 years. Apparently, I wasn't quite as big of an asshole as all that.

The next film Bruce and I made (with Sam's help), was a straightforward, Hitchcock-style thriller entitled *Holding It*, that does not have Scott or John in it, nor did they work on it, nor did Mike help with the lighting. I called Bill Kirk (a truly nice, bright, funny guy who died several years ago), whom I really didn't know very well, and asked where he stood on this rift? With a wonderfully succinct snort Bill dismissed the whole thing, saying it all meant nothing to him, and if I had a part for him he would be happy to play it. So I offered him the lead and he took it (Bill's only lead in any of our movies, by the way). The film was shot entirely in the course of one long weekend. This was my first fully-functional, completely conventional film, and it basically worked just like it was supposed to. My biggest gripe looking back after all these years later is that is should have been cut faster. It's sixteen minutes and ought to be twelve or thirteen. Bill Kirk plays the "wrong man," Bruce plays both the right man, as well as the James Mason-like bad guy. Sam plays one of the two thugs (his specialty in my films) who abduct the wrong man, then lose him, and end up chasing him for a fair amount of the film (set to electronic disco music, a very hip score for 1979). The action culminated in a big bloody shoot-out where everyone got killed, except the good guy, in hyper slow-motion. This was achieved by not only speeding up the film while shooting, but also having everyone act like they were in slo-mo, too. We used a mustard bottle connected to a length of rubber hose for the squirting blood effects and it worked great. In the finale, Bruce has been shot and lies on the steps. Bill kneels down to him and Bruce hands him the gun, which Bill takes. Bruce's character then dies and spits a big mouthful of blood up all over his own face, in slo-mo, which always got a huge reaction.

I then moved back to L.A. for the second time, and when I returned to Detroit in October of 1979 we all went down to Tennessee to make *Evil Dead*. All, that is, except Scott, John and Mike, who were still out on strike (John and Mike did subsequently show up on the set for a couple of days, grumbling and mumbling, but Scott never made it).

Soon after principal photography of *Evil Dead* was completed and we returned to Michigan, Scott, John and Mike made the short horror film, *Night Crew* (that Scott later remade as the feature, *Intruder*). Scott came to me and asked if I would help him complete the shooting of the film (and oh, yeah, could I bring my camera). I said sure, and ran camera and worked on the lighting with Mike for the final two nights of shooting. John starred in the film as a crazed killer in a grocery store, and Sam played one of the hapless store employees who gets his head sawed in half on a band-saw. I then helped Scott with the sound effects and the scoring, and it all went together pretty well. Scott and I both saw that we could actually work together rather harmoniously.

So Scott and I were out having coffee, discussing the idea of making a Super-8 short together, when we began kicking around the idea of a nearsighted waitress. This evolved into a short script called "The Blind Waitress," that ultimately became the film *The Blind Waiter*.

"The Blind Waiter," 1980: Bruce Campbell as the Blind Waiter, Sam Raimi as the Stuttering Busboy, Rob Tapert as the Deaf Manager, Scott Spiegel as the Clumsy Chef

We all—meaning Bruce, Sam, Scott, John and Mike, but not Bill Kirk—made the short film *The Blind Waiter* together. Bruce played the visually-challenged lead role, Sam as the stuttering busboy, Rob Tapert (producer of *Evil Dead, Xena* and *The Grudge*) as the deaf manager, Scott Spiegel as the silly chef, and John Cameron as the angry customer (the part he was born to play). Scott Spiegel and I wrote, produced, and directed together. I photographed and edited the film (with lighting help from Mike Ditz, as well as Tim Philo, who had just shot *Evil Dead*), Scott was the art director, and, if I do say so myself, it's quite a funny little film. Sixteen minutes of non-stop slapstick and verbal gags.

The co-directing concept, in my opinion, immediately didn't work. I had suggested a number of times to Scott that we get together and storyboard the film together, or at least do a shot list, but Scott kept putting me off and it never occurred. So, the night before we shot, in something of a panic, I sat up late and storyboarded the entire film. Since I was also the cameraman, I simply followed my storyboards and everything went very smoothly. Scott basically kept everybody entertained while they awaited their turn to shoot, then I shot all the scenes. It seemed to me that what I was doing was directing (and shooting) the film, while what Scott was doing, along with being an actor, was producing, but not directing.

The next film I made was *Stryker's War*, my biggest Super-8 film, which I wrote and directed, and both Bruce and I produced. Bruce starred as the embittered Marine veteran Jack Stryker, Sam played the Charles Manson-like cult leader, Cheryl Gutteridge played Sally the pretty-girl-in-distress, and Scott played one of the Marine buddies (the other two Marine buddies were played by Don Campbell, Bruce's older brother, and David Goodman, later the co-producer of *The Man With the Screaming Brain*). *Stryker's War* was 45-minutes long, shot at 24 frames per second (for better picture and sound quality and easier video transfer capabilities), at a whopping cost of $4,500 (a big portion of this came from the unemployment checks I was then receiving from having recently been laid off as a security guard—I considered it my State Film Subsidy). This was to be the pilot film for a proposed feature version. Bruce and I again meticulously planned the whole production. It was shot over the course of eight hot, beautiful summer days in 1980, and everything went very smoothly.

Josh with Ted Raimi on the set of *Stryker's War* (photo by Mike Ditz)

All except our first attempt at shooting the Vietnam scenes in the woods. This scene had to be reshot because it came out too dark since I had mistakenly used ASA 40 film stock, which was too slow to expose in the dark woods. The reshoots on ASA 160 turned out particularly well, and I like them better than the feature version that was to come four years later (improbably re-titled *Thou Shalt Not Kill . . . Except*). The day we shot was both rainy and foggy making the forest really look like a jungle. I then used a terrific cut of Jerry Goldsmith's music from *Patton* to score it and the scene is surprisingly effective—for a second you completely forget you're watching a Super-8 movie. The opening shot is of the forest across a green, murky swamp. Between the grainy film stock, the low exposure, and the diffusion of the fog and misty rain the image is literally crawling with movement. It holds on an empty frame for about 10-15 seconds, with this great low, ominous Jerry Goldsmith music, then there seems to be a little extra movement in the forest at the center of the shot, and suddenly a platoon of Marines in camouflage uniforms and face paint seem to appear out of nowhere. It's one of the best shots I've ever done, on Super-8 no less, and it was due to a confluence of circumstances, several of which were entirely out of my hands. As a personal note (and with all due respect to the various actors), having Bruce Campbell as Sgt. Stryker makes this version *much* easier for me to watch than the feature, although I actually like all the other Marine buddies better in the feature.

On location in the mud shooting *Stryker's War*, 1980
(photo by Mike Ditz)

I then sublet part of the office where Sam, Bruce and Rob were doing the post-production on *Evil Dead* (it had once been a dentist's office and was broken into many small cubicles). I then spent the next year attempting to raise money for a feature version of *Stryker's War*. Sadly, I wasn't able to raise any money at all.

During this time, Scott suggested that we make another comedy short together, and I counter-suggested that we take the big step up and shoot it in 16mm. We agreed, then began sniffing around for an idea. Scott and I were driving past the cemetery in Franklin Village, where I grew up, that has a steeply inclined front lawn leading down to Franklin Road. A guy was vainly trying to mow the grass, except gravity kept pulling him down toward the road and he was in a valiant battle with his lawnmower trying to keep it horizontal. Scott and I both burst out laughing, and our next comedy short, *Torro, Torro, Torro!*, the story of a lawnmower gone mad, was born. We shot the opening in the same exact location at the cemetery, now with Scott as the poor schmuck lawn maintenance guy. Once the lawnmower goes out of control it doesn't stop wreaking havoc for the next six minutes. The finale was the lawnmower arriving at the Franklin Bake-Off, where there's a twenty-five foot long table of pies, that the lawnmower runs over and spits out at all the guests. The film involved a whole variety of special effects, like stop-motion (done by Bart Pierce, who did the animation effects on *Evil Dead*), fast-motion, reverse-motion, wires, and dummies. Scott and I again took the co-credit of "written, produced and directed by," but I now felt even more strongly that that really wasn't working out. *Torro!* has a few good laughs, but was rather sloppy in its execution. This was mainly due, I think, to our inexperience with 16mm, but was also partially due to having two squabbling directors.

Our next short production, shot in 1981 and completed in early 1982, was a nine-minute, 16mm, black-and-white *Raiders of the Lost Ark* parody called *Cleveland Smith Bounty Hunter*, starring Bruce as Cleveland Smith, Sam as the evil Nazi, and Cheryl Gutteridge once again as Sally the-pretty-girl-in-distress. The film was shot in four days entirely around mine and Bruce's parents' houses. This time I solely directed, Scott produced (we both did, but he took the sole credit), and we both wrote it. Kurt Rauf (who would later be the DP on my films *Running Time* and *If I Had a Hammer*) was the art director, Bart Pierce once again did the effects, and I shot and edited. I believe this is the best of all my short films.

I was able to score 4,000 feet of black and white, 16mm Tri-X negative film stock for free from a local film teacher, Ron Teachworth, because it was past it's expiration date. Having complete faith in the Eastman Kodak Company that the film would still be good, I had Bart, who worked the night shift at one of the local film labs, Producer's Color Service, break the four, 1,000 ft. rolls, down into forty 100 ft. rolls, and that's what I shot the entire movie with. When Bart gave me the 40 rolls back he said that there had been a lot of "static-flashing" as he wound the rolls, due to the silver content in black and white film stock that becomes highly-charged with static electricity. I asked, "Did it ruin the film?" Bart shrugged, "I don't know. It did something." So I went and shot the whole movie with it anyway. The static-flashing did indeed effect the film—it gave it the look of being an old movie.

Dissolve to some point a year or so later, and I was in New York

City visiting my old friend, Steve, and I showed he and his hip, sophisticated friends the film. They all laughed at the sophomoric, slapstick humor, which I took as a triumph. Afterward, Steve asked very seriously, and rather impressed, "How did you achieve that great, old-looking, black and white look?" I lied, saying we did the static-flashing thing on purpose, and they all bought it.

I edited the film with rewinds and a viewer on the pool table in the basement of my parents' house. I also cut all of the soundtracks there, too. I did all the post in a fairly leisurely fashion, and I found the process very calming, and I really didn't want it to end. I'd never lavished such attention on each individual cut before, nor have I since.

Also during this time, Bart and I shot all of the special effects in his basement. Bart was in charge and I assisted him. We animated a clay dinosaur in front of a rear screen, with a projection of a jungle background that was actually a 35mm slide of the woods behind my parents' house. We also animated a two-inch Indiana Jones toy on fishing line, in front of the rear-screen, jumping off the dinosaur, and falling into the Grand Canyon. Bart and I shot the titles and superimposed them over a shot of Bruce lighting a match by using a Bolex camera as an optical printer, and a process called "bi-packing," where you load the camera with a print of the shot you want the titles on, as well as unexposed negative squished right against each other. Scott's sister, Pat, painted the title cards on canvas, with white lettering on a black background. I also cut the negatives for *Torro* and *Cleveland Smith* down in Bart's basement, with his helpful supervision.

I shot *Cleveland Smith* with a Canon Scoopic 16mm camera, borrowed from fellow local filmmaker and Bart's buddy, Rick Merciez, who had a basement full of old movie equipment, both 16mm and 35mm. Very soon after the film was completed and Bart ran the first prints for us, Rick Merciez dropped by the lab late one night to visit Bart and see the film. Bart showed Rick the film, and Bart said that Rick laughed a lot, then left. He drove his van a few miles north on Woodward Avenue, the main street of Detroit (and the first paved road in America), which is also the main street of Highland Park (where the original Ford Factory was located), a city caught within the borders of Detroit, that actually has a higher crime-rate than Detroit. Apparently, when Rick stopped to pick up a hooker on

Woodward, a guy jumped into his van, robbed him and stabbed him to death. The next day the hooker turned in the murderer. Bart and I attended Rick's funeral, which is still the only open-casket funeral I've ever been to.

The postscript to this story is that a few months later I called Bart and asked, "What do you suppose Mrs. Merciez is going to do with all of that film equipment?"

Bart said he didn't know, but she certainly didn't have much money and would probably be pleased to sell it. I asked him if he'd call her and find out, and Bart said he would. I spoke with Bart a few weeks later and asked if he'd called her and he said no, he couldn't do it. So I called her myself and asked if she was interested in selling the equipment? She said yes, she was very interested, she really needed the money and she wanted to get rid of the stuff. I got Sam, Bruce and Rob to put up the money, and we bought everything for a couple of thousand dollars. There were quite a few lights, a 16mm projector, the Canon Scoopic, a 35mm Arri-C (a silent, multi-speed 35mm camera that ended up being used to shoot parts of Sam's film *Crimewave*), and a bunch of other junk. This was a lot of the equipment I later used to shoot *Thou Shalt Not Kill . . . Except*.

About ten years later, having already made two feature films, an actor acquaintance asked me to direct a short video production of him performing various scenes playing Muhammad Ali. It was fun to get in and shoot a ten-minute film covering all of Muhammad Ali's life in two days, but I don't think it holds together as a movie with a story, it's just an actor's showpiece.

Making short films trained me for making features. The reasons those early short films of mine kept not working out are the same problems me and all other filmmakers still face all the time—faulty conception, poor planning, not enough money or time to do it right, and not enough imagination to properly fake it. But if you can't ultimately pull it all together for a short film, you'll never do it for a feature.

Confessions of a Movie Geek

I loved cartoons so much as a child of four or five that I went out of my way to learn to tell time, then had my parents buy me an alarm clock, specifically so I could get up early enough so as not to miss *any* of the cartoons that were being broadcast. The idea that there were cartoons showing while I slept was entirely unacceptable to me. So, I would get up at 5:00 AM when they would show *Clutch Cargo*, a very poorly-animated cartoon, with weird, real-looking mouths, that was shown on half the screen while they ran the news in tele-type form on the other half. But since *Clutch Cargo* was a cartoon, I simply couldn't miss it (meanwhile, I still get up at 5:00 AM, but I don't watch cartoons anymore). My very favorite cartoons were those made by Warner Brothers, with Bugs Bunny, Daffy Duck, Fog-horn Leghorn, and Porky Pig, because they were funny *and* beauti-fully animated. My second favorite was *Rocky & Bullwinkle,* and all of the cartoons that were included on that show, like *Fractured Fairytales, Aesop & Son, Peabody and Sherman,* and *Clyde Crash-cop,* which were all *very* funny, but *not* terribly well-animated. How I knew the difference between good and bad animation at five years old is an interesting question, but I absolutely *did* know, and I clear-ly had discriminating taste (and time has proven that what I thought was good when I was a kid, continues to be good for me as an adult). I also enjoyed Tom Terrific and Felix the Cat, but I especially liked the older, Fleischer Brothers cartoons, like Popeye, Betty Boop, and Superman, that were extremely well-animated, yet so strange they seemed other-worldly. Interestingly, I think, I never much cared for Disney cartoons because I never found them funny, even though they were always beautifully-animated. There are some oddball Dis-ney cartoons I do like, however, like *The Old Mill* (winner of the 1937 Oscar for "Best Cartoon"), which is just gorgeous, and very dramatic. Honestly, I've always loved *Bambi* and *The Jungle Book,* too, but not much else by Disney.

I was already obsessed by the visual storytelling medium from my very earliest memories. I think most people, if they can remember being or four or five at all, have flashes of memories with their families in various places; I, on the other hand, distinctly remember Popeye punching all of the animals in the jungle, and when they landed the alligator has become several pairs of shoes, and the other animals came down as coats on a rack; or Betty Boop singing and dancing in "The Old Man of the Mountain" with Cab Calloway ("Hi-Dee-Hi, Hey-Dee-Hey, it's the old man of the mountain").

The decade of the 1960s was the very end of the era of road show engagements, when big new movies were opened with great dignity and respect, as though they were Broadway plays. Your tickets were for specific seats, you dressed up in your nicest clothes, and there was a bowl of punch, but no candy. When I was four my parents took my older sister Ricki, but not me, to the road show engagement of *Lawrence of Arabia*. When I found out that I wasn't going I pitched the worst fit of my entire life, swatting a big glass of milk right off the table that shattered against the wall covering everything in milk and broken glass. My dad smacked me, then they all left without me (and my Grandma Olga). A few months later, however, when I was five, my parents did take me to see the road show engagement of *How the West Was Won*. This film was shot in the very short-lived wide-screen process, "Three-Screen Cinerama." There were only two dramatic feature films ever made in this process: *The Wonderful World of the Brothers Grimm* in 1962, and *How the West Was Won* in 1963, and that was it. The whole process was then dropped due to being too expensive and unwieldy. Three-screen Cinerama was as crazy as wide-screen filmmaking ever got. The screen was 146-degrees wide, using three projectors running in unison, seven-track stereo sound, that took three projectionists, a sound-mixer, as well as a master controller. The movie completely blew my still-forming five-year-old mind. This seemed way better than real life in all possible ways. Particularly when the buffalo herd stampeded and knocked over a water tower with a bunch of guys on top of it. The tower came falling down from the right side of the screen all the way across to the left side, then crashed to the ground and exploded with all the guys tumbling off to now be trampled by the buffalo. My jaw was on the floor. They also had the camera in a hole in the ground and the buffalo stampeded right over it. I was completely overwhelmed. My parents purchased a hardcover program for the film that I immediately appropriated and still have (I wrote in crayon on a few of the pages). Then I made such a stink for the next week or two that my parents were compelled to take me back to see the movie again at a weekend matinee. This time as a souvenir I got a bolo tie with a silver cowboy boot. I was standing on the driveway swinging the bolo tie around and around when it slipped out of my hand, flew up in the air, landed in the gutter and I never got it down.

My obsession with live-action movies had begun. Luckily for me, my parents liked going to the movies and took the whole family every week or two. The nearest theater to where we lived, and close enough to ride my bike to, was The Berkley Theater, an old, run-down, 1930s second-run movie house, and this is where I saw the second-runs of such terrific 1960s epics as: *The Longest Day, It's a Mad, Mad, Mad, Mad World* and *The Great Race*. I also distinctly remember going with my family, excluding my little sister Pam who still too young at the time, to see the road show engagement of *The Sound of Music* in 1965. The scene where the Von Trapp family was hiding behind the gravestones while Hans, the young Nazi, searched for them with a flashlight still stays with me as being so horribly suspenseful that I could barely breathe.

When I was six or seven I saw an afternoon matinee of *Abbot and Costello Meet Frankenstein* with my cousins, Gary, Paul and Eric, at an old theater in Detroit called The Royal. The film is a comedy, and very possibly Abbott and Costello's best film, but I was completely terrified. There was Dracula, the Wolfman, and Frankenstein, and they were all trying to kill Abbott and Costello. At the end the Wolf-man is chasing Dracula who turns into a bat and flies out the window. The Wolfman falls out the window and plummets to his death about fifty feet down into a moat. It scared the living hell out of me, and I had nightmares about it.

So, naturally, I made models of all the monsters, like Frankenstein and The Creature From the Black Lagoon, and they frightened me so badly at night that I finally had to keep them in a cupboard.

I've also always loved old movies, and my earliest fascination was with Warner Brothers films (hey, I liked their cartoons, why wouldn't I like their movies, right?). One of the first movie books I ever got was a filmography of Humphrey Bogart. Luckily for me, Detroit's movie host, Bill Kennedy, also loved Warner Brothers movies and showed them all the time. By the time I was ten or twelve I'd seen all the really famous Warner Brothers films, like: *Casablanca, High Sierra, White Heat, Public Enemy, Little Caesar, Gentleman Jim, The Adventures of Robin Hood*, etc., and I knew the names of all of the Warners stock actors, like Frank McHugh, Alan Hale, Joan Blondell, and Jack Carson.

But I watched any old movie that got a decent review in the books. I was particularly interested in the Oscar-winning movies (I now have every Oscar-winning Best Picture on video, so no one can say I've wasted my life). It seemed like a real triumph when I finally saw *Grand Hotel* (Best Picture 1931-32), which I didn't even like (Wallace Beery was ridiculous as a German). It wasn't until 30 years later that I completed seeing all of the Best Pictures by finally getting a chance to see *Broadway Melody* (Best Picture 1928-29), at a screening in Hollywood with the star of the film, Anita Page, attending (needless to say, she was *very* old at the time).

In 1968 when I was ten my family took a trip to Toronto, which is just three hours north of Detroit. We saw the film *Oliver!* at a big theater in 70mm and I experienced an epiphany. The kid who played Oliver, Mark Lester, was exactly same age as me. The only difference between us was that he got to star in this big movie (and he was cute and could sing and act), whereas I only got to watch it. As I left the theater I had my first realization of how movies must be made, that actual kids stood on a street singing "Consider Yourself" and were photographed with a camera. I decided right then and there that I had to be in the movies, although I wasn't entirely sure in what capacity.

My whole family went and saw *Easy Rider* in 1969. I walked into the film a little kid, and I walked out a rebellious little adult. The first thing I did was to get an American flag and sew it on the back of my army jacket.

Somehow in 1970 my sister Ricki and I talked my dad into taking us downtown to see the film *Woodstock*, which we knew he wouldn't like, but he took us anyway. Well, he didn't like it, and actually walked out and smoked cigarettes in the lobby. I thought it was just about the greatest thing I'd ever seen. I became a hippy on the spot and I didn't cut my hair again for the next four years.

1970 was a big year for me. Somewhere between seeing *Patton* five times, *2001: A Space Odyssey* (on a re-release, but in 70mm),

Women in Love, Five Easy Pieces, M*A*S*H and *Airport*, I became clear about the roles of the director and the writer, and decided that's what I must do, write and direct.

Meanwhile, another early movie book of mine was "The New York Times Guide to Movies On TV" Edited by Howard Thompson, published in 1970 (when I got it), with over 2,000 entries (that seemed like a lot at the time). I still have the book, of course, and it's just loaded with snotty little reviews. Soon thereafter I got my first Leonard Maltin book (with over 10,000 entries—now it's over 18,000), with his much less caustic reviews, and it's still the book I use daily. But I guess I've always preferred the more opinionated and pithy form of review.

After everybody in my family went to sleep each night, I would sneak back downstairs and watch The Late Show. I had to be very quiet and keep the TV very low. One night I watched Preston Sturges's *Unfaithfully Yours* and I laughed so hard I woke up my whole family. Preston Sturges blew my cover.

So then I built a wall in the basement of my parents' house that separated a corner into a room, and I moved down there. It was kind of creepy living down in the basement at first, with a sump-pump dripping all the time, then sucking itself dry every fifteen or twenty minutes, and heat vents clinking and clanking all the time, but I got used to it. Now I could watch The Late Show, *and* The Late, Late Show, which was when the really good, old movies were shown, and I could even smoke cigarettes, and I wouldn't be bothering anybody. This was when school really went to hell for me because I was stayed up all night every night to watch movies.

I subscribed to TV Guide, and as soon as it arrived each week I'd scour through it searching out every interesting and unfamiliar movie title, which I would then look up in one of the various reference books, then I would notate it's rating in the margin. I continued doing this for over the next 30 years, and I actually just stopped because with TiVo it's easier to do it on-screen.

I frequently skipped school on Wednesday afternoons because that's when the new movies opened and I'd attend the first matinee showings. I saw *The Godfather Part II* on its very first matinee screening in Detroit at the enormous, 2,000 seat, Northland Theater, and I was the only person there. I thought it was the best movie I had ever seen in my life. When it was over I looked around the huge empty theater and thought, "This film is *all* mine. It was made just for me."

When I was a teenager it was an astounding period for movies, and I was at a particularly formative age. There were so many terrific movies that it was very hard to choose just five nominees for best picture each year. Within a thirty-six month span, 1972-74, here is an example of the films released that I went to the theater and saw:

Slaughterhouse-Five, Play it Again, Sam, Murmur of the Heart, Minnie and Moskowitz, The Life and Times of Judge Roy Bean, Lady Sings the Blues, Junior Bonner, Joe Kidd, Jeremiah Johnson, The Heartbreak Kid, The Godfather, The Getaway, Frenzy, Fellini's Roma, Everything You Always Wanted to Know About Sex, The Emigrants, The Effects of Gamma Rays on Man-in-the-Moon Marigolds, The Discreet Charm of the Bourgeoisie, Deliverance, The Cowboys, The Candidate, Cabaret, Fat City, Ulzana's Raid, Westworld, The Way We Were, Walking Tall, Two English Girls, A Touch of Class, Theater of Blood, Such a Gorgeous Kid Like Me, Sounder, Sleuth, The Sting, Soylent Green, Sleeper, Sisters, Serpico, Scarecrow, Save the Tiger, Payday, Pat Garrett and Billy the Kid, Papillion, Paper Moon, The Paper Chase, The New Land, O Lucky Man, Mean Streets, The Long Goodbye, The Last Tango in Paris, The Last Detail, The Iceman Cometh, The Homecoming, High Plains Drifter, The Harder They Come, The Exorcist, A Delicate Balance, The Day of the Jackal, Cries and Whispers, Cinderella Liberty, Bang the Drum Slowly, American Graffiti, Young Frankenstein, A Woman Under the Influence, The White Dawn, The Towering Inferno, The Texas Chainsaw Massacre, The Taking of Pelham One Two Three, Playtime, The Phantom of the Paradise, The Odessa File, Murder on the Orient Express, The Longest Yard, Hearts and Minds, Harry and Tonto, The Groove Tube, Going Places, The Godfather Part II, The Gambler, Earthquake, Death Wish, Day For Night, The Conversation, Claudine, Chinatown, California Split, Butley, Blazing Saddles, Billy Jack, Badlands, The Apprenticeship of Duddy Kravitz, and *Alice Doesn't Live Here Anymore.*

My brain was being filled with the art of filmmaking, I believe, at the very peak of its sophistication. Movies seemed like they simply

n," said the guard, "they threw those out. Columbia moved to
nk, y'know."

ook my head sadly. "I know, but they couldn't have taken the
es with them?"

e guard shrugged, indicating very clearly, "Who gives a shit?"
out this same time, MGM moved out of their Culver City lot,
e they'd been located since the early 1920s (it had originally
the Triangle Pictures lot, run by D.W. Griffith, Thomas Ince
Mack Sennett). I drove by and saw the crane remove the big Leo
Lion sign from the top of the main building. It was replaced by a
that said, Lorimar Tele-Pictures, which was eventually replaced
ony.

1977 I worked for four days as an extra in John Cassavetes's
Opening Night. There had been ads on an L.A. rock & roll
io station that said if you wanted to be an extra in Cassavetes's
, go to the Pasadena Civic Auditorium on a certain day wearing
ss clothes, and you'd also get a free lunch, but no pay. I had been
Hollywood for three months and this was the best offer I had
ard yet, so I went. There were about a couple of hundred other
ople there and we all sat in the audience clapping all day long
hile watching John Cassavetes and his wife Gena Rowlands per-
rm a scene from a fake play that was within the movie. By lunch
y hands were bright red and aching from all the non-stop clapping.
Nevertheless, unlike many others, I went back in for the second half
f the day and clapped until my hands were swollen and throbbing.
When I got into my car to drive home I could not make a fist or
ightly grab the steering wheel with either hand.

Several days later I received a call from a 2nd assistant director
asking if I'd like to do some more extra work on Opening Night,
and I said sure. Luckily, the next location was much closer to my
apartment. It was a theater on Wilshire Blvd. between LaBrea Ave.
and Vine St., I believe was called The American Theater, which has
long since been torn down. This was a night shoot and I was instructed to arrive at about 5:00 P.M. As the crew set up outside the
theater, the extras, all dressed in warm coats since it was supposed to
be in New York in the winter, just hung around for hours. I attempted to strike up a conversation with a German fellow who seemed to
have absolutely nothing to say. I asked if he liked any German films
and he shrugged. I said, "Fassbinder? Herzog? Wim Wenders? Fritz

couldn't be any better than they were, and everyone just expected
to get a good new movie every week, and a great new movie every
month.

I began college in 1974 and immediately began writing for the
school newspaper, The Oakland Community College Recorder, and
naturally became the film critic. I think back on some of my earliest
reviews that were so badly-written I'm still ashamed. My weekly
column was called "Becker's Bijou Review," named by the pretty
editor, with the eponymous name, Meymo Sturgis.

I then went to Eastern Michigan University and became their film
critic. I panned so many of the movies showing on-campus, and attendance was so low, that they banned me from reviewing further
on-campus films. When I panned the film Lenny, a woman in a class
of mine angrily stomped up to me, stated, "Lenny is a great film!"
then soundly slapped my face. I also won the "Best Article of the
Month" award for my review of John Cassavetes' A Woman Under
the Influence, a film I thought was brilliant.

I attended the University of Michigan in 1976. Oddly, U of M had
a retrospective of the still photographs and movies of Karl Struss,
winner of the very first Oscar for cinematography in 1927-28 for
Sunrise. There was a big article in the newspaper and a picture of
Karl and his wife, Ethel, who were both in their eighties. On opening night I went and saw the film The Story of Temple Drake, and
the 1932 version of Dr. Jekyll and Mr. Hyde, both of which were
beautifully photographed by Struss. After the films I went directly
to the showing of his photographs of New York City in the teens
and '20s that were stunning. I turned around and there stood Karl
and Ethel Struss. The president of the university was about to have
his picture taken with them and Karl was fumbling with a very old
Leica 35mm camera that he seemed to be having difficulty putting
back into it's case. To Karl Struss's utter astonishment, the president
took the camera right out his hands, turned and handed it to me,
saying, "Here, hold this." The photo was taken, the president shook
Karl and Ethel's hands, then promptly turned and left.

I stepped up to them and handed Karl Struss back his priceless
camera. He said thank you, clearly pleased to have it back. I said, "I
just saw The Story of Temple Drake and Dr. Jekyll and Mr. Hyde,
both of which were gorgeously photographed. How on earth did
you do the transformation effects of Jekyll to Hyde?"

Both Karl and Ethel smiled in delight and Karl eagerly explained, with Ethel regularly joining in to remind him of details. The effect was done with a series of colored filters, combined with the hairs and make-up on Fredric March being of various colors, and since it was a black and white film the filters disguised the hair. As they pulled out the filters one by one the hair and make-up seemed to appear. I'd never seen anything like it and congratulated him on a brilliant effect. Karl and Ethel both smiled warmly, were ridiculously pleased that I'd enjoyed the films, and thanked me. I assured them it was entirely my pleasure.

At the end of the semester I moved to Los Angeles. In the first week of July, 1976, I moved into my very first apartment, at 666 N. Van Ness just off Melrose, kitty-corner from Paramount Pictures. A big movie at that time was *The Omen* and Damian the evil devil child had 666 on his scalp, the sign of Satan. Anytime I said my address someone always commented on it. The apartment cost $65 a month, including utilities.

That August I turned eighteen years old. The joke on me was that at the time you had to be twenty-one to drink in California, but only eighteen in Michigan.

So there I was, eighteen and living by myself in a tiny apartment in Hollywood, across the street from Paramount Pictures, where Billy Wilder and Joseph Von Sternberg had made many of their great pictures, like *Sunset Blvd.* and *Shanghai Express*.

From my desk, peering out the window at Van Ness Street, I looked directly across a parking lot to Producer's Studio, a much smaller film studio across from Paramount. On the bricks on the side of one of the sound stages, the name "Clune" could still be faintly read, one of the film studio's names back in the early silent days. Producer's Studio has long since become Raleigh Studios. That was where Sherwood Schwartz, producer of "Gilligan's Island" and "The Brady Bunch," had his office.

Between the old "Clune" soundstage and Melrose Avenue was a 1940s strip mall with a liquor store, a revival movie theater called The Encore Theater, and Jerry's Market (an old Los Angeles grocery store chain that can still be seen in Billy Wilder's film *Double Indemnity*). They would frequently shoot the Charmin toilet tissue commercials with Mr. Whipple ("*Please*, don't squeeze the Charmin") in this Jerry's Market, and I ran into the actor who played Mr. Whipple

there several times, which was always odd, I mu
They would shoot a lot of TV shows and mo
too. I came by one day and in front of the movi
shooting a very short-lived TV show of the mid
Cop with Ernest Borgnine as the human partner to
gnine was just sitting there on a car hood in a pol
drinking a cup of coffee. As I passed by I offhan
"What'dya wanna do tonight, Marty?" He smiled
familiar gap-toothed smile and replied, "I don't kn
want to do?"

My first film job in Hollywood was as a projectionis
Theater. The very friendly old man who owned the thea
to train with the projectionist for a week, then just ha
The theater was equipped with very old, Simplex, ca
projectors, and you had to forever be diddling with th
to keep the flame fully illuminated. I projected the Mosc
forming "Swan Lake" and "Sleeping Beauty" for abou
which was kind of fun, although I quickly grew weary
scratchy prints of ballet films. Finally, the old theater-own
back to his place after work, gave me a drink, then made
When I politely rebuffed him, I promptly lost the projecti

Late one night as I was going out to my car an old m
up to the car parked behind me and we began to talk.
locksmith at Paramount Pictures, and had been workin
50 years, since the 1920s. He proudly told me about all
he had let movie stars like Marlene Dietrich and Gary Co
their locked dressing rooms because they'd lost their keys,
ing the locks for Adolph Zukor or Jesse Lasky, two of the
pioneers of cinema who had founded Paramount in the teer

At that time Columbia Pictures was still in its original
on Gower Street, beside what used to be known as Povert
the home of all the *really* low-budget studios, like Produce
leasing Corporation. On either side of Columbia's front door
two black marble bas-reliefs of Harry and Joe Cohen, the fou
of the studio, which I had stopped and inspected many times
sauntered past one day both reliefs were gone leaving disco
squares on the stucco walls. I went inside and asked the sec
guard, "What happened to the plaques of Harry and Joe Co
outside the doors?"

couldn't be any better than they were, and everyone just expected to get a good new movie every week, and a great new movie every month.

I began college in 1974 and immediately began writing for the school newspaper, *The Oakland Community College Recorder*, and naturally became the film critic. I think back on some of my earliest reviews that were so badly-written I'm still ashamed. My weekly column was called "Becker's Bijou Review," named by the pretty editor, with the eponymous name, Meymo Sturgis.

I then went to Eastern Michigan University and became their film critic. I panned so many of the movies showing on-campus, and attendance was so low, that they banned me from reviewing further on-campus films. When I panned the film *Lenny*, a woman in a class of mine angrily stomped up to me, stated, "*Lenny* is a great film!" then soundly slapped my face. I also won the "Best Article of the Month" award for my review of John Cassavetes' *A Woman Under the Influence*, a film I thought was brilliant.

I attended the University of Michigan in 1976. Oddly, U of M had a retrospective of the still photographs and movies of Karl Struss, winner of the very first Oscar for cinematography in 1927-28 for *Sunrise*. There was a big article in the newspaper and a picture of Karl and his wife, Ethel, who were both in their eighties. On opening night I went and saw the film *The Story of Temple Drake,* and the 1932 version of *Dr. Jekyll and Mr. Hyde,* both of which were beautifully photographed by Struss. After the films I went directly to the showing of his photographs of New York City in the teens and '20s that were stunning. I turned around and there stood Karl and Ethel Struss. The president of the university was about to have his picture taken with them and Karl was fumbling with a very old Leica 35mm camera that he seemed to be having difficulty putting back into it's case. To Karl Struss's utter astonishment, the president took the camera right out his hands, turned and handed it to me, saying, "Here, hold this." The photo was taken, the president shook Karl and Ethel's hands, then promptly turned and left.

I stepped up to them and handed Karl Struss back his priceless camera. He said thank you, clearly pleased to have it back. I said, "I just saw *The Story of Temple Drake* and *Dr. Jekyll and Mr. Hyde,* both of which were gorgeously photographed. How on earth did you do the transformation effects of Jekyll to Hyde?"

Both Karl and Ethel smiled in delight and Karl eagerly explained, with Ethel regularly joining in to remind him of details. The effect was done with a series of colored filters, combined with the hairs and make-up on Fredric March being of various colors, and since it was a black and white film the filters disguised the hair. As they pulled out the filters one by one the hair and make-up seemed to appear. I'd never seen anything like it and congratulated him on a brilliant effect. Karl and Ethel both smiled warmly, were ridiculously pleased that I'd enjoyed the films, and thanked me. I assured them it was entirely my pleasure.

At the end of the semester I moved to Los Angeles. In the first week of July, 1976, I moved into my very first apartment, at 666 N. Van Ness just off Melrose, kitty-corner from Paramount Pictures. A big movie at that time was *The Omen* and Damian the evil devil child had 666 on his scalp, the sign of Satan. Anytime I said my address someone always commented on it. The apartment cost $65 a month, including utilities.

That August I turned eighteen years old. The joke on me was that at the time you had to be twenty-one to drink in California, but only eighteen in Michigan.

So there I was, eighteen and living by myself in a tiny apartment in Hollywood, across the street from Paramount Pictures, where Billy Wilder and Joseph Von Sternberg had made many of their great pictures, like *Sunset Blvd.* and *Shanghai Express*.

From my desk, peering out the window at Van Ness Street, I looked directly across a parking lot to Producer's Studio, a much smaller film studio across from Paramount. On the bricks on the side of one of the sound stages, the name "Clune" could still be faintly read, one of the film studio's names back in the early silent days. Producer's Studio has long since become Raleigh Studios. That was where Sherwood Schwartz, producer of "Gilligan's Island" and "The Brady Bunch," had his office.

Between the old "Clune" soundstage and Melrose Avenue was a 1940s strip mall with a liquor store, a revival movie theater called The Encore Theater, and Jerry's Market (an old Los Angeles grocery store chain that can still be seen in Billy Wilder's film *Double Indemnity*). They would frequently shoot the Charmin toilet tissue commercials with Mr. Whipple ("*Please*, don't squeeze the Charmin") in this Jerry's Market, and I ran into the actor who played Mr. Whipple there several times, which was always odd, I must say.

They would shoot a lot of TV shows and movies on this corner, too. I came by one day and in front of the movie theater they were shooting a very short-lived TV show of the mid-70s called *Future Cop* with Ernest Borgnine as the human partner to a robot cop. Borgnine was just sitting there on a car hood in a policeman's uniform drinking a cup of coffee. As I passed by I offhandedly asked him, "What'dya wanna do tonight, Marty?" He smiled warmly with his familiar gap-toothed smile and replied, "I don't know, what do you want to do?"

My first film job in Hollywood was as a projectionist at The Encore Theater. The very friendly old man who owned the theater allowed me to train with the projectionist for a week, then just had me take over. The theater was equipped with very old, Simplex, carbon-rod, arc projectors, and you had to forever be diddling with the carbon rods to keep the flame fully illuminated. I projected the Moscow Ballet performing "Swan Lake" and "Sleeping Beauty" for about two weeks, which was kind of fun, although I quickly grew weary of watching scratchy prints of ballet films. Finally, the old theater-owner invited me back to his place after work, gave me a drink, then made a pass at me. When I politely rebuffed him, I promptly lost the projectionist job.

Late one night as I was going out to my car an old man stepped up to the car parked behind me and we began to talk. He was a locksmith at Paramount Pictures, and had been working there for 50 years, since the 1920s. He proudly told me about all the times he had let movie stars like Marlene Dietrich and Gary Cooper into their locked dressing rooms because they'd lost their keys, or changing the locks for Adolph Zukor or Jesse Lasky, two of the original pioneers of cinema who had founded Paramount in the teens.

At that time Columbia Pictures was still in its original location on Gower Street, beside what used to be known as Poverty Row, the home of all the *really* low-budget studios, like Producer's Releasing Corporation. On either side of Columbia's front doors were two black marble bas-reliefs of Harry and Joe Cohen, the founders of the studio, which I had stopped and inspected many times. As I sauntered past one day both reliefs were gone leaving discolored squares on the stucco walls. I went inside and asked the security guard, "What happened to the plaques of Harry and Joe Cohen outside the doors?"

"Oh," said the guard, "they threw those out. Columbia moved to Burbank, y'know."

I shook my head sadly. "I know, but they couldn't have taken the plaques with them?"

The guard shrugged, indicating very clearly, "Who gives a shit?"

About this same time, MGM moved out of their Culver City lot, where they'd been located since the early 1920s (it had originally been the Triangle Pictures lot, run by D.W. Griffith, Thomas Ince and Mack Sennett). I drove by and saw the crane remove the big Leo the Lion sign from the top of the main building. It was replaced by a sign that said, Lorimar Tele-Pictures, which was eventually replaced by Sony.

In 1977 I worked for four days as an extra in John Cassavetes's film *Opening Night*. There had been ads on an L.A. rock & roll radio station that said if you wanted to be an extra in Cassavetes's film, go to the Pasadena Civic Auditorium on a certain day wearing dress clothes, and you'd also get a free lunch, but no pay. I had been in Hollywood for three months and this was the best offer I had heard yet, so I went. There were about a couple of hundred other people there and we all sat in the audience clapping all day long while watching John Cassavetes and his wife Gena Rowlands perform a scene from a fake play that was within the movie. By lunch my hands were bright red and aching from all the non-stop clapping. Nevertheless, unlike many others, I went back in for the second half of the day and clapped until my hands were swollen and throbbing. When I got into my car to drive home I could not make a fist or tightly grab the steering wheel with either hand.

Several days later I received a call from a 2nd assistant director asking if I'd like to do some more extra work on *Opening Night*, and I said sure. Luckily, the next location was much closer to my apartment. It was a theater on Wilshire Blvd. between LaBrea Ave. and Vine St., I believe was called The American Theater, which has long since been torn down. This was a night shoot and I was instructed to arrive at about 5:00 P.M. As the crew set up outside the theater, the extras, all dressed in warm coats since it was supposed to be in New York in the winter, just hung around for hours. I attempted to strike up a conversation with a German fellow who seemed to have absolutely nothing to say. I asked if he liked any German films and he shrugged. I said, "Fassbinder? Herzog? Wim Wenders? Fritz

Lang?" Shrug. "*M? Metropolis? Ali: Fear Eats the Soul? Aguirre,
the Wrath of God?*" Nothing. Finally, a bright, bespectacled, blond,
collegiate-looking fellow in a long wool coat stepped up and said,
"I've seen all those films."

I said, "All of them?"

He nodded. And indeed he had, too, plus thousands and thousands
more. His name was Rick Sandford and he was my good friend for
the next eighteen years until he died in 1995. (Rick wrote a book
called "The Boys Across the Street," published posthumously in
2000 by Faber & Faber, and I'm a character in it).

My friend, Rick Sandford

Rick and I talked movies non-stop all night long on the set of
Opening Night, then we went back to my place, talked movies all
day, then we went back to the set and continued shooting and talking movies all the next night, too. Over thirty-six straight hours of
movie talk. The scenes we were in not only had John Cassavetes and
Gena Rowlands in them, but also Ben Gazzara, Joan Blondell, who
had been in many of the 1930s James Cagney pictures, as well as
Paul Stewart, who had been in *Citizen Kane*.

I was called back in for one more day of work, but Rick wasn't.
This was apparently based on zip codes and proximity to the new
location, which was a restaurant in downtown L.A. All of the scenes
were being shot inside the restaurant between Gena Rowlands and
Ben Gazzara, who were sitting in a booth with their backs to a big

window. Since this was supposed to be New York in the winter, the people passing back and forth outside the window, including me, had to be dressed appropriately. An assistant director was stationed at either side of the window, and would choose which extras to send through and when. Being a ham, every time I went through and knew I would be seen by the camera between the actors, I'd pause for a second, shiver, and shake my arms like I was freezing (of course it was really about eighty-five degrees out). The ADs loved my little performance and sent me back through over and over again. Each time I'd do a little variation on my frozen routine, and each time the ADs would smile in approval, then send me back through again.

At lunch that day, which was served inside the restaurant, I saw Gena Rowlands sitting all by herself. No one was eating with her. I summoned all of my courage, walked over and asked if I might sit down? She shrugged and said sure. I told her that I had written a very positive review of *A Woman Under the Influence* for my college newspaper a few years earlier and had won an award for the best article of the month. She seemed mildly interested. I then mentioned that my friend Rick Sandford had written her a fan letter a few years earlier analyzing her entire career and I wondered if she remembered it. Ms. Rowlands held up her finger, then reached into her purse and retrieved Rick's letter, saying, "This one?"

I was astounded. "Yeah, that one." It was all dog-eared and covered with smudges, clearly having been read a hundred times.

Rick wrote similar letters to many of his movie heroes, including the great director George Cukor, analyzing all of the films in his career. Rick liked and respected most of them, but he despised *A Double Life* (for which Ronald Coleman won an Oscar in 1947, as did the wonderful composer, Miklos Rosza). George Cukor wrote back on his personal "G.C." stationary and said, "Thank you for the nice letter. Sorry about *A Double Life*. GC." Rick had gotten a great director to apologize for making one of his classic films, which I thought was pretty audacious.

Rick kept a list of every movie or play he had ever seen and every book he'd ever read. Rick goaded me into keeping a list of movies and books, too. Rick collected many different series of award-winning book, like the Pulitzer Prizes, the National Book Awards, and the Nobel Prize-winners. So I started to collect the Pulitzer Prize-winning novels, too (I took it a lot further than him, though. He had all of them in paperback, I have them all in hardcover first-editions).

Rick and I began going to the movies together constantly, and we saw about a thousand movies together in the theater over the next eighteen years. Every morning Rick would read the newspaper, then he would call me up and tell me what interesting movies were playing, and which ones he intended to see. What this meant was, I could go to the movie with him or not, but this was what he was doing. Occasionally I would choose the movie, but very rarely. Also, first thing in the morning Rick would inform me of which famous people had died. His theory was that if he told me a famous person had died, as he did with Joan Crawford among many others, that when I then thought of that person forever after I'd have to think of him, too. And it's true. Rick's goal was to see in a movie theater every film that had ever been *nominated* for an Oscar. That's not just the winners, but all of the nominees, which is an enormous amount of movies. That's about twenty-five categories times five nominees each, times eighty years, equaling nearly 10,000 movies. There were several years (like 1939) when they had as many as ten nominees in some categories. I went to see quite a few of these movies with Rick, including *Aloma of the South Seas*, which was nominated (but didn't win) for best color cinematography in 1941 for Wilfred M. Cline, Karl Struss, and William Snyder. I told Rick as we walked to the County Art Museum on Wilshire Blvd. that I had met Karl Struss the year before in Ann Arbor and Rick was sort of impressed, since Struss won the very first Oscar for cinematography for *Sunrise* (1927-28, with Charles Rosher). "He must've been old?" said Rick. "Yeah," I said, "He was pretty old. In his eighties. But he was very nice." When we got to the museum they had the same old photos of New York by Karl Struss up on the walls. I saw an old man at the other end of the lobby and it was in fact Karl Struss.

I pointed, all excited. "That's *him*. That's Karl Struss."

He came walking toward us, saw me, smiled and put out his hand to shake mine. "You're that nice boy I met in Ann Arbor, Michigan, aren't you?"

I nodded, grinning hugely, and shook his hand. "Yes, I am."

"I'm so pleased you could make it. Thanks for coming," he said in a kindly voice, then walked away.

Rick looked at me and was now honestly impressed.

Journal entry: "May 25th, 1977, I went to the movies with Rick and saw the very first showing anywhere in the world of *Star Wars* at the Chinese Theater and it was really a lot of fun. It's story is a bit shallow, and the reasoning for the action wasn't the best, but they way it was done—wonderful."

On Friday, May 11, 1979, Rick and I went to the very first public screening ever of *Apocalypse Now* in Westwood. This was months before the film was actually released. I arrived at 3:00 PM for an 8:00 PM show and Rick had already been there for five and a half hours, since 9:30 AM. He had the very first place in the line that was already stretching around the block. Rick, my friend Sheldon, and I were interviewed by reporters from *The LA Times, The Herald-Examiner, The Chicago Tribune*, National Public Radio, and David Denby from New York Magazine. Bill Graham (who owned the Fillmore East and West and was in *Apocalypse Now*) was walking around making sure everything was cool in the long line. We saw Francis Coppola go by a few times looking very haggard. In the *LA Times* that Monday (May 14, 1979) it said: "But by 9:30 AM, nearly *11 hours* before showtime, Rick Sandford was on line reserving a spot for himself and five friends–Christopher Isherwood, Don Bacardy, Joshua Becker, Jeff Capp and Sheldon Lettich."

Christopher Isherwood was one of the foremost writers of the 20th century, a contemporary of Aldous Huxley (with whom he collaborated with) and W. H. Auden, and Chris's story, "Sally Bowles," was the basis for the musical, *Cabaret*. Chris and his lover, Don Bacardy, were very good friends with Rick. Chris and I spoke more that day standing in line for hours together than we ever had before, or afterward. I asked him whatever happened to Sally Bowles? Chris said she had married a British man, moved to England, had kids, and had written him a few letters, but eventually stopped. He also told me about a picnic lunch he took in the 1930s at the L.A. river basin with Charlie Chaplin, Greta Garbo and George Cukor. A cop showed up and Chris went to talk to him. The cop said they couldn't picnic there. Chris said, "But that's Charlie Chaplin and Greta Garbo." The cop replied, "What do you take me for? Some kind of idiot? Get outta here!"

After the screening of *Apocalypse Now*, which was stunning for the first two-thirds, then completely dropped dead for the final third with Brando, Sheldon and I went into the McDonald's in Westwood and there was Gray Fredrickson, producer of *The Godfather Part II* and *Apocalypse Now,* eating a hamburger with his girlfriend. Sheldon and I talked with him for about fifteen minutes. We both did many impersonations of lines from *The Godfather Part II,* that he and his girlfriend found highly amusing. "Yeah, buffers, there were a lot of buffers."

"Monday, July 16, 1979–
This evening I went and saw a series of silent comedies with Rick, Don Bacardy, and Christopher Isherwood. We all agreed that the Buster Keaton films, *Our Hospitality* and *The Navigator,* were brilliant. I thought the Harold Lloyd films, *Dr. Jack* and *The Freshman,* were the next best, then the Harry Langdon film, *Tramp, Tramp, Tramp,* which had some funny bits, but I just didn't like him. Both Rick and Don took exception to my comments. They felt that Langdon was superior to Lloyd and began to verbally rip me to shreds. Well, they're both such intelligent, well-spoken guys that I couldn't hold up my end of the discussion, and began to sort of stutter. Finally, Chris joined into the conversation with, "I agree with Josh. Harold Lloyd is *much* better than Harry Langdon." And that was that; my side won. We all accepted that Chris's opinion outweighed all three of ours."

Over the course of the next ten years both Rick and I became seriously disenchanted with Hollywood movies that seemed to get dumber and more formulaic every year, relying more and more on remakes, sequels and comic books. Rick stopped seeing most Hollywood films, but I just kept right on going to see everything, and Rick started to get really mad at me. His theory was that if you saw a film when it opened you were actively supporting it, and telling the producers to make more like it. He also prescribed to the idea that if anyone is holding a gun on the poster, don't see the film. Rick continued seeing old movies, Oscar nominees, but otherwise completely switched to seeing nothing but documentaries, which kept him busy.

My filmmaking career finally began to happen in the mid-'80s, and by the '90s I was working regularly directing TV. Subsequently, I had a lot less time for movie-going.

The last movie Rick and I saw together was *The Bridges of Madison County* in 1995, the year he died of AIDS. Before every single movie that Rick and I had ever seen together, and no doubt all the films I wasn't there for, too, the last thing he would do as the lights went down was to take off his glasses, thoroughly clean them, put them back on, then cross his arms and settle back to watch the film, his expression and posture saying, "Okay, what have you got?" This time, however, since Rick was nearly blind from the disease, he didn't bother to clean his glasses. I glanced over at him and I could see perfectly in the projector's back-light that there was dirt and smears all over both lenses, but he didn't know it.

Rick was in a coma for a couple of months before he actually died. They moved him from L.A. County General Hospital (the building in the first shot of King Vidor's 1928 film *The Crowd*) to a hospice in South-East L.A. As far as I know Rick hadn't spoken a word in several weeks. There were four or five of us in his room, talking amongst ourselves, when Rick suddenly blurted out, "*The Magnificent Ambersons?*" phrased as a question. We all turned and looked at him and everyone shook their head. No one had mentioned *The Magnificent Ambersons* (a film that Rick and I had seen together and we both loved). As far as I know, those were his last words.

Going to the movies lost a lot of its appeal to me. But of course I haven't stopped *watching* movies, just going to them. And I continue to keep the list of all the movies I see, the list that Rick goaded me into starting nearly 30 years ago. I recently passed 4,000 films (that's only films I've seen all the way through, by the way), and I am in fact at 4225. Like Rick, I've also turned to mainly watching old movies and documentaries now. With the improvements in digital video cameras these days, being so small, ubiquitous, and able to shoot with almost no light, the documentary form seems to be improving all the time. Regarding old movies, luckily there are tens of thousands of them I still haven't seen, either.

Being a P.A.

A production assistant, or P.A., is the lowest position on a film crew, and is also often referred to as a "gopher" or a "runner."

I began my career as a P.A. in 1977, when I was nineteen, in Detroit on a Ford commercial. I was working with my buddy, Bruce Campbell, who had gotten me the gig. Detroit pitchman Bob Hines was shooting a series of local Ford spots for the entire country. Six new Ford cars drove right at the camera as Hines stepped forward between them and said, "So, come on down to your local Detroit Ford dealer for the Labor Day Sales-a-thon . . ." Cut. Back up a half dozen new Fords, start again, "So, come on down to your local Boston Ford dealer for the Labor Day Sales-a-thon . . ." Cut. Back up the cars, etc. I was so useless on my first day that they pulled a gag on me, having me go further and further away for a "focus test," and then just leaving me there. I knew they were making fun of me, but I didn't care—I was working on a film crew and being paid, even if I was the very lowest guy on the totem pole.

Hey, you gotta start somewhere, right?

I began working regularly around Detroit as a P.A. I generally worked on car commercials, automotive industrial films, or "spots" (what we in the business call commercials) for a now defunct Detroit appliance store chain called Highland Appliance, all of which were conceived by the W. B. Donner advertising agency and produced by the same company, Magic Lantern, owned and run by Bob Dyke (who has since written and directed two feature films, *Moontrap*, with Bruce Campbell and Walter Koenig, and *Nobody Knows*). This series of Highland Appliance commercials were all very well-done movie parodies, and were considered to be a true highlight in Detroit commercial production.

One spot was based on a short film that Bruce, Sam Raimi, Scott Spiegel, and I had already made called *Cleveland Smith Bounty Hunter*, a *Raiders of the Lost Ark* parody. Bruce and I were hired by Bob to do the costumes and the props, Kurt Rauf did the effects, and the big-time Hollywood cinematographer, Matthew Leonetti (*Fast Times at Ridgemont High, Breaking Away*), came in and shot it. It's a pretty hot little spot, too.

There was a black-and-white James Cagney parody, which I believe was the one and only time that Ted Raimi ever worked as a P.A. It was very hot on the stage and it was getting late and the end did not appear to be in sight. The production manager told Ted to go get some cheese and crackers for the crew. Three boxes of crackers and three blocks of cheese would have more than handled it, although I'd say cheese was a poor choice in that heat anyway. Ted returned with twenty blocks of cheese and ten boxes of crackers. Within minutes the cheese was mushy and unappealing and nineteen blocks were left over unopened, as well as nine boxes of crackers. Ted never worked as a P.A. again, feeling unsuited for the job.

On a science fiction *E.T.* parody spot, Sam Raimi worked as P.A. for one of the very few times in his life. He was no better suited for it than his brother. We were shooting in the woods near Cass Lake and, at one point, Sam was sent out to buy some paper towel. He returned two and a half hours later, furious and fuming at having been lost for so long. Luckily for Sam, he's much better, not to mention far more successful, as a director.

There was a particularly good spot produced in this series, this time for the Detroit Optimetric Center. It was a musical number in a 1950s diner set to the song "Pretty Little Angel Eyes." Rob Tapert worked as a P.A. on this shoot (and was quite good at it, too). William Dear, who has gone on to direct the films *Harry and the Hendersons* and *Angels in the Outfield*, directed the spot, and did many of the other Highland Appliance spots, as well. I got stuck with the mind-numbing job of transforming this actual diner's black tile floor into a black-and-white checkerboard by use of squares of white contact paper. This process took me all night long. When the crew showed up in the morning I was still at it. We then worked all day and all night shooting the spot, running the song "Pretty Little Angel Eyes" on playback over and over and over again. Bill did a great job directing it and it's a terrific little musical number.

Meanwhile, the next day I was booked to work for Bob Dyke and Bill Dear again, this time on a Canadian Tire spot. This was tabletop shoot, with paint cans as houses and Matchbox cars parked in front. Kurt Rauf was working on the art crew, sticking down little trees and shrubs with a hot glue gun. He, too, had been up all night—although I had already been awake for two nights—and at one point, as a joke, Kurt squirted hot glue on my arm. It was like having a dime-sized glob of burning napalm caught in the hair on my arm. I tried to grab it and burned the ends of my fingers. I still have a scar to commemorate the event. I also had the most embarrassing moment of my life so far on this commercial. As shooting stretched on all night long, my third night up, I sat down in a chair and quickly fell asleep. Although I was asleep, I could sense something going on around me. I opened my weary eyes to find the entire crew surrounding me, with the director, Bill, looming over me.

Bill casually said, "Y'know, if all these lights and cameras and things are bothering you, I can get rid of them."

I worked on a General Motors presentation film for the Epcot Center in Florida. We shot most of it at the GM Tech Center outside Detroit. The production company was out of L.A., the crew was from Detroit, and the camera crew was made up entirely of Mormons from Provo, Utah. The director of photography was Reed Smoot, who was a good DP. Smoot's 1st and 2nd assistant cameramen, however, were snotty pains in the ass. All the non-Mormons on the crew had been ordered to not swear in front of the camera crew. The production coordinator was an inexperienced girl from L.A. who had never worked on a film crew before. Not knowing what her job entailed, she decided to spend all day picking on the one P.A. on the show—me. After she had dogged my heels for a day, I finally turned to her and asked, "Don't you have something else you can do?" She became furious, pointed in my face and said, "You'll never work in this town again!" This was the first time she had ever been in Detroit. Luckily, she said this in front of two highly amused Detroit grips, Donny Allen and Tim O'Day, with whom I had previously worked many times. For the remainder of the shoot, Donny or Tim would whisper to me, "Y'know, you'll *never* work in this town again," then burst out laughing.

I never liked being a P.A. I really wanted to be a director and working as a P.A. only reminded me how far I was from my goal. As I began to resent the situation more and more, naturally I got more and more work as a P.A. Finally, I was the highest-paid P.A. in Detroit, making $150 a day in 1983, which was damn good money at the time.

I worked on a GM spot directed by Ralf Bode, a terrific Hollywood cinematographer who photographed *Coal Miner's Daughter* and *Saturday Night Fever*. I spent many days out in the hot sun in the studio parking lot prepping new cars to be photographed. You get a cart with every kind of cleaner and solvent ever invented, and an endless supply of rags, and you clean every visible part of the car until it shines. This can take forever. And then grips with dirty hands push the cars onto the sound stage, and the process begins again, but now in a panic.

Before and after each shoot on a sound stage the floor had to be painted. I liked this a lot better than prepping cars because you could see the end of the job. A car could *never* be clean enough.

So, I finally grew to hate being a P.A., and would vow after each and every job that I would never work as a P.A. again. Then I'd get offered another P.A. job and, of course, I'd take it.

I moved back to Los Angeles for the fourth time in 1989, having already written and directed two feature films, *Thou Shalt Not Kill . . . Except* and *Lunatics: A Love Story*, and thinking I would now somehow naturally slide into the film business and begin working at my proper job, that of feature film director. Instead, to my utter chagrin, I now began working in Hollywood as P.A.

I worked on one of Mariah Carey's very first music videos which was shot on the New York street on the Paramount lot. It was a night shoot and it was raining and cold. The grips stretched tarps across the top of the set, which quickly filled with water and began to bulge precariously. I had to locate every 55-gallon trash drum on the lot, roll them over to New York Street, and set them up underneath the bloated tarps. A grip would then go up on a cherry-picker and punch holes in the tarp so that it would drain into the drums. It was darn chilly that night, but young Mariah Carey, wearing a scant little sexy outfit, did take after take after take all night long, never complaining or losing her smile. I was impressed.

I did parking lot patrol for an Amnesty International show at the Wiltern Theater. I had a list of celebrities who were to be allowed to park in a cordoned-off area, and the list included Bruce Springsteen (which had me giddy at the prospect) and Jackson Browne, but the only one who showed up from the list was David Crosby, who seemed quite pleased that ten parking spaces had been saved for him. I heard (since I was never inside the theater) that the host of the show, Rosanne Arnold threw a conniption fit when she was announced as "Rosanne Barr," an honest mistake since she had just recently married Tom Arnold at that point.

I worked on a music video for the band Damn Yankees, with fellow Michigander Ted Nugent on lead guitar. First, there was a day of shooting in a sound studio in L.A. where Ted and the band pretended they were recording the song. At one point in the little lunch room, it was just myself and Ted Nugent having a coke. Nervous to be near a childhood hero, I told him that I was from Detroit and one of the very first records I'd ever bought was the 45 of "Journey to the Center of the Mind" by the Amboy Dukes, Ted's first band.

Ted said, "That's one of the first records I ever made." Since we didn't have much else to talk about, Ted decided to confide in me. "You wanna know what I *really* want to do?"

"No, what?"

"I wanna kill a black rhino with a compound bow."

"Really?" I said, trying not to look revolted. "Aren't black rhinos an endangered species?"

"Oh, yeah. But I'm paying the South African government ten thousand dollars to let me kill one. They don't think I can with a bow and arrow; they don't think it's possible. But I'm gonna take that arrow and put it right into that rhino's pump!" Nugent poked his own (miniscule) heart for illustration.

I stood up, "Well, I've got to get back to work. Nice talking with you."

At the end of the day, Ted came up to me and gave me a copy of the magazine he publishes, *Bowhunter*, as well as a bumper sticker that said, "Bow hunters do it deeper."

The remainder of the shoot was at Mile High Stadium in Denver, where there was an all-day heavy metal concert, and Damn Yankees were the headliners. Also playing were REO Speedwagon and King's X, among others.

My buddy and I drove an 18-foot Ryder truck full of movie lights from L.A. to Denver, which took all day and most of a night. We arrived in time to help set everything up, including ten 35mm cameras. My job from there on out was to run freshly loaded magazines of film to the camera, then run the exposed film back to the camera truck, each time making my way through over 50,000 heavy-metal fans. I was getting severely weary of being a P.A.

My last gig as a P.A. was on a series of Domino's Pizza commercials starring Bronson Pinchot. It was a five-day shoot with a lot of location changes: first a house in Brentwood, then a house in Alta Dena, then somewhere in Pasadena, and finally on a stage at Culver City Studios. There was an enormous amount of equipment and props to move around, like scaffolding and hundreds of potted trees, plants, and flowers. Also, the 1ˢᵗ A.D. was short, big-mouthed prick who was always yelling at everyone on the crew. Driving a truck full of something from the San Fernando Valley to Brentwood, I got caught in a terrible traffic jam on the 405 freeway in the Sepulveda Pass because there were raging brush fires all over the hills. Everything was at a dead standstill as fire trucks and police cars wended their way to the fires, frequently going the wrong way up the shoulders of the freeway. When I finally got to the location the 1ˢᵗ A.D. promptly ripped me a new asshole in front of everybody. Of course, I should have quit right there, but I needed the money and there was only one more day left, so I smiled and took it. I snuck off and ate ibuprofen tablets like candy. The last day of the shoot was on a sound stage and involved several horses. First thing upon my arrival I was handed a shovel and I spent the next eighteen hours shoveling horseshit into a wheel barrow and hauling it out of the stage. Fresh steaming piles of it, one after another after another, all day long and well into the night. *Ah, show business!* I was absolutely certain that I would vomit three or four times during this job, but I'm pleased to report that I refrained.

As I dragged myself home at dawn on that day in 1991, weary, bruised, beaten, and reeking of shit, I waved my fist in the air once again and vowed, "As God is my witness, I will never work as a P.A. again!"

And I never have.

Knock on wood.

The *Evil Dead* Journal

I was the only person to keep a record of the making of the film *Evil Dead*, which was then called *Book of the Dead*. This is that journal, unedited, but with a few additions to fill things in.

On location in a swamp shooting *Evil Dead*, 1979: L to R Rob Tapert, Steve "The Dart" Frankell, Sam Raimi, Tim Philo, Josh Becker.

"Friday, November 9, 1979–

Last night I was invited to Sam's house to "sign my contract," which the guys were making a big stink out of. However, when I got there I found that the contracts had not been Xeroxed, so we could only look at them and see what we thought. We were also supposed to receive our first week's pay.

This was all done in a mildly odd, ritualistic way. As myself and the rest of the cast and crew sat in the living room watching *Jaws* on videotape, we were called in one by one to get our checks. I was first.

As an interjection, the rate of pay that I'd heard several times already over the past month was $175. a week for cast members and

$50. a week for the crew, which I felt was a big disparity. Also, I was going to be doing the lighting and getting the same rate of pay as the production assistants? It didn't seem right to me, but I didn't say anything.

So, I arrived in Sam's dad's office and Rob wrote me a check for $38.66. I was told that $1.34 was deducted for workman's comp.

I was shocked. "But I was *supposed* to be getting $50. a week."

"What?" Rob exclaimed. "Say's who?"

"Said Bruce and Sam, several times," I said handing Rob the check back.

Meanwhile, Bruce sat behind Rob saying nothing. I don't know where Sam was.

"Well, the whole crew is getting $40. a week," Rob stated flatly, "so here," and he handed me back the check, but I didn't take it.

I shook my head. "I was told fifty and fifty it'll be."

"Look," said Rob with weary impatience, "just take the check."

I smiled. "You hang onto it and when it's rewritten I'll take it."

Rob and Bruce went silent and both lowered their heads with oppressed expressions as though I had just ruined their whole lives, although I continued to smile.

"Give him fifty," Bruce mumbled quietly.

Rob handed Bruce the old check which he slowly shredded, then wrote me out a new one. "Don't tell anyone you're getting fifty," Rob said, "'cause they're still getting forty."

"Sure thing," I said as I put the new check for $46.88 (minus workman's comp) in my pocket and went back into the living room to see the end of *Jaws*.

Later that evening, after everyone else had gotten their money and left, I found myself back in the office talking with Rob, Bruce and Sam.

"I have one question, " I said. "Why aren't we shooting the interiors here in Michigan?"

"We may be," said Bruce.

I looked at the three of them quizzically. "Then why are we going to Tennessee for six weeks?"

Rob looked to Bruce and Sam, then said, "We spoke with the Tennessee Film Commission today and our location may have been yanked out from under us. So we may still shoot the interiors here. Don't tell anybody, okay?"

I agreed and departed. This took place on Thursday (yesterday) and we were supposed to leave the next day, today. But we haven't."

Later . . .

I'm sitting in Ricki's car in the parking lot of the Showcase Cinema Theater in Sterling Heights awaiting the start of *The Rose*, which, I assume, must be about forty-five minutes off.

Tomorrow I shall be leaving for Tennessee. I'm pretty much indifferent to the whole situation now. Last night Sam, Rob and Bruce informed me that I would have no creative input into *Book of the Dead* in any way, but will merely be a production assistant and nothing more. Of course I had been told that I would be collaborating with Sam on the lighting design, but that's not to be since apparently I can't be trusted. And this is because I demanded the full $50. a week that had already been offered to me several times for doing the lighting on a feature film. I can't be trusted? They're the ones that reneged, not me! My attitude toward "the boys" is one of annoyance and aggravation for A). Setting up the production in an amazingly haphazard way, and B). Very intentionally now putting me into a totally subordinate position. I *know* I could have been a great deal of help on planning the production and I also could have brought some good things to the lighting, but they will not allow me any input at all. I take this as a major slight to my abilities and to their interpretation of my abilities, as well being just plain old spiteful. And who's going to do the fucking lighting now? Sam? Give me a fucking break! He doesn't know shit about lighting, for Christ sake! Sam ended this horrible meeting by saying, 'I'll be glad to listen to any suggestions you might make.' I told him bluntly I wouldn't make any."

* * * * * *

Eighteen of us in the cast and crew all drove down to Tennessee in a caravan of six or seven cars and a rental truck. I drove with David Goodman, also known as "Goody," whom I knew vaguely from camp. Goody and I had never really spoken before. He reminded me that when, at camp in 1971, he had been called to the office to find out his parents had died, the last person he saw was me coming out of my cabin and it had always stuck with him. I clearly remembered it as well.

"Sunday, November 11, 1979–
Ah, Tennessee . . .
We of the cast and crew of *Book of the Dead* are presently residing in an extremely large house (6 bedrooms, 3 full baths) somewhere outside Morristown, which is about an hour outside Knoxville. We were told it was once a whore-house.

Getting here wasn't particularly difficult, other than the instructions we received were completely wrong. The location at this writing is a wonderful exterior (I've only seen stills), however the interior is unacceptable to those in the know. We may still be shooting in Marshall, Michigan.

We all moved into our rooms (although I haven't spotted Rich and Theresa yet) and I got a bed (most everyone else is on army cots or the floor). Goody and I are in the same room. He took the mattress and I got the box springs.

Sam spoke for our first production meeting and made a good show; he was adroit, yet funny (at the expense of Gary Holt, our local location manager, who is from Morristown, owns a limo service, and once drove Elvis around). Sam used a camp counselor attitude to the whole thing, seemingly covered *all* the points and that was that.

Gary Holt then played us a song he had written and recorded that was very strange. It was about 10-minutes long with a guy talking about the horrors of a Vietnam vet. Some of the lines were, '. . . He was the real Deer Hunter . . .' and '. . . It's like that Fonda-woman said . . .' and '. . . Under the constant threat of mentacide . . ."

It was too weird.

Later . . .

I don't have any idea as to what time it is. I have gotten twice as much sleep as anyone here. I awoke today to dinner being made (spaghetti that was okay), then dope smoking and beer drinking wiped me out in a few hours and I went back to sleep. When I awoke this last time I found Sam and Tom still up working on the actual Book of the Dead (Sam was having a rubber cast of his palm made to use as one of the pages of 'human skin').

So now everyone is asleep and I'm up. Sam said it was about 6:30 AM, then said it was 1:30 AM, then came back with 6:45 AM and since there isn't a clock around I really don't know.

It's a real strange grouping together of people. I'll wait to see how everyone functions as a team.

Nevertheless, we're all here, all the equipment is here, props galore, and we do have car exteriors to shoot and we have a car, so I guess we're making movies.

"Tuesday, Nov. 13th, 1979–

We now have a location, which is about a mile from here, that is almost totally demolished and needs to be rebuilt. This is expected to take eight days, during which time we shall be filming driving scenes.

I drove to Knoxville airport to pick up the film but it hadn't arrived yet. It's supposed to be in later tonight.

I don't feel like part of this happy family.

I don't feel like writing right now.

Later . . .

It's about 4:30 AM and I can't seem to get past my old sleeping habits. I went to sleep at 9:00 PM and woke up at 3:00 AM. This gives me quite a few hours to myself to read and write (I finished 'Commander 1' a few minutes ago). Also, I haven't been having a terrific time becoming one of the 'family,' so I just sleep it out.

Bruce picked up the film so I suspect we *could* shoot tomorrow—that would be nice. And although 'they' are trying to be democratic about who works where, I simply do not want to be doing clean-up and carpentry on the cabin when I could be assisting the shoot. I will undoubtedly end up on clean-up anyway.

Of the cast and crew, here's how I see it: Theresa is an air-head but well-meaning and is trying to be motherly, Betsy just is, Rich is okay, Don is okay but a little wacky on destroying things, Ellen is distant and seems troubled (she seems to have had difficulty with her face mold tonight), Tim (camera) seems to know what he's doing, John (sound) is a good guy, Goody is Goody (loud & goofy), Dart (Steve Frankell) arrived today and he's a good guy, Tapert seems to be enjoying his power-position, but hasn't become annoying, Bruce is either ALL BUSINESS or ALL SHTICKS and Sam, though a bit harried, is just his plain-old self and everyone seems to adore him. As for me, I'm the recluse.

Last evening, as I was trying to get the dishwasher going, Theresa said to me, 'You know, you're not as bad as they made you out to be.' I asked her what this meant and she wouldn't reply.

I forgot Tom Sullivan–he does his job and enjoys himself, but otherwise is barely apparent."

"Thursday, Nov. 15th, 1979–

So, yesterday was our first day of filming. We were out at this fairly large, creaky old bridge filming the car driving across and boards dropping out from beneath.

My job was slating and setting up the fake beams beneath the bridge (which was done by threading fishline through the fake beams, then running the line across the bridge at a height so that when the car drove past it would break the line. At the same time Rob and I were also tossing real logs off).

Things went quite well, if slow. My first job of the day was attracting the attention of some bulls that were attacking Tim and Sam as they shot a long shot of the car driving by from a field across the street. I just sang some songs and the whole herd moved to the other end of the field.

Later . . .

Today's shooting was chock full of exciting things. The very first event of the day after we left in three vehicles for the location is that the van got lost and we spent a half hour trying to locate it.

Our location at Clinch Mt. was very panoramic and we did some follow shots of the subject car that should look terrific. We then got to this dirt road beneath a highway overpass and within the first hour of setting up Sam drove his car into a ditch and we had to get a tow truck to get it out.

About two hours later Rob and I set out to find Don Campbell, who had gone out to scout a location, and found him standing high atop a wooded cliff. We called to him, then he disappeared only to reappear moments later sliding off the cliff. Don made one last try at grabbing a tree, missed and went sailing down about twenty feet.

I dashed up the hill to where he had landed and called to him, but he didn't respond. I lost my footing and tumbled back down. On the next try I clawed my way up and found Don sitting in a daze. I asked if he thought anything was broken and it wasn't.

We've now taken him to the hospital for some tests."

"Friday, Nov. 16th, 1979–
Today's shoot was rather boring. All of the shots were of sequences taking place in the car. Rob was busy today so I kept the log. That entailed waiting for the car to get back, then coercing the information out of Sam and Tim. It wasn't particularly taxing.

Things are running well. The cast does what they're told, the only bitching coming from Theresa, but no one ever listens. Sam is funny and has been giving some first-rate direction, Bruce is funny and keeps Ellen particularly always laughing, Rob is dealing with the problems and not giving anyone grief, while always wanting the best for the production, Dart and Goody are digging fixing up the house, Don is a psycho and always firing guns, and I do what needs to be done–as does Tim and John.

I've been going to sleep directly after dinner and finding that I'm *just* getting enough sleep. I'm in bed now."

"Sunday, Nov. 18th, 1979–
I just returned from watching Tim and Rob do some 'evil entity POVs' through the woods by means of attaching the camera to a five-foot 2x4, the camera at one end with Tim holding it, Rob holding the other end for stability. Theoretically it's not a bad idea, although in practice Rob kept smashing into trees.

Yesterday I spent the day working on the cabin: peeling old wallpaper, plastering, painting, etc. The place may look okay depending on how it's dressed-up.

Last night Gary Holt took us to a performance of 'The Good Doctor' at a local theater that was pretty awful. The setting of the play is supposed to be Russia but no one could handle the accent, so it ranged from Liverpudlian to Ohio to southern USA/Russian. Before the show began an ugly, overweight girl got up and made some announcements: no smoking, try-outs for 'The Twelfth Night,' thanking people, then saying that the bathroom was in the dressing room and if anyone used it please don't flush because it would ruin the mood of the play.

Anyway, I could barely keep my eyes open.

Later . . .

I'm finding it increasingly more and more difficult dealing with the women on this production. I feel intentionally alienated and even to the point that I am an object of ridicule. As usual I figured this was exclusively my problem, but yesterday Goody said exactly the same thing.

Last night Tim and I talked for about an hour about a script idea of his that I found exciting and rather unique. I'll bring it up to him again later.

I lapse back and forth between simply not caring what my function on this film is to despising my lowly position. To Sam, Bruce, Rob, Tim and Tom this is a dream-come-true, for the cast it's a chance at fame, for Don, Goody and I it's merely something to do. I really don't mind the chores I've been doing, but they're menial and uninteresting, and the idea that five weeks of this remains is a tad unsettling.

Three ounces of pot has been lost (or so I've been told) so staying stoned is not even a possibility anymore.

Five more weeks–Lord God this is going to be trying."

"Tuesday, Nov. 20th, 1979–

I'm not exactly sure it's either Tuesday or the 20th, but it doesn't really matter.

Today was spent at The Old Bridge location about 45 miles from here. Scenes of styrofoam 'It's Murder' beams falling onto the camera below and the car wheel dropping through the planking were shot and both looked terrific. And then the welder and the wrecker showed up to tear the metal structure of the bridge apart and make it look like a clawing hand. It's almost finished (which took all day and night) and it looks amazing.

Upon arriving at the bridge in Bruce's car, Sam realized he had the keys to his Olds (the subject car) with him, so I had to drive 45 miles back home, then back *again*.

Walking on the rotting planks totally freaked me out. It was something like a 35-foot drop into fast-moving water, however Dart bounded around on the beams like a ballerina.

During tonight's construction, the winch was drawn around the left side of the bridge to bend the little finger to the left. Unbeknownst to anyone the cable was also around a large tree-branch that snapped when tension was applied to the cable and landed on Sam. The limb must have weighed 50 lbs., but didn't knock him over. He merely staggered back and sat on the wrecker. Everyone thought he was okay, however I went over to him and found him pale, his eyes completely bloodshot, his lips white and crusty and a small amount of blood dripping from his left nostril. I offered my assistance and he shook his head slightly declining. About ten minutes later he was functional but seemed groggy and passed out on the way home.

The first footage comes back tomorrow.

It's 1:15 AM and I've been up since 4:30 AM and I have to be up at 7:00 AM."

"Wednesday, Nov. 21st, 1979–

So far today has been a fiasco–not for me actually, but . . .

I drove Rob around today as he checked on, and had done, all that needed doing for tonight's shooting of the bridge/claw scene.

We went out to the bridge and found that the end knuckle of the ring-finger had been amputated at Dart's decree. It doesn't ruin the claw effect, but it is a definite detraction.

The electrician that was supposed to rig the cable from the 5000 watt light to the generator arrived drunk. As he guzzled another beer he told us he was too busy and couldn't do it today. I listened to him mumble 75% incoherently, then left assured of his complete and total stupidity.

Goody drove to Atlanta, GA. to pick up the new film from Kodak and his truck broke down, and although I'm not certain, it seems quite serious. His truck was the only vehicle equipped with a trailer hitch to pull the generator, so now they're considering renting a U-haul van to put the generator in.

A moment ago Bruce and I heard a crash, went into the garage and found that Sam had just broken a 5000-watt bulb which cost $75.00.

So, we don't have a truck, the use of the 5K, new film, several knuckles on the bridge fingers, or Goody.

We leave for the bridge very soon."

Friday, Nov. 23rd, 1979–

Yesterday was probably the nicest Thanksgiving I've ever had. After shooting the gnarled-hand/Bridge scene all night until 6:30 AM, with two generators, a thirty-six foot cherry-picker, three fog machines and 4000 watts of light, we then got up at 11:00 AM to go to Gary Holt's mother-in-law's house for the Thanksgiving meal.

It was sunny and warm, the colors wonderfully vibrant, the setting rural and rustic. The meal was extravagant, the people folksy and hospitable, we rode around on Gary's son's go-cart, we played football, played with the two Dobermans, three tiny kitties, and two Pekinese dogs, watched Detroit vs. Chicago on TV, showed *Within the Woods*, actually helped a neighboring farmer herd some cattle that had wandered astray, then came home and watched the rushes–some of which are great, the rest good, then I went to sleep and awoke today at 6:00 AM and am presently defecating my Thanksgiving meal."

"Saturday, Nov. 24th, 1979–
Once again we are about to leave for the dirt road location at Clinch Mt. Yesterday we filmed the scene with the subject car swerving in and almost hitting a logging truck and I filmed a couple of shots. It never looked as good as it should have, though.

Dissension among the cast and crew seems to be building. Some of the gripes are: Sam never shoots a master-shot of anything, therefore the cast never gets to play out a whole scene, he'll spend hours filming an insert, then not have time for three other shots, he spends very little time telling the actors what he wants, he'll do a few run-throughs, but mainly for the camera's sake, not the actors, he films everything from every angle, except the really important things like the bridge scene where he got very few shots (which bugged the shit out of Tom). Supposedly we are three days behind, but I'm not sure whether to believe it or not since Campbell, Tapert, Raimi seem to think it necessary to withhold or lie about certain things. For instance, Rob told me the bridge scene cost $2,300.00, whereas Bruce said $1,200.00–that's a big discrepancy.

My neck has hurt for four days, and yet, even with all this I'm still enjoying myself.

My tape recorder keeps getting taken out to the cabin, left overnight in the cold, which kills the batteries, then I track it down (since no one returns it) and if I want to use it I have to buy new batteries which runs me $5.00.

This production is depressing me again. It rained last night so we can't go to the dirt road and alas we're just sitting around.

I guess that it must be a reflection of my comportment, but I do not like the way I'm treated by several people here. Betsy gives me upward of four dirty looks and snide comments a day, always to statements of mine not directed toward her. Theresa simply doesn't deal with me at all and Sam (this is the major one) appears to not only not want my suggestions on open questions, but is more than a shade reticent to let me do anything that takes any amount of thought or creative input. When he decided to go with multiple cameras yesterday, he immediately asked John to run camera #2, then began wondering aloud who had the ability to run camera #3, and only after I asked and he gave it some thought would he *let* me run it. Today he was thinking of a method for a fake shot, opened it up to suggestions from Dart, didn't like what he heard then just left it to Dart.

This sounds like paranoid ravings, and maybe it is, but I'm still mildly bugged.

I talked for a long time with Tom Sullivan last night and rather enjoyed myself. Mainly we talked movies and I told him the story of *Bloodbath* and he liked it, then he told me this totally bizarre idea of his about other dimensions, ghosts, 'actual demons,' and 'actual sea-serpents,' that just went on forever.

So far, if I did a film, of these folks I wouldn't mind using John Mason in some capacity, Tim Philo as camera operator, both Goody and Dart as carpenters and PAs and possibly Tapert as producer– but, that's just jerk-off thoughts.

Later . . .

Speaking of paranoid ravings, this production is making me paranoid. I've got this odd, unfounded fear I'm going to get fired–I'm assuredly replaceable, as a matter of fact, I'm totally expendable. I have no basis for this fear, yet it persists.

These guys are freaking out with all this money, they can't stop finding ways to spend it. Now they're having Dart build a slanted, twenty-foot ramp running from the edge of the porch out in front of the door to get another crane effect. It's ridiculous.

Why am I in this absurd position? The idea of working on a movie is great, but the grief just isn't worth it. To be on a production with good friends and intentionally and continually placed in a lower position is maddeningly insulting. I really want to tell them to fuck off, but it won't accomplish anything. I've tried to keep a good attitude throughout but it's difficult–I have ideas that I have to force on people just to get them to listen, not even accept them.

And, I think I'm sick, too.

Fuck!

And yet a little while later . . .

It appears as though this production is running into some trouble.

The high brass is in a special conference this very moment discussing it; how to keep going with exteriors while it's raining, or to go interior with a cabin that is as yet unfinished and unfurnished.

At this point, this is what I would do: stop shooting for a couple of days, get everyone out to the cabin, rehearse every move, every lighting set-up, finish fixing the place, dress it, wait for it to stop raining, then keep shooting (the rain is supposed to end on Thursday) but now do the long tracking takes that comprise so much of the footage, then get the inserts and go home.

Tom asked if I suggested this to them and I hadn't, nor will I. I've made as many suggestions as I'm going to.

This meeting is taking place in the room adjoining mine so I can't even go to my room.

The question is: why is all of this bothering me so much? It's not my film, why should I care? I'm back-assed on both points. I want to care, but I don't really, and it's not my film, yet I wish it were—at least in some part–then someone might take heed of my words.

But why do I want them to take *my* word? Isn't theirs enough?

No. It's not.

We are now four days behind and there is a good chance tomorrow will make five. Sam does not have a firm control of the situation at all.

Of course I never thought he did, but his movies always turned out well. That was super-8 though, this is 16mm and a *lot* of money. There are a million variables in this business. Someone once said that being a good director mainly consists of answering better than 50% of the questions right. This has always made sense to me but I've never seen it so intensely illustrated. Everyone bombards Sam with questions continually and I'm not sure if his average is better than 50% at this point. We are fourteen days into a forty-three day shoot–one-third of the way in–and *Book of the Dead* is theoretically one-ninth shot (if it was ever going to run ninety minutes). The big answer now is 'once we get to the cabin things will *really* move.' As far as I can see it's not too much different from shooting in the car, and that took forever. Sam doesn't *really* know what he wants. I'm convinced.

I saw part #2 of *Salem's Lot* on TV and it was drek. *Texas Chainsaw Massacre* was a fluke. Tobe Hooper is bad–not even mediocre– bad."

"Sunday, Nov.25th, 1979–

Today I worked out at the cabin painting. Don and I painted the trim around the doors and windows battleship grey (as instructed by the Almighty One). When this was accomplished Sam decided he wanted all the trim brown, so the rest of the day was spent re-painting.

Just previous to Sam's original decision to paint it grey, I suggested it all be painted brown and was ignored. I'm getting to be an extreme I-told-you-so.

Today's shooting consisted of a few fake driving shots in the afternoon. The morning was spent getting the subject car out of the ditch Sam drove it into while attempting a stunt that had been filmed possibly twenty-five times previously.

This now puts us six days behind.

After work on the cabin, myself, Dart, Don, Rob and Sam piled into the rental truck and attempted to drive back to the house, however yesterday's and today's rain has almost made the long driveway to the cabin impassable. Four of us had to push to get the truck up to the road.

In a few minutes I leave for the Knoxville airport to drop off the film. This is the second time we've sent out our film on Sunday, the day when the only freight service open is Delta which happens to be the most expensive."

"Monday, Nov. 26th, 1979–

It's about 10:30 A.M. and Rich and Tim just left to get a couple of second-unit driving shots. Later today, and supposedly all night, we'll be in the cabin.

Last night, while I drove to the airport, everyone else was out at the cabin working. Scuttlebutt has it that the middle bedroom is painted yellow and the back room white. Yellow? For a horror movie?

The furniture is to be purchased today, interior shooting tonight.

The Arriflex-S busted and now Bruce is calling equipment rental places in Atlanta to get another. Ivan Raimi [Sam's older brother] was going to bring one down, but he doesn't want to make the drive. The footage of the car and truck stunt didn't run through the Arri-S, however it was covered by the Arri-BL and the Bolex, nevertheless, there are a few more shots lost."

"Tuesday, Nov. 27th, 1979–
We did shoot all last night at the cabin and got some real nice shots. The front room was absolutely filled with lights, about 7000 watts inside and 3500 outside, and we did a 90-degree dolly from the porch to in front of them and an upward ramped pull back/zoom back that should be interesting.

There are more fakery fog shots tonight and I don't know what else. I'm rather bored of this whole deal and having no one to talk to.

I figured going in that if nothing else I could always talk to Bruce, however that is not the case. Bruce is either all business (which I'm not part of) or shticking for everyone, which I find rather tedious.

At first I tried to sit in on the business end of this thing, but found that I was neither a part, nor wanted. I have ceased this practice.

Early the next morning . . .

Shooting ended about an hour ago, at 7:00 AM, and we got six shots in total: a straight-on shot of the car (approaching the bridge) tilted to about 4:00, the camera tilted to 4:00 and Bruce and Ellen getting out at a normal angle. [A storyboard is drawn]. I like it."

"Thursday, Nov. 29th, 1979–
Things have gone topsy-turvy. We all changed over to a night schedule that would permit filming from when it got dark at about 6:30 PM to dawn, however within two days things have gotten pushed to the point of beginning to film last night at 2:00 AM, then going until noon. It's 1:00 AM now and we have yet to begin, nor does it appear as though we will for another hour or two.

Winter has come, the muddy driveway to the cabin has frozen allowing access to it, and the cabin itself is now always astoundingly cold inside, even with a big fire and two space heaters. Last night, on the seventeenth take of an exterior dolly shot the sync cable froze and we were forced to go in and let it thaw.

Our director is a first-rate mess. He is sleeping at the cabin (someone has to since all of our power tools were stolen: a skill-saw, saber-saw, drill, chainsaw) and he seems to get more frazzled and less organized by the day.

After completing the filming at noon yesterday, Sam and I put away two-thirds of a bottle of scotch and smoked four doobs until we were stumbling idiots. I awoke a few hours later in total pain from sleeping on the floor, as well as being severely hung-over, and drove back to the house. I awoke at 10:30 PM and went right back to the cabin. I'm back at the homestead now taking a shit (actually leaving one) and awaiting the return to the cabin for filming.

Everyone including myself, is a fried-out wreck. This production is taking its toll."

"Saturday, Dec. 1st, 1979–
We've just returned from another all-night shoot, then breakfast and it's about 9:30 AM. Early into last evening's proceedings I began drinking Rebel Yell bourbon, smoked a doob, then switched over to scotch and in no time felt incredibly bad. I tried to sleep on the couch in the main room and couldn't, then moved to the freezing back-room and crashed on a cot for several hours. When I awoke the sun was just coming up and Sam was still shooting the same shot as when I retired.

I feel like a total scum-bag. My only consolation is that Sam looks worse and assuredly feels worse.

We looked at the second load of rushes yesterday and among some real nice shots (the tire dropping through the bridge) the big events of the truck scene and the night-time gnarled-hand/bridge scene were both let-downs. A bunch of the footage of the truck scene just wasn't there, and what was there didn't look very good. As for the bridge, well, it's almost a total waste. the gnarled hand effect isn't there, the crane shot doesn't work and the whole thing looks like a cheap, backyard set.

Sam is now considering shooting both scenes again–which is obviously insane since there is possibly twenty-minutes of film shot.

I entirely understand Sam's directorial technique now: he breaks *every* scene down to *every* possible angle and films them *all*, thus giving himself total latitude in the editing room. It's a viable method, but not rational for a low-budget production like this one."

"Sunday, Dec. 2nd, 1979–
Once again I have just returned from an all-night shoot. Although things were still slow, they went appreciably faster than usual.

Sam looks like he's on his last leg. Now he *really* looks like a punch-drunk boxer. Nevertheless, he's still right on top of the action (as he says quite often) and he's getting some nice footage.

Aside from the fact that I still have serious doubts about the completion of this film and that neither Betsy, Theresa nor Bruce is giving a particularly good performance, this film will be slick as shit and have some great things in it."

As the pressure increased, so did Rob's smoking. He already smoked a lot before we got there, as did I, but he really kicked it into high-gear when we got to the night shoots. He got up one day, looking like hammered shit, and croaked, "The angel of death has been jumping up and down on my chest all night long," then lit a cigarette.

And Sam, who loved to torture people (as the shoot was proving), began calling Rob "Red" because of his red hair, which Rob didn't appreciate at all. Sam then began to regularly chant, "Red, Red, who shit on your head?" which *really* annoyed Rob, but amused the hell out of the rest of us.

"Wednesday, Dec. 5th, 1979–
Tonight is going to be another all-nighter for two scenes: Ellen running through the woods and Rich walking into the cabin looking through all the rooms.

Last night I picked the optometrist up at the airport. He had the white 'monster' contact lenses with him for the girls that are just repulsive-looking–very effective. An interesting sideline is that they can only be kept in for fifteen minutes, five times a day. This seems like it ought to effect Sam's shooting style just a bit, and the whole end of the movie has these contacts in.

On the way back from the airport with the optometrist I took the wrong fork on the Andrew Johnson Hwy, realized my mistake immediately, turned around on the hwy, cut across the median and was pulled over by the police. I showed him my license and he informed me I had just broken about three laws, then asked what I was doing in Tennessee anyway? I told him I was part of the production of a horror film called *Book of the Dead* being shot in Morristown, that I had just picked up the optometrist from the airport who had the white contact lenses for the monsters and I wasn't sure of my way back to Morristown. He seemed a little incredulous, smiled, and told me to just keep going the way I was going and that was that. No ticket.

Also, we (although not I) were on TV yesterday. The Knoxville news filmed this press conference that Gary had set up, then they all went out to the cabin. It was kind of funny.

The shit hit the fan yesterday finally and everyone voiced their gripes–and there were a lot of them. Rob and Bruce (not Sam) listened to them all, said something would be done, mainly with getting Sam to straighten out his act, get the schedule normalized, give someone the job of production manager, and someone the job of assistant cameraman, keeping the house clean and many, many more. Once everything was aired it was all promptly forgotten and things continue exactly as they were.

I am tentatively considering just not going back to Detroit. I'd like to meet Sheldon somewhere between here and LA and figure out what we can do with *Bloodbath*. I'll call him. I would like to rewrite it myself first, but going home will just cause me grief and despair–that

I can count on.

We would either have to sell it, which would be okay, but I would rather make it myself. That would entail a lot of time and money and shooting a short version which this script doesn't really lend itself to. Also, that much time with Sheldon would drive me insane.

Much later . . .

The shooting has ceased (it's 7:00 AM) and one scene was filmed–Ellen running through the woods. It was nicely done: 120 feet of dolly track (particle board), four 1000-watt lights and the 5000 watt light on the driveway, with access to a high angle shot on one side and a low angle on the other. We did twenty-two takes of her running in a nightie and undies (it was about 40- degrees out), then two takes of her falling in front of the camera.

On the second take she fell hard and scraped her leg, got pissed, began cursing and said she couldn't film anymore—shooting came to a halt. I don't blame her, either, I was freezing cold in a winter coat and gloves.

Right now upstairs there is a discussion about upcoming scenes, many of which are with the contacts which can only come in and out five times a day, fifteen minutes at a time. For Sam that pretty much means no exact run-through and probably about two quick takes. Not because I said so, but out of necessity he will have to rehearse his actors and go for the big takes–or he will be fucked.

Book of the Dead is three full days behind schedule, with no contingency days. Rob mentioned staying beyond the 22nd today, just in passing."

"Saturday, Dec. 8th, 1979–

I just returned from seeing *Star Trek: the Motion Picture* and am exceedingly unimpressed, however I did get off from work for a while so I'm still rather pleased to have seen it.

Ivan, Rob's sister, Dorothy, and another fellow arrived today and are presently out at the location filling Don's and my shoes–fine, I need a break.

Shooting continues with increased fervor now that the horror scenes have begun and for most of it the contact lenses are in. Out of necessity we must begin shooting this film rationally.

Later . . .

I finished 'Nine Stories' by J.D. Salinger and they were terrific. I've heard rumors that there are more of his stories extant, I must check it out.

I have an inkling of an idea as to how to adapt the Glass family stories into a single film

–something to think about."

"Sunday, Dec. 9th, 1979–

After shooting all day and night we all came home and watched our movies. Only Tom, Theresa and Ellen saw *Holding It*, but they liked it. The big success was *The Happy Valley Kid*, which it ought to be."

"Monday, Dec. 10th, 1979–

I spent today watching and logging the rushes. It took me eight hours to watch eight reels (three remain) and after that my mind was numb. The ulterior motive for my spending the day watching the rushes is that 1200 feet of film is missing. I did not locate any of it.

Anyway, I slept for four hours, felt amazingly refreshed and have been up since reading 'Altered States' by Paddy Chayefsky.

I dreamt last night that I was in love and holding her close. Upon awakening I attributed this woman to Renee, but I'm not so sure it was.

Yesterday Dart came up to me out of the blue and said, 'Stop trying to get even, get ahead.' He didn't seem able to explain this comment very well, but related it to things I had said to him and repeated it a few times. And it's stuck with me. I *am* trying to get even a lot of the time; to do and outdo what Sam has done, to prove myself. But I really can't do it alone and those I want help from won't do it. They'll let me work *for* them, but not *with* them. I will *not* work *for* them ever again. It's been a gainful experience, but also a compromising position. Next time it's either with them or without them. I'll even work with Cameron if I have to."

As all of the women in the cast began playing their monster roles, covered in rubber latex make-up, with white contact lenses in their eyes, they would invariably freak-out at some point and just tear off their make-up. This was often accompanied by cursing and tears, as well, and came to be known as "The Latex Point."

"Saturday, Dec. 15th, 1979–
I skipped out of the shoot this evening without asking and with no particularly good reason. Ivan and his friend came back down here and are playing PAs so I'm less than needed, I'm in the way. Well, I won't intentionally be in the way, that's for sure.

Things are progressing at an increasingly slow rate (since all of the difficult things were saved for last) and the quality seems to be dropping, although Sam continues to come up with a lot of interesting shots. It seems apparent to several people now that the final film will be rather short, or, as Tom Sullivan said this evening, 'Short of an hour,' which is very short.

Sam seems to be going through some kind of phase in which he has to prove his manhood. It's done seemingly in jest, but not in totally. He and Dart are constantly playing catch with the two-bladed ax, where they toss it spinning into the air and hopefully catch it by the handle. Or, the two of them drank an entire Mason jar of moonshine– which is enough moonshine to strip all the paint off a car–then slept on the driveway. Not on the nearby soft grass, the driveway.

Last night we were shooting Betsy popping her hand out of the grave and grabbing Bruce's arm. Aside from the fact that it's *too* much of a rip-off of *Carrie* to deal with, it was an insert of a hand grabbing an arm and we actually completely buried Betsy in the frozen ground. To compound this stupidity it was 15- degrees out and piercing cold and Sam once again went into a hyper-meticulous state and spent *five hours* shooting the insert."

"Monday, Dec. 17th, 1979–
Soon we'll be leaving for the location again and once again I'm dreading it. Last night was unquestionably the coldest yet, possibly zero, and just absurd weather to be doing extensive exterior shooting in. Aside from the fact that it's awful to be out in personally, both lights and cameras resent it, too–the Arriflex-BL freezes up regularly now and has to be thawed by the fire.
The night before last the tension between cast, crew and head honchos almost came to the boiling point. I can't finish this now, Sam just told me I have to go."

Bruce was constantly drenched with fake blood, made from Karo Syrup, which is pure sugar, and food coloring, which would then freeze. Between shots we would huddle inside the unheated cabin by a big industrial kerosene heater. Between the freezing and the heating, Bruce's shirt turned into rock candy and just broke off of him. This happened several times.
We were shooting a shot where a fake hand gets cut off. My job was "blood-blower," meaning I had to fill my mouth with fake blood and blow it through a rubber tube at the proper moment. So, we got all set to shoot the shot, I filled my mouth with the pure sugar syrup (you could actually feel it rotting your teeth), drooled it into the tube until it was full, then refilled my mouth to capacity, put the tube between my lips, and then no one was ready to shoot. Lighting was being adjusted, the lens was being replaced, and suddenly I couldn't breathe. I could have just pulled the tube out of my mouth and spit out the fake blood, but instead I grabbed the fake hand, tore it off the wrist, then blew the blood through the tube, thus ruining the effect. Everyone looked at me on the floor panting, my face covered with blood, the rubber hand dangling from the wrist. Sam pointed at me and stated, "You panicked!" Which in fact I had.

"Tuesday, Dec. 18th, 1979–
I'm not exactly sure it's Tuesday or the 18th, but anyway . . .
Yesterday's filming was dreadful: it was astoundingly cold, long

pauses between every stage of filming, then Sam did another of his fourteen takes a shot business.

When everyone got home Sam, Rob, Bill (their friend and ex-professor from MSU) and myself sat around smoking pot, discussing LSD and movies. When everyone else had retired and I was attempting to draw Sam's storyboards for him (this was at 8:30 AM), Sam decided to let me in on how to make it in the directorial world– 'make a ten-minute gem.' This is to show everyone that I can direct. He said that he and Rob and Bruce would gladly help me.

I was awakened today at noon and just ignored whoever did the waking and was not re-awakened. It's now 10:00 PM.

With all of this unexpected time on my hands I read Strindberg's "The Stronger" (I finished 'Altered States' last night), then watched Sam's 'ten-minute gem' *Clockwork* which is fun, has one terrific shot and is immediately forgettable. I also watched his Shakespeare film, which I had never seen, and was quite impressed–it's very funny.

Even though I haven't got the money I think I will do as he says. Now to think it up.

Later . . .

Several hours ago Betsy called from the location to get Ellen out just as Tom was completing her make-up. Betsy had mentioned that she had had her contacts in nine times already, four more than allowed, and there were still shots to do. I called and spoke with Rob about it and was told to mind my own business. Tom went out with Ellen to straighten things out and has yet to return.

So, with *all* this time on my hands I read 'The Jaws Log' by Carl Gottlieb which was interesting."

"Friday, Dec. 21st, 1979–

This filmmaking epoch draws to a close tomorrow for many of us on *Book of the Dead*. Ellen and Betsy both left today, Sunday Rich, myself, Don and Tom will leave. I'm kind of sad to see it end even if it has been a major source of grief it's also been very educational. And of all of Sam's drawbacks and inabilities as a director he never forgot the point of the film and may very well succeed on technique alone. Early this morning after we had watched *Holding It*, Sam's 'Shakespeare Film' and some rushes, Rob, Sam and I smoked some pot and talked and Sam related filmmaking to being a magician. He said the only thing a magician is thinking about while performing is, 'do they know how I'm doing this trick?' If they don't, he's succeeding– period. The point also isn't just to make the film, it's to amaze yourself and everyone at the same time. If you think what you're doing is neat, chances are everyone else will, too.

Nothing says I have to leave Sunday, I could stay the next two weeks, but I don't think it's a real good idea. My services are not particularly needed and feeling unneeded I become aggravated and despondent, so maybe leaving is the best thing–but going home certainly isn't.

Later . . .

If everything works out right I'll be going to the movies tomorrow–hopefully I'll catch two.

Sam and Rob asked me to stay on and run sound and I agreed. I have no reason to go home, so why not spend Christmas and New Year with the boys.

And they asked me."

"Saturday, Dec. 22nd, 1979–

I'm presently seated in the Capri Terrace Theater in Knoxville, Tennessee awaiting the beginning of *The Black Hole* which is in about a half hour. Surprisingly enough this isn't a bad theater: mildly large screen, reclining seats, decent sound system, this should be okay. After this I'm going to see *1941*, then I've got to get to the airport at 10:00 PM to get a ride back. Because of the late date I may be better off calling in my reviews to Ricki and have her transcribe them.

Scott Joplin rags are playing pleasantly as I wait out the purgatory of sitting in a movie theater before the film.

Later . . .

I'm sitting on the side of the road in Knoxville waiting for Ivan Raimi to pick me up. The instructions on how to get here were pretty easy, but Ivan'll never find it. Aside from having no sense of direction, he didn't pay much attention to me when I explained. I'm sitting here for naught."

"Sunday, Dec. 23rd, 1979–

Early this morning Rich, John, Don and Tom all left for home and now just the rot-gut cast and crew is left–and Ted Raimi [Sam's younger brother]. What he's doing here I couldn't say, however within an hour of Ted's arrival I wanted to kill him. I was vainly attempting to re-write my reviews and Ted did almost everything within his means to distract and annoy me, and thoroughly succeeded.

At this point I still have two reviews to do and my only recourse will be to read them to Ricki over the phone.

So now I'm the sound man. Although I haven't yet used the mixer, everything else is fairly simple. The stuff I did last night sounds fine."

Local kids wandered down to the cabin on occasion while we were shooting, generally asking, "Wanna smoke some wacky-tabacky?" which we always did.

Late one night a drunk, pot-bellied, snaggle-toothed hillbilly with the improbable name of Fats Derringer came wandering in, and asked, "Can I be in the movie?"

Sam looked at him and said very seriously, "Yes, of course you can." Sam turned to the rest of us and began barking orders, "Swing over those lights, get the camera over here, for God's sake, someone give him his lines!" We all jumped into action. Fats was utterly awestruck as he suddenly found himself the star of the movie. I quickly wrote out a few lines, Sam handed them to Fats, told him to speak them with real feeling, then we slated the shot, Sam called "Action!" and we shot it. Bruce played the scene with him, and Fats delivered the memorable line, "I don't want this damn shit!" Sam beamed with happiness, called "Cut! That was perfect! Print it!" and we turned back to what we were doing.

"Dec. 28th, Friday, 1979–
Another long night of shooting. It's 8:00 AM and I'm just going to bed.

Cameron and Ditz are here adding a new, dryer flavor of humor to the scene. John is apparently very bitter about this whole thing and has said that he hates Sam.

Interestingly enough, Sam and I are getting along rather well. He's a zombie, of course, bearded, dazed and confused, but he keeps it all going.

Tom Sullivan returned, a fresh, self-produced contract in hand, demanding the rights to all his creations, $100.00 a day for being here after his old contract expired (although that was amended) and an assurance that he leaves the 29th. After that we do our own make-up and effects.

Goodnight."

"Saturday, Dec. 29th, 1979–

Lately Tim Philo has been rather pointed with me and any others who don't immediately respond to the call of duty with sarcastic quips. Several times I have found appropriate moments to use his quips right back at him, which always makes him smile. He and I just went out to breakfast and talked and happily there are no hard feelings at all.

Tom Sullivan leaves today, which should add some major obstacles to filming. What's left is almost all special effects and make-up and the most difficult aspects of both. Although I almost totally agree with Tom's POV, his leaving us in the lurch with his effects on the line is rather self-defeating. His point that this film is an 'effects film' and he wasn't entrusted with his job until the last minute is valid, he should have been in on the proceedings from as early as possible. Anyway, his departure is going to make this last bit of filming a bigger chore than it already is.

And, this just occurred to me, if my reviews do not appear in this month's 'Magazine' I will be compelled to quit.

"Monday, Dec. 30th, 1979–

Actually, it's the last day of the seventies, but I'm running a day behind. The eighties will be ushered in as myself and my *compadres* frantically attempt to finish *Book of the Dead* before hell freezes over. The idea of working on a film through the decade change appeals to me, although more in concept than in reality.

Ellen left today for good. Theresa arrives tonight, Rich leaves Friday, Ditz and Cameron left yesterday, Ivan and Tom Perlman will be back tonight and immediately leave, Tim leaves Friday, and all that will be left will be Sam, Rob, Bruce, Goody and myself.

As for money, I've got $70., upon completion I should get between $250-300. and I have $100. at home. We're talkin' about $400.00 once I'm back in Detroit. I immediately owe $40.00 on the phone. The rest may get my car fixed and get me away for a while. Even better would be, if the dope drought in Detroit continues, stopping in Atlanta and scoring through Goody's connection and making a bit more."

"Tuesday, Jan. 1st, 1980–
Another long night of shooting, but not too bad since there was just the necessary people on the set.

Last night, in celebration of the new year, I ate some speed, drank beer, bourbon, and champagne, began feeling very lousy but had to work and after four or five bad hours made a comeback. The highlight of this New Years was getting into a massive firecracker war, not unlike the way Sam, Bruce and I spent New Years 1977-78.

Tonight I pushed Bruce to the breaking point. I kept squirting him with the shpritz bottle again and again until he gave me a the ultimatum that if I did it one more time he'd throw his cup of orange juice in my face. I squirted him again and lo and behold he threw his OJ in my face. For some inexplicable reason I totally enjoyed the whole exchange, even the OJ, possibly because once he'd done it he was totally off guard and the Bruce Campbell of old resurfaced."

Goody did all of the cooking and some of his concoctions were horrifying. He made pizza and mistakenly used baking soda instead of baking powder, and the crust rose six inches. We called it "pizza cake" and after a bite, most of us tossed it in the fire. Bruce, on the other hand, was so hungry he just ate it, saying, "It's not so bad."

Another time Sam, Bruce, Rob and I returned from the cabin and ate Goody's disgusting chili. One by one we slid off of our chairs and collapsed to the floor beneath the table. We all felt drugged and nauseous. We were convinced that Goody had intentionally drugged us so he could now come over and sexually take advantage of us and we wouldn't be able to struggle.

"Sunday, Jan. 6th, 1979 [year crossed out]–1980
Sam, Rob, Bruce and I went out to the set about 6:00 P.M. today, cleaned up, cut wood, set-up and got one shot, then came home for dinner. Afterward, Sam crashed and wouldn't get up so it's another night off.

We've all been talking a lot in the last several days, mainly about *Book of the Dead*, but also about other things. We discussed me at great length last night and Rob seems to think I'm lazy (as does

Goody). As a PA, that's true. But now that I'm recording sound, doing the lighting, and loading the cameras, I don't think so.

Tim left a few days ago, and since he was the one that borrowed
the Arri-BL from Wayne State University, he felt that he had to take
it back and return it. Sam wouldn't hear of it, and kept saying over
and over again, 'I need it for back-up. What if the Arri-S breaks?'
(Which, of course, it has). After Sam had continually pestered Tim
for several days, and at the last possible moment Tim finally relented, stating flatly, 'But you're not going to use it, it's only for back-
up.' Sam agreed heartily, 'Absolutely, just for back-up.' The second
Tim left the cabin, got in his car and drove out of sight, Sam turned
to me and said, 'Load the BL.'

Also, Sam offered me the job of helping him edit, and he and I
will begin cutting this film upon our return while Rob and Bruce get
more money. That's great.

And also, I think I may be able to adapt *Bloodbath* into a compact
half hour super-8 film. I think I'll also do a ten minute chase film,
too."

"Monday, Jan. 7th, 1979–[all crossed out] Tuesday, Jan. 8th,
1979–[the year is crossed out] 1980–

Today was ridiculous. In fourteen hours we got two shots. It's
finally gotten to the point where I consider *Book of the Dead* to be
partially mine. The first shot today was going to be a dolly from
Bruce's profile to his front. Now it's from profile to front, then back
and down for a low angle. The additions were mine. The shot of
Betsy lifting Bruce up is mine as well as the zooms from outside at
the stump through the window, as well as part of the tracking shot
of the van up Clinch Mt. and . . . the last shot of the film, when it's
shot, is all mine. I'm quite pleased about contributing. There's also
some inserts of Ellen running that I shot, although they probably
won't get used."

Friday, Jan 11th, 1979 [date crossed out]—1980

It's raining, it's pouring. It's 12:30 PM and not only are we not out
at the set, Rob and Sam aren't even awake yet. If we get anything
done today I'll be surprised.

Things have been going along fairly well, although slow. Each day
Sam or Rob is sure to say, 'We'll get twenty-five shots today.' I'd say

we're averaging about six or seven.

Yesterday, Rob was saying since he hasn't any written documents with Gary Holt he's not going to give him a percentage, which Gary is expecting. I asked how much of a percentage was Gary expecting and Rob replied 'I can't tell you.' Well, it's really no big deal and I actually don't care what Gary gets, but the fact that I'm here three weeks beyond my contract with no pay increase, I'm doing the lighting, loading both cameras, recording sound and most anything else that needs to be done (which is quite a bit), I really don't need any reminders that I'm merely an employee of Renaissance Pictures and not a partner. Everyone but Goody and Don Campbell made more than me and stands to make more if the film goes anywhere and *none* of them saw fit to stick this thing out–well, I'm kind of pissed. My only ulterior motive was that I might become part of the company, but now (and I've been feeling this down in the core of my being for several days now) I don't think I'll ever become one with these guys. I wasn't with them from the beginning and I'll never be allowed to forget it. As Rob is never wont in reminding me, I simply can't understand how difficult it was getting the money.

Fine.

Later . . .

Sam gave me the day off, although I certainly didn't ask for it. Along with the day off he also gave me a list of things to get and told me to go to the airport and drop off the film, which I just did and now I'm at the Big Boy across the street.

Back in the days when I was a PA and rather paranoid about being fired, Goody informed me today that my fears were justified and they were planning on firing me. Goody said he talked to Sam in the workshed and persuaded him not to.

Now I'm at Howard Johnson's having just seen *Going in Style*, which was interesting, but oddly written and paced and didn't really go anywhere. What was really neat was seeing the trailer for *The Shining*. There was more blood in it than all of *Book of the Dead*. Very effective.

Once again I get the odd impression I may be fired. I'll return to Morristown and be asked to leave–politely, yet firmly. It would be exceedingly asinine considering I'm nearly the whole crew, yet it's imminently possible.

Why am I unable to broach the subject of joining the company?

Because I'll be rejected, that's why. It's a stupid attitude and thoroughly in keeping with my past performance.

Now an hour drive back to grief."

[Written on the back of a folded script log form]

"Wednesday, Jan. 16th, 1979–[Though really 1980]

I'm going insane! Nothing makes any sense! I can't keep my mind focused on a single thought! My mental processes have no continuity at all! I just want to have one uninterrupted day of thought, but *Book of the Dead* will not end!"

"Thursday, Jan. 17th, 1979–[year crossed out] 1980–

We're presently watching rushes (I was, but I've escaped to the W.C.) and I don't much care (aside from the very few shots I did or lit on my own).

Yesterday, out at location, I began going crazy. I felt it coming, then awoke with the same persistent headache of the past four days, felt my stomach gurgling and wound up breakfast with a twenty-minute, gut-wrenching bout of diarrhea. The rest of the day was spent trying vainly to focus my mind on some thought other than 'B.O.T.D.', but it was impossible. Everyone thought I was acting nuts so I played it up a bit and practically did nothing the whole day.

My psyche is damaged. My health is damaged, and for what? $50.00 a week? Certainly not. Fame? Even if this thing hits huge I won't get any notoriety. Companionship? Possibly, however they have *their* projects and I mine and I just can't see them really coming together.

All day yesterday I was thinking of resigning and both Pam and Ricki called telling me that mom and dad were gone, the house is ours, school is great, etc.

However, if I quit now both Rob and Sam will label me as they have labeled everyone else–a quitter, and an asshole for abandoning them. This shouldn't bother me too much, but I want to make movies too and these guys could help me a lot, but not if I'm an asshole.

I can't go back to the cabin, though. I would if I were doing just this or just that, but that's not how things go. The only person who gets any personal enjoyment is Sam and what he enjoys tortures the shit out of me.

What to do?

And now, after watching rushes, Sam has even more things to re-shoot, aside from all that still needs to be shot for the first time. Two more weeks of this will ruin me.

Later . . .

The bulb on the projector blew and Bruce and I went to get a new one. On the way I told him of my feelings of bitterness and hostility and that I simply did not want to go out to the location anymore. He said he'd bring it up when we returned, which he did, like this, 'Josh wants to leave,' the topic immediately changed to: who can we get to replace him.

I broke in and explained just what was on my mind–again–said all that I needed to say, which was mainly directed at Sam and was agreed with, although first Sam got pissed, then insulting, then quiet. Sam has some splendid arguing techniques, but I was right and mad and he backed down.

And so, we're leaving next Wednesday (they say) and we have sixty shots to get and things as Sam says (for about the fourth time) are 'going to move.'

Why is it that it's always me that locates and elucidates the problems? Everyone else surely knows them, they just won't say anything. So why do I?"

"Tuesday, Jan. 22nd, 1980–
Things are coming to a close here on *Book of the Dead*. Tomorrow we are supposed to be out of this house, although we may not. The plan is to shoot until Friday. I was pretty sure this evening's shoot would merge with the next three, but luckily it hasn't.

As of Jan. 18th I have been *entirely* in charge of lighting and have been having a swell time. I'm trying a lot of extremely directional lighting and keeping everything at 5.6. This footage I can't wait to see. When Rob finally came to me and asked me to be in charge of the lighting, I said, 'Fine, but no else gets to touch the lights. That way it'll look better and I'll be done four times faster.'

Rob was hesitant, 'Uh, I don't know.'

I said, 'Yes, you do know. You're the producer. Make it happen.'

And so it was. And just as I said, it all started moving *much* faster."

"Wednesday, Jan. 23rd, 1980–
I just can't seem to keep it in mind that it's actually 1980. Maybe

after we leave Tennessee it'll become real.

We have almost exclusively exteriors to shoot and it's raining. Very poor luck. As things stand the shots we lack are all seemingly necessary for the film to cut.

It's rather interesting, although I'm not exceedingly well-versed in the art of lighting, what I've done so far does look visibly better than Philo's work and it plainly tortures Rob that it *all* could have looked better. Fine, he ought to be tortured.

We shall be leaving Friday or Saturday, I assume, but I'm not sure I can remember what life was like previous to 'B.O.T.D.' and I'm not sure I want to find out.

Even though Sam and I agreed I would assist him in editing (and we shook on it) I'm still a little skeptical as to whether I'll be editing or not. We'll see.

Anyway, I've got $116.00 in my possession, and about four weeks pay coming (if they have the money) which would be $200.00 and I've got $75.00 at home = $391.00. That should get me a little way.

Today's shoot was plain stupid. In about ten hours we got two shots. One shot took one hour, the other took nine."

I stepped on a nail protruding from a board in the cabin and it embedded about an inch into my foot. My whole body sort of curled up into a version of the fetal position, although I just kept working like a dog, lighting, running sound, loading the cameras, and finally operating camera more and more frequently. I had to do a panning shot of the car, driven by Bruce, to two fishermen on the side of the road waving, played by Sam and Rob. For one brief moment I lapsed into my own world of pain, then suddenly realized the car was coming and I hadn't even turned on the camera. I pushed the button in a panic, then performed possibly the worst panning shot in the history of motion pictures. Luckily, the next take went much better.

We ended up shooting straight through the final three days and nights to achieve all of the missing shots. At some point Sam stepped away from the camera, only he was still attached to it by the battery-belt he was wearing, and pulled the Arri-BL right over onto the 16mm Schneider lens, crushing it. At another point Sam fell asleep standing up behind the camera. I shook his shoulder and offered him a cigarette, which he took. I lit for him, then it fell out of his mouth and fell asleep standing up again. And at yet another point Sam, Bruce and I heard a thud and a groan outside somewhere. We went out to find that Rob had passed-out and collapsed into a half-frozen mud puddle. He was curled up in the fetal position, soaking wet, shivering, but sound asleep.

Those last three days were the toughest part of a very difficult shoot.

[These pages are folded and crinkled]
"Saturday, Jan 26th, 1980–
I just awoke at the cabin, along with Bruce, Sam, Rob and Goody, and could barely move on account of a headache developed from mental and physical abuse, beer, pot and sleeping on the floor. I took some aspirin (the staple of my diet over the past two weeks) and some vitamin C, drank some tea and improved somewhat–now I just feel awful.

In the very near future, probably less than ten hours, we shall be headed back home. This may have been the most difficult and the most rewarding experience of my life. I began this shoot bitter, unhappy and a PA. I end it fairly happy, exhausted, in mental and physical pain as lighting and sound man.

I've been thinking endlessly about *Bloodbath*. It's such a natural, yet warped idea — six marines take on the Manson family — that possibly a totally American, John Wayne treatment might be perfect."

Sam drove his car into a ditch for about the tenth time. He told Rob he couldn't shoot for a while and had to go up to the road and wait for the tow-truck. With a less than a day left to shoot at this location, Rob got completely furious that Sam thought his car was more important than getting the remaining shots. We had just moved outside to get the shot of Bruce leaving the cabin for the final time, but Rob, Bruce and I watched as Sam just walked away up the long driveway and disappeared from sight. I figured we were going to take a break now that the director had left, but Rob turned to me and asked, "Where would Sam shoot this shot from?" Having set up the camera and changed lenses for him for the past several weeks, I felt like I did know where he'd shoot it from. I walked over to the corner of the cabin, pointed at the ground and said, "From right here, on the ground on the high-hat, with the 18mm lens."

Rob looked at Bruce and I and resolutely said, "Set it up."

Bruce and I looked at each other, shrugged, and did as we were told. We ran a rehearsal and I suggested that Bruce stop on the porch, blind his eyes from the brightness, then keep going. It looked okay so Rob said, "Let's shoot it." We shot two or three takes of it and it seemed fine.

Sam came driving back to the cabin in his rescued car. I quickly moved the camera to another spot beside some other equipment, then we all played innocent like we'd simply been waiting for him the whole time. Sam suggested that we now get the shot of Bruce coming out of the cabin. We all shrugged and said sure. I asked Sam, "What lens would you like?" Sam thought for a second, then said, "Put on the 18." Rob, Bruce and I threw each other a look, then got on it. I brought the camera out and asked, "Sticks, baby legs, or the high-hat?" Sam said, "Put it on the high-hat," which I did. I then asked, "Where would you like it?" Sam looked around, then chose the exact spot where I'd just had it. Rob, Bruce and I nearly burst out laughing, but didn't. Now it had become a joke. As we ran a rehearsal Bruce suggested to Sam that he stop on the porch, blind his eyes from the brightness, then keep going. Sam nodded, saying, "Sure. Do that." So we shot it a few more times. And no one ever told Sam that we'd shot it without him, nor were any of us sure which take made it into the final film.

The last shot we did in Tennessee was the shot I thought up for the ending. Sam tried to avoid shooting it at all costs, but every time Rob would ask Sam what the last shot was, Sam would respond, "I don't know, but I know I need a crane." So Rob kept the cherry-picker for an extra week hoping Sam would tell him what the shot was, but Sam never thought of anything. Finally, on the last day of the shoot, Rob demanded that we shoot something for the ending, since there was a very good chance we would never be back at that cabin ever again. So, with no other recourse, Sam agreed to shoot my shot. It starts on a leaf, looks up at the cabin, goes racing toward it, then bursts through the back door going inside, knocks down the middle door, blows the front door to pieces, then goes right into Bruce's face. I set the whole shot up, too, since Sam didn't believe it would work. I hinged the middle door to the floor so it would fall properly (and I ran it), then I sawed the front door in half in a zig-zag pattern and attached ropes to both sides so you could just pull it and the door would fly apart. Rob and a local kid did that. Sam ran the camera, and it all worked like a fucking charm, too, and we were able to repeat it a few times. And that's the last shot of the movie.

When we were done shooting, we took all of the scrap lumber, broken props, garbage and extra sheets of glass, and burned it all in a giant bonfire. The fire got so big that burning ashes began to rain down all over the place and started fires in the dry grass and woods all around us.

We spent the next couple of hours running around like crazy men putting out one fire after another after another, and for a while it looked like we might set the whole forest ablaze.

Bruce and I drove the rental truck back to Detroit. As Bruce drove down the long driveway from the cabin for the last time, a low-hanging branch caught the top edge of the truck and tore the entire corner off. For the entire drive back we could hear the dangling ribs on the interior of the back of the truck banging from the wind getting in through the giant gash. Bruce and I spent most of the drive completely reworking *Bloodbath* into the story that became *Stryker's War*, which ultimately became my first feature film, *Thou Shalt Not Kill . . . Except*. We worked out the whole story, then Bruce fell asleep. I stopped at a restaurant and wrote out the whole outline on the back of several placemats. I shot *Thou Shalt Not Kill . . . Except* in 1984 and it was finally released in 1987. Sam played the Charles Manson-like killer in the film. But that's another story.

"Tuesday, Jan. 29th, 1980–
Back in Detroit."

When Bruce and I got back to Detroit, the first thing we did was return the equipment to the rental houses. First we got yelled at by the folks at Jack Frost Lighting Rental, since every light was damaged, several no longer worked at all, and all of them were coated and sticky with fake blood. Next, we both got severely reamed-out by the people at Victor-Duncan Camera Rental because the Arri-S was also covered with fake blood, and wasn't working properly (during the final week or so of the shoot we couldn't find the crescent wrench, so when Sam or I would mount the Arri-S on a piece of 2x4 for him to do the 'evil entity' or 'force' shots, we'd just tighten the bolt up as much as we could by hand, then twist the camera around until it was tight. When the technicians at Victor-Duncan took the camera apart to clean it, then attempted to put it back together, none of the pieces would fit. But we didn't know that just yet). What *really* pissed them off royally, though, was the crushed 16mm Schneider lens. Bruce and I got seriously hollered at, then informed that we would *never* be allowed to rent equipment at Victor-Duncan ever again. They eventually did rent to us again for the reshoots, but now there had to be a professional assistant cameraperson that was acceptable to them along on the shoot to supervise us.

By the way, once we got back to Detroit I was not asked to help with the editing of the film. And though I had vowed otherwise, I ended up working for them many, many times in the future.

There were extensive reshoots and pick-up shooting throughout the rest of 1980. Perhaps as much as 40% of the film was shot at that time. We shot for a week in Marshall, Michigan, at the Tapert family cottage, where we did all the basement scenes, as well as all the shots around the fireplace that had been rebuilt there. We shot for another week in Gladwin, Michigan, at the Campbell's summer cabin, where we did a lot of the vine-rape scene, as well as a second failed try at the film's opening of the evil force POV moving through a swamp (the first try was down in Tennessee, and it completely didn't work). Finally, at my insistence, we shot the opening for the third time in Hartland, Michigan at a vacant piece of land my father owned, and that came off perfectly. Sam was in a rubber boat, pushed by Bruce, and he took the Arri-S camera, grabbed it, then literally taped it to his hand to the camera with half a roll of black camera tape, thus allowing him to go right in and over stumps and glide along the swamp's surface. My job, by the way, was tossing giant chunks of dry ice into the swamp. We also shot for days in Sam's backyard, where we got all of the inserts for the vine-rape scene; in Sam's garage, where we shot the whole sequence that takes place in the cabin's basement, tracking Bruce along a fake brick wall until Rich jumps out and scares him. I did most of the lighting for these shoots. On the last night of shooting in Gladwin, which went all night, Tim and I drove straight back to Detroit to catch the very first matinee of *The Empire Strikes Back*, then we both fell asleep during the screening.

There was also a lot of special effects shooting by Bart Pierce, in his basement and in his garage. I assisted Bart and the others on a lot of this shooting. Bruce and I drove up to MSU to get a cookie jar full of live cockroaches to be used when the monsters melt down. A science professor took us to a storage closet that was lined with white plastic 10-gallon buckets filled with thousands upon thousands of various kinds of live cockroaches, including Madagascar cockroaches, which are the size of a bar of soap and hiss at you. The odor in that storage closet was perhaps the single worst thing I've ever smelled in my life. The professor reached into a bucket and grabbed handfuls of cockroaches and threw them in to Bruce's cookie jar until it was full. Bruce stood there frozen as roaches ran out of the jar and up his arms. I courageously and quickly backed out of the storage closet and as far away from the proceedings as I could get.

Book of the Dead was retitled *Evil Dead* and was released in 1983 to universal acclaim, and is now considered a classic in the low-budget horror genre.

Although I didn't realize it at the time, at some point during the shooting of *Book of the Dead* my childhood ended and my adult life began. Making full-length feature films that cost hundreds of thousands of dollars of investor's money is certainly an adult's game, and not something kids do. During that production, which still remains the most difficult shoot I've ever been on (and Bruce, too, and he's been on four times more shoots than me), we all put away our childish things and stepped into adulthood.

Josh Becker and Sam Raimi at the premiere of *Book of the Dead,* later retitled *Evil Dead* (photo by Mike Ditz)

The Japanese video cover of *Thou Shalt Not Kill . . . Except*

FX man, Gary Jones, applies fake blood to the leg of Brian Schulz, on the back of Robert Rickman, while shooting *Thou Shalt Not Kill . . . Except*, 1984.

July, 1979.

I sat on the brown vinyl, cowboy-themed couch embroidered with cowboy hats and cacti (that I had pilfered from a friend's backyard), in my cheap, tiny, poorly-ventilated apartment (with a Murphy bed), located at the foot of the Hollywood Hills, thinking very seriously to myself, "What's a good idea?"

At that point in my life, a month shy of my twenty-first birthday, I had written four full-length screenplays, and I was painfully aware that all of them were inept in one way or another. I had not yet in my life gotten a reasonable idea from which a rational, workable screenplay could be written, so just exactly what was a good idea was still a mystery to me.

I began thinking about bad guys. Why must everybody use Nazis or terrorists as the bad guys in their stories? Aren't there any other bad guys in the world?

The Manson family jumped into my mind. They certainly were bad. So, who fights them? The cops? They'd just arrest them, as they did. But who would really *fight* them? The Manson murders took place in 1969, what else was happening that year? The Vietnam War.

What if some soldiers got back from Vietnam, battle-hardened and trained to kill, and *they* fought the Manson family? Or, better yet, some Marines.

Hmmm? I mused about this for a while, then put it all out of my head.

The next day my friend Sheldon, a Marine vet who'd fought in Vietnam, picked me up to go out to lunch. The Marines versus the Manson family idea came back into my head and I pitched it to Sheldon. He laughed and jokingly said, "It should be called *Bloodbath*." We both chuckled and dropped it.

Later that night, Sheldon called me and said that he hadn't been able to get the idea out of his head; it wasn't a stupid idea, it was a pretty good idea. I suggested that we work on it together and Sheldon agreed. Sheldon, at this point in his life, had only written one inept screenplay, to my four, but we were in approximately the same early place.

Sheldon and I spent the next couple of months working on the story and writing the script. The end result was a 185-page script that was very, very serious and not much fun to read. I was displeased and told Sheldon so. He didn't really care because he had already moved onto a another script, an even more serious Vietnam War story.

I moved back to Michigan and subsequently worked on *Evil Dead* down in Tennessee. Throughout that whole shoot my mind kept drifting back to *Bloodbath*.

When *Evil Dead* was over, on the drive from Tennessee back to Michigan in a big Ryder truck (which, having gone under a thick, low-hanging branch, Bruce had managed to tear the roof off of within 10 yards of our location), Bruce Campbell and I discussed the *Bloodbath* story idea at length. I already had an approach that I wanted to explore—since the idea of the Marines fighting the Manson family was so warped, why not tell it like an all-American John Wayne movie? Attempt to get a rooting interest going for the Marines instead of just feeling bad for them, then ashamed of them as the first draft had done.

Bruce and I kicked the story around for hours as we drove north, accompanied by a giant, metallic, clunking noise coming from within the back of the truck, caused by the metal ribs being blown around through the new hole in the top of the truck. When we finally had the entire story worked out, and Bruce had fallen asleep, I pulled into a restaurant, had coffee, and wrote everything down on the back of a placemat (that I still have somewhere).

Back in Michigan I got a job as a security guard at a construction site from 5:00 P.M. to 5:00 A.M. A lot of time to do very little. So I brought a little, portable typewriter with me each night and began writing the 2nd draft of *Bloodbath*. My intention was to write a short script that I could potentially shoot in Super-8 making a 30-45 minute pilot film to use as an investment tool to help raise money for a feature. After several weeks of work, I had a 38-page script that I rather liked. Wanting to differentiate this version from the last one, I renamed it *Stryker's War* (Stryker is John Wayne's name in *The Sands of Iwo Jima*). I made copies, gave it to all my buddies in Michigan, and sent a copy to Sheldon. My Michigan buddies all liked it and agreed to help me make it into a movie. Sheldon, on the other hand, blew a gasket. He yelled at me for a solid hour about how bad it now was and how terribly I had ruined a good idea.

I then put together $5,000 dollars to shoot the pilot film. Luckily for me, right at this time I got laid-off from the security guard job. For the one and only time in my life I received unemployment benefits, which I viewed as my state film allotment.

Principal photography began on the Super-8 pilot version Aug. 25, 1980, with Bruce Campbell starring at Stryker and Sam Raimi as the Manson-like bad guy, and we finished shooting on Sept. 2. While shooting the biggest scene in the movie, where the Marines come to free the hostages at the Manson-held campground, it began to pour rain, thunder and lightning flashing and crashing all around. A bolt of lightning struck a tree about 100 yards away, severing a limb. Scott Spiegel, playing one of the Marines and wearing his uniform, ran perhaps 50 yards to his car, started the engine, burned rubber screeching away up the road and disappeared as 30 people watched. The storm blew over and about 20 minutes later Scott returned, his whole body visibly trembling. Scott said, "I panicked."

We then shot inserts and pick-ups whenever people were available for the next three weeks. As Bruce and I were shooting inserts on the front lawn of his parents' house, Bruce's older brother Don (who plays one of the Marines in the film) stood by watching, occasionally poking Bruce in the side with his toe. Bruce told Don to stop it and Don persisted. Suddenly, Bruce turned around and stuck Don in the arm with a screwdriver, embedding the point deep into Don's flesh. Don went insane, kicking Bruce as hard as he could, then chasing him all over the neighborhood holding his wounded arm and screaming bloody murder.

Armed with the 45-minute pilot version of *Stryker's War*, I then attempted on my own to raise several hundred thousand dollars to make it into a feature film. In the course of the next year I got absolutely nowhere. I did write and rewrite the feature version of the script many times, but was once again unable to raise any money.

Undaunted, I took the pilot film and the feature script to Hollywood, got an agent at ICM who (honestly) said, having neither watched the film nor read my script, "This kid is the next Steven Spielberg." I began hanging around Roger Corman's New World Pictures. I bothered Corman's assistant, John Schouwieler (now a producer), so often for the next several months that he finally let me in to see Roger Corman. As I stepped into Roger Corman's office it finally struck me that he was one of the senators in *The Godfather Part II*, which I hadn't realized until that moment, and I said so.

He smiled. "Yes, I was. I'm sorry, I don't have a job for you."

That was that with Roger Corman.

I took a number of meetings, but they all came to naught. My agent at ICM never called me back once in five months.

So I dropped *Stryker's War* and moved on with my life . . .

Four years went by. Scott Spiegel and I, now partners, had spent the previous year and a half vainly attempting to raise money for a slapstick feature called *Cleveland Smith Bounty Hunter* (we'd shot a 16mm pilot this time) that we knew we couldn't produce for a penny less than $600,000. After two grueling years of hundreds of meetings with prospective investors, we had raised exactly $18,000. On August 17th, my birthday and the day we were *supposed* to start shooting, it was totally apparent to both of us that we had failed. Desperately, I suggested going to L.A. Scott countered, suggesting, "Then let's shoot the feature version of *Stryker's War*.

"With $18,000?" I queried.

"How much did the Super-8 version cost?" asked Scott.

"Five grand."

"So, we've got almost four times that much."

I seriously considered what he said, then uttered the fateful words that have launched so many other great and foolish enterprises, "Sure! Fuck it! Why not?"

We planned to start shooting Oct. 1, come hell or high water. To prove our point we purchased $5,000 worth of film stock from Kodak and left it sitting in the middle of the office floor so everyone had to step over it. (As a technical note: I chose 400 ASA color 16mm film stock, the highest-speed film available at the time. This goes against the common wisdom for a 16mm film that one intends to blow-up to 35mm. The idea being, keep the grain fine by using low-speed film stock [and a lot of lights] so when the grain is magnified to four times it's size it won't be too grainy. All the scenes that took place in the woods, which was a lot of the film, would need lighting and I didn't have the money for a lot of lights or a generator, certainly not a real movie generator that was quiet. With 400 speed film I could easily get an exposure in the woods or anywhere else for that matter with very little lighting, so I decided that the grainy look in 35mm would be part of the gritty aesthetic of the film. Quite frankly, I think this worked out fine. The high-speed film stock blew up to 35mm without a problem).

In the next six weeks Scott and I put together our gigantic cast (there are about 100 different actors in the film), our small, completely untrained, crew, and a million period props and vehicles from the 1960s. (In retrospect *Stryker's War* was an insane movie to make with so little money).

We began principal photography on the feature version of *Stryker's War* on Oct. 1, 1984. Here is my one journal entry for the month of October, 1984 (the top left corner of this page of yellow legal paper is torn off and taped back on).

"Mon, Oct 7, 1984

It's 6:00 A.M. and I'm taking a shit before shooting today. We have all of the Vietnam battle footage except four shots and a few inserts. Today we do interior car dialog. My crew is inexperienced, generally unprepared, but dedicated and having a good time I believe. My cast is also inexperienced, but dedicated and look good together. Presently Brian Schulz who portrays Stryker is the weakest link. Robert Rickman as Jackson is the best and is doing a swell job of stealing the picture out from under Schulz, who is so busy with character interpretation he can't see it. I am directing, shooting, producing (with Scott), managing, running, and starting today, lighting this film. Oh my . . . It's all working, but I could use some help. Michelle Poulik is doing pretty well at wardrobe and props, Pam [my younger sister] is panicking as coordinator, Scott is getting by as co-producer, Ann and Brian Belanger take up a little slack as A.D.s, etc. I just have to remember every single detail. Right now we are about to film a scene and the Marine's uniforms have no rank insignia. "

Robert Rickman, who played Sgt. Jackson, was Detroit's Mr. T impersonator, and was working at the state fair when Scott and I first saw him. He was as muscular as is humanly possible, and far more ripped than Mr. T. We contacted him and got him to come into our office. Robert arrived acting very tough, wearing a baseball cap to cover his Mohawk haircut. I told him, "If I cast you in this part, which is the second-lead in the movie, you have to promise to give me 100%." Robert said, "If I take this part I will absolutely give you 100%." He did take the part, and as it turned out he was as sweet as could be and did a very good job. Since Robert needed to keep his hair in the Mohawk for upcoming Mr. T gigs, we had a make-up FX artist named Roger White make hair pieces that fit into the slots, which he called "T-tops."

By Oct. 10 we were completely out of money. After the first week the film lab, Producer's Color Service in Detroit, continued to process our negative, but no longer printed dailies. For the next six weeks I would call the lab, speak to our sales representative (a very nice guy), and ask, "Is there an image on the negative?"

"Yes," he would reply. "When are you going to pay your bill?"

"Soon."

Then I would proceed to shoot as though everything were fine.

Desperate, and ready to close down the production, I asked my father for some money. He had already turned me down before, and after I explained my situation, he flatly turned me down again. Luckily, though, my mother slipped me $3,000 on her own. Scott weaseled another couple of grand out of his little brother and his mother. Then we both begged Sam, Bruce and Rob and got another $5,000. Now we could feed the cast and crew and even make some half-assed attempts at paying people.

Regarding my younger sister, Pam, who was working as coordinator and panicking, every time I came into the office she seemed to be yelling about something or at somebody. I finally took her aside and told her she was no longer allowed to yell under any circumstances. Pam said, "I do everything around here!" I replied, "No, you don't. If I get rid of you, within fifteen minutes everything will just keep moving along and no one will even remember you ever worked here." Well, Pam wigged-out about something else and began screaming, so I fired her. Except that we were both living in the same house with our parents. When I got home my mother said that Pam was sorry, she promised not to yell anymore, and I really should hire her back. So I did, and she didn't yell anymore, either.

Or biggest stunt was pushing a motorcycle over a cliff. We managed to finagle four cameras—one at the top, two on the side, and

the main camera at the bottom, operated by me. We then loosened
every screw and bolt on a Honda 350 that we had gotten for free to
its final thread and pushed it over the cliff. The motorcycle stayed
100% together, and three of the four cameras missed the action—all
except the main camera, that is. But, we had a tow truck standing
by with a very long cable and winch, and hauled the bike back up to
the top and did it again. This time parts flew off and all four cameras
got the action.

I had a scene of Stryker leaving the veteran's hospital. I called the
Detroit office of the Veteran's Administration and attempted to get
permission to shoot at the veteran's hospital, but they said I had
to get permission from the Washington office. Yeah, right. I took
the camera and Brian Schulz in his costume and we went to the
Veteran's Hospital. I explained the shot to him in the car—go in
the front door, wait one minute, then come out the door and walk
slowly down the steps looking all around. I had the camera set up
in about a minute, Brian went up the steps and through the door. I
zoomed all the way in on the front door, on the Veteran's Administration logo, rolled the film, the door opened and Brian stepped out.
I slowly zoomed back as he walked down the steps until I could see
the entire front of the old hospital. Brian exited frame, I cut, we got
back in the car and got the hell out of there. The entire maneuver
hadn't taken ten minutes.

There's another scene of the Marines leaving a military base. I
didn't even try to get permission from the military. We simply showed
up at this little military installation, I got out with the camera, Scott
with a few others in the car drove right through the open gate, did a
slow circuit inside past lines of camouflage military vehicles, I shot it
through the fence, the car drove out the gate, I grabbed the camera,
got in the car and we split. We never saw any military personnel at
all.

Sam Raimi as the Manson-like cult leader is mainly seen riding
a Kawasaki 750 that we had borrowed from an old friend. At the
end of the first take with Sam actually operating the motorcycle, he
tried to slow down and turn and ended up just dumping the bike on
its side. Well, a 750 is a big heavy bike, and the weight of it falling
crushed the entire side of the bike, the handlebar bent, the mirror
shattered, the gear shifter mushed in—total disaster! We had to have
all of that fixed, too.

Meanwhile, I only had Sam for one week, so I made sure to get every shot facing him, then we picked up all of the shots behind him with doubles. In the scene where Sam is being shot repeatedly in the chest, all done by Gary Jones with his own homemade squibs, the reverse shot of Sam's back is really me. I had six of Gary's squibs go off on my back, then I had to fall down a cliff. When I did this stunt I twisted my leg so badly I thought it would break off at the hip. Anyway, when Sam saw the reverse angle of the stunt he began yelling, "Who is that? That's terrible! Who is that?"

I said, "Sam, it's me."

He was horrified. "*You?*"

"Yeah, and I really hurt myself doing it, too."

Sam was also doubled by Danny Merritt, our exuberant 1st AD, and also by Ted Raimi in a few shots, too, and Ted's about six inches taller than Sam. Ted's performance as Sam from behind particularly amuses me because Ted appears to be playing Sam as some sort of a monkey. When Sam saw that footage he was also doubly horrified. "Now who's *that*? They're even worse!"

"That's Ted."

We found this great old log cabin about a mile from my parents' house and used it as Stryker's cabin exterior. There's a scene in front of the cabin of Stryker chopping wood, then his buddy walks up, they do some dialog, then enter the cabin. But no matter how hard Brian Schulz tried he simply couldn't chop the wood. After about his tenth failed attempt, Brian broke down and began to cry. He said, "I never chopped wood as a kid. I didn't play with guns, either. I'm just not right for this part." Well, I'd already been shooting with him for a week, so there was no way I was changing lead actors at that point. This was my first real test as a director. I took Brian aside and calmly assured him that his performance up until then had been just fine with me, that he was certainly a good enough actor to play this part, and it wasn't necessary to have lived it. I also said that he didn't have to chop the wood, either, just embed the ax in the stump like he'd just finished, then play the scene. And that's what he did, and it all went great. After everyone else was gone I got a series of close-ups of the ax splitting several logs and I cut those in at the head of the scene.

Our last location was Bruce Campbell's house in Southfield. Bruce and his wife and kids were out of town, so we took over the house and built our sets in the garage. Some of the last scenes we got there were the interior bunker scenes, supposedly in Vietnam, but actually in Michigan in very cold, late-November weather. I had to have all the characters smoking cigarettes and cigars to hide the steam coming out of their mouths. I also lost my 1st assistant cameraperson, Bridget Alexander, somewhere before the end and so I wound up directing, shooting, loading and lighting. At one point at night, shooting inside Stryker's cabin, which was really Bruce's garage, it was freezing cold and I was standing in the back of the grip truck with my hands inside a changing bag trying to load film into a magazine and I just couldn't do it. My hands were too cold and I was just too tired, but I had actors and a crew inside and I had to keep going. And as hard I tried I could not get the film through the sprockets in the magazine. I finally did load it, though, and we kept on shooting.

Another of these last scenes shot in Bruce's garage was the conclusion of Act II, when each of the Marines has seen the cult members committing various crimes, then they all return to Stryker's cabin, tell what they saw, then they decide to "Go clean 'em up." We ran the scene a few times and it simply wasn't playing very well or coming to life. Oh well, time to shoot. We shot the scene a few times and it still wasn't playing very well, but I honestly didn't think I could get it any better, so I said, "Okay, moving on." Robert Rickman got mad for the one and only time during the shoot and stated, "I didn't feel it."

I nodded, "Me, neither."

"Then why are we stopping?"

"Good question. What do you think the problem is?"

Robert pointed directly at Brian Schulz. "He is. I don't feel anything from *him!*"

Brian's eyes lit up for the very first time that day and he said to Robert, "Oh, yeah? Fuck you!"

Robert said, "No, fuck you!"

I said, "Going again."

And the next take, which in fact finally had some life in it, is the one in the film. Thank you Robert for doing my job for me.

Somehow or other we wrapped principal photography on Nov. 21.

At the wrap party, Robert Rickman came up to me with a beer in his hand and said, "You never asked for a 100%." And it's true, I never did.

Scott, Bruce, Gary Jones, Paul Harris and I just kept shooting and picking up inserts with a Canon Scoopic camera for months—rifles cracking open, shells being loaded into chambers, bottles exploding, Asian hats being squibbed, Asian extras getting shot in the head, hand grenades flying through the air. My favorite insert is a tight close-up of a switchblade snapping open during the bar fight, that was actually shot in our office against black velvet with a star filter on the lens so that when the blade appears it glimmers in a star-shaped flare.

But this was all in an attempt to try and fill in what was clearly a deficient production. Scott and I had truly pulled this production out of our asses out of sheer and utter desperation, and we never had anywhere near enough money to make this script properly. But we made it anyway.

My mother and father, having just watched us pull off damn close to a miracle, now amazingly stepped in and financed post production. They put up $80,000 between them. Sadly, I couldn't help thinking, and still do, that if I'd just had half or even a third of that money when I was shooting I could have made a *much* better film.

I edited the film myself on a 16mm KEM flatbed editor with just my pal, Paul Harris, there as the one and only assistant, synching sound to picture and keeping track of all the film. This took about four months. All of the scenes cut together in one way or another, but man, what a cheesy production.

Then Bruce Campbell stepped in as supervising sound editor. We hired a half dozen Wayne State University students to edit the sound, among whom was Wendy Stanzler who went on to edit *Roger & Me* (which was shot with a lot of the same crew as *Stryker's War*). Wendy also edited half of all the episodes of *Sex and the City*, and she's now a TV director.

Joe LoDuca, who had previously scored *Evil Dead*, came aboard as composer. Joe's score, in my opinion, is the single best thing about this entire film. It's a full orchestral score with a five-piece ethnic accompaniment (Asian flutes and drums). I own a lot of soundtracks to war films: *Patton, 1941, MacArthur, The Great Escape, The Sand Pebbles, The Battle of Neretva*, etc. Joe LoDuca's score for this film stands up there with the best of them. I only wish it was available on CD (and it will be soon, along with three of his other scores for my films).

I am particularly pleased with the front title sequence, edited together from actual Vietnam news footage. Since you pay by the second for stock footage, I purchased 60 seconds, then had it all double-printed into slow-motion making it two minutes, then printed the titles on top of it.

The sound for the film was mixed in Toronto, Canada at Filmhaus Sound, where we got a very good deal due to the U.S./Canadian exchange rate. It was fun hanging out in Toronto with Bruce and Scott for a week, too.

Our film was then taken on by Irvin Shapiro and his company, Films Around the World, an overseas sales agency that also handled *Evil Dead*. Irvin, who was then about 85 years old (and one of the founders of the Cannes Film Festival in the 1930s), didn't like the title *Stryker's War*. "It sounds like people are on strike and at war." Irvin had changed *Book of the Dead* to *Evil Dead*. So, in an attempt at appeasement, we changed the title to *Sgt. Stryker's War*, which nobody liked.

The film premiered at the Universal Theater in Warren, Michigan to a standing room only crowd of 700 people on Sunday, Oct. 13, 1985. We had listed not only every actor, but every extra in the credits, which was literally over a hundred names. Right after the film ended, Tom Davis, the actor who played the speaking role of the sheriff, came up to me and said, "My name's not in the credits," and it's not. We'd somehow missed it. I didn't know what to say because I certainly wasn't going to replace the titles.

Irvin Shapiro called one day soon thereafter and said, "The new title of your picture is *Thou Shalt Not Kill . . . Except*."

I said, "That doesn't sound like a title, that sounds like a tagline."

"Nevertheless, that's the new title of your picture."

I was flabbergasted. " *Thou Shalt Not Kill . . . Except?*" I repeated, certain I must have heard him wrong.

"Yes."

I considered it for a moment, then said very honestly, "I don't think I can live with that, Irvin."

"Do you want me to represent your picture?" he asked flatly.

"Yes." I most certainly did.

"Then the new title of your picture is *Thou Shalt Not Kill . . . Except.*"

And so it was.

With the new title Irvin began selling the film to all of the territories of the world. He set up a video deal with a now defunct company, Prism Video, and I received an advance of $50,000, which completely paid off my mother's investment, and a quarter of my father's, too.

Everything was starting to go pretty well, when sadly Irvin became too ill to run the company anymore. He sold out to man who will remain nameless here, but from this moment on I never saw another cent.

Thou Shalt Not Kill . . . Except had a 25-print, 20-city theatrical release. It played in eighteen theaters in metropolitan Detroit. I saw it at an old theater, The Norwest, in a crummy part of Detroit, in a double-bill with another Michigan-made feature, *The Rosary Murders* (written by fellow Michigander, Elmore Leonard). After the movie I followed two black teenaged girls out of the theater to hear their comments.

One of them said, "It was funny."

The other said, "It was stupid."

The film moved slowly across the country, opening in fewer and fewer theaters in each city. Eventually, every single one of the 25 prints was lost.

After not receiving anymore money back for a couple of years, and consistently being treated like a jerk, my father began to really get mad at me. He'd say, "Make that guy give you the money he owes you." I'd reply, "Oh, yeah? How do I do that?" Then I'd get a lecture on how a real businessman works. So, one day when my dad was around, I called the sales agent and asked if he'd speak to my father, then I handed my dad the phone. The sales agent treated my dad exactly like he treated me, like a jerk, and when my dad hung up he was furious. "We'll sue the motherfucker!" said dad.

Which we did, and won, but it was in the wrong venue, so we got no money. Then we sued him again, this time in another venue, and won again, but we still got no money. So we sued him yet again in yet another venue (New Hampshire, I think), won again, and still didn't get any money out of him. The only satisfaction we ever got was making him fly from New York to Detroit in a snowstorm for a deposition. And my dear old dad ended up dropping about $50,000 in legal costs over several years.

Finally, in 1995, I was able to get my film elements (meaning the negative and the soundtrack) back from Technicolor in New York, where of course the sales agent had left a $5,000 unpaid bill, that I had to pay. At least I was then able to make a new video master and make a new deal on the film, which I promptly did with Anchor Bay Entertainment, who already handled *Evil Dead*.

I just recently signed the contract for the film to begin it's fourth video/DVD release (first was Prism Video, then Good Times Video, then Anchor Bay, now Synapse Films), so it has stayed in constant release for over 20 years, since it was made. Since most movies completely disappear off the face of the Earth within a year or two of their initial release, this is something of an accomplishment, particularly for a film that was literally shot in my backyard.

Thou Shalt Not Kill . . . Except plays at The Harris Theater in Times Square, NYC, 1987, a true grindhouse that's long gone.

The Life Span of Creativity

I'm sitting here listening to Paul Simon's album *Graceland* for the eight millionth time, and it's still as impressive as it ever was—catchy tunes, infectious rhythms, and very witty lyrics. I purchased his new CD, *You're the One*, yesterday and it's just awful. There isn't one catchy tune, nor a single interesting lyric. This is the worst album of Simon's long career, and I didn't think he was capable of such poor work. But the fact of the matter is, not only is Paul Simon capable of such a thing, everybody is. The difference between Paul Simon and most other people is that he did so much distinguished work. That the great work will stop is inevitable; that it ever begins is the giant hurdle.

Age will ultimately extinguish creativity, generally a long time before physical incapacity or death. Some guys, like Orson Welles, for instance, are over the hill when they're twenty-six years old. Others, like Alfred Hitchcock and William Wyler, keep making quality product into their seventies. Rarely do any filmmakers make anything of value once they're in the eighties. At that age just staying alive and defecating regularly are apparently big enough jobs.

But something makes certain people need to create, as opposed to merely procreate. Of the six billion plus people on the planet right now, most will live out their lives without ever creating something new or unique or interesting.

Perhaps creativity is simply a manifestation of a very strong sense of self-expression—*I did this! Me! Nobody else!* Or perhaps it's a form of curiosity—*What if there were one of these?* Or maybe it's just one more meaningless enterprise to amuse ourselves during our allotted life spans, and really nothing has any meaning.

Well, who wants to deal with that? So we arbitrarily choose things that do matter to us: I like movies, my buddy likes James Bond books, my Dad likes golf. *La!* What's the difference? There isn't any. For some reason the films of William Wyler or Alfred Hitchcock seem more significant to me than the adventures of James Bond or the career of Arnold Palmer (although the life of golfer Ben Hogan made a pretty good film called *Follow the Sun*).

But, should you decide to create stuff, the chances are you won't be able to keep it up for any length of time. Should you have the ability to create art for any length of time, the chances are it won't be very good after a point.

Alfred Hitchcock and William Wyler's careers represent the longest examples of sustained commercial creativity in the film industry. Hitchcock's first hit film was in 1926, *The Lodger*, and his last hit was in 1972, *Frenzy*, which is forty-six years of making commercial and critical hit films. Wyler's first hit film was in 1929 with *Hell's Heroes* (after five years of directing silent westerns), and his last hit film was in 1968 with *Funny Girl*, which is thirty-nine years. Both men made one film after their last hit that completely dropped dead.

The shortest important film career is probably still that of Jean Vigo, who made two classic films in a row, *Zero For Conduct* in 1933 and *L'Atalante* in 1934, then died at the age of twenty-nine just as the latter film premiered. Bummer. There was also Steve Gordon, who wrote and directed the big hit film *Arthur*, then promptly dropped dead right after the film was released in 1981. It's not as though Jean Vigo or Steve Gordon's creativity inexplicably stopped, their lives stopped, and that fate lurks around every corner for everyone.

But what about Francis Ford Coppola? The dynamics of his career have been plaguing me for most of my adult life. He was considered the film *wunderkind* in the 1960s for some reason, even though none of his films from the 1960s are all that good (*You're a Big Boy Now, The Rain People, Finian's Rainbow*). But in the '70s Francis Coppola was legitimately the hottest, most creative filmmaker there was, and that was a particularly good period of filmmaking. In 1970 he won an Oscar for "Best Adapted Screenplay" for *Patton*, (with Edmund H. North, who had previously written *The Day the Earth Stood Still*), in 1972 he directed and co-wrote the "Best Picture," *The Godfather*, and in 1974 he produced, directed and co-wrote the "Best Picture," *The Godfather Part II*, and also had another film nominated for "Best Picture," *The Conversation*, that he had written, produced and directed. Mr. Coppola finished off the decade with *Apocalypse Now* in 1979. That's a seriously impressive run of films.

But Francis Coppola hasn't made one really good film in the following twenty-five years, although he's made quite a few films. The best of the bunch is probably *Peggy Sue Got Married,* and that was certainly no cinematic milestone.

So what happened to him? Was it too much cocaine in the Philippine jungles while making *Apocalypse Now?* Too much sustained stress? Perhaps it was finally having too much money and success? Does it matter? I don't think so. His creative period ended for whatever reasons, and it hasn't come back. Nor should we expect that it ever will.

When creativity ends, it never returns. You may be able to sustain it for a period, but when it's dead it's dead. You simply have to be thankful that you ever had it to start with. What about one-hit wonders? Every time I hear "Spirit in the Sky" by Norman Greenbaum or "Nah Nah, Hey Hey, Kiss Him Goodbye" by Steam, I can only think: they sure sound like they know what they're doing, why couldn't they do it again?

Duke Ellington wrote and recorded sharp, intelligent, interesting music from the 1920s through the 1970s, with the same guys in his band for most of that time. Admittedly, there were stretches of his career when he wasn't very popular, but he weathered them. The Duke's biggest selling album, *Live at Newport,* came out in 1956, twenty-five years into his career, and man, it swings.

Carlos Santana's biggest-selling record, *Supernatural,* came thirty years into his career. But neither Ellington nor Santana ever stopped. They just kept on making music their own way, and the audiences came and went and came and went.

Seventy doesn't seem all that old anymore, but there are damn few working seventy-year-old filmmakers. Sidney Pollack, Sidney Lumet, and Norman Jewison and none of those guys has made a good film in years. Their films are all professionally produced and generally okay, just like Coppola's, but they're all unexceptional.

What about seventy-year-old writers? Novelists, seemingly yes, but not screenwriters. Probably the only working screenwriters in their seventies are William Goldman and Alvin Sargent. There are probably aren't all that many working screenwriters in their sixties. This to me seems like the biggest error the film business continues to make. Screenwriting is so hard and so elusive that anyone who has ever displayed the ability ought to be courted and showered with money until their dying days.

There have been a few playwrights, novelists, composers, and conductors who kept it up until they were old but not many. George Bernard Shaw and Groucho Marx both still had a few sharp barbs left in them in their eighties, just as Aurturo Toscanini and Herbert Von Karajan were still kicking orchestras' asses into their nineties. But we're down to counting on fingers and toes at this point.

The man whose career I am spiritually attempting to emulate is John Cassavetes—who by financing his own movies got to make exactly the movies he wanted to make—and he worked steadily right up to his death at age fifty-six. At this point I would be hard-pressed to write and direct as many films as John Cassavetes did, forgetting all the films he appeared in.

Very few people escape the precedents of history. Sure, there are a few Gandhis and Alexander the Greats, but only a few. For the most part we are buried far too deeply and quickly in our own mundane circumstances to ever become another Gandhi or Alexander or Mozart. By the time we figure out what we want to do, let alone how to do it, we've already used up a great deal of our allotted years. We all just didn't get started early enough.

Precedents prove that seventy years old is the absolute creative dead-end in the film business—Hitchcock was seventy-three when he directed *Frenzy* and Wyler was sixty-six when he did *Funny Girl*. In the film business, where youth is idiotically venerated, *sixty is old!* Realistically, TV and movie writers rarely get hired past fifty.

So, here I am, already forty-three (forty-nine now) years old. I got to Hollywood when I was eighteen, sneezed, and *wham!* it's twenty-five years later. What the hell happened? I feel like I've hardly gotten started.

I am asked with some regularity who is my favorite filmmaker? I always reply without hesitation that it's William Wyler. Sadly, most young folks no longer know who Wyler was—unlike his contemporaries, John Ford, Howard Hawks or Alfred Hitchcock. Nevertheless, for nearly forty years William Wyler was probably the most respected director in Hollywood. His films received twice as many Academy Award nominations and wins as the next two biggest directors combined. Charlton Heston, near the peak of his career in 1958 (1959 was the *real* peak), took fifth billing in *The Big Country* just to work with Wyler. This was a very smart move on Heston's part for two reasons: (1) it's the best part and best performance of his entire career; and (2) it got him the lead in Wyler's next film, *Ben-Hur*, for which Heston won the Oscar for "Best Actor" (that is truly a tribute to Wyler's abilities, since I don't think any other director who ever lived could have gotten an Oscar-caliber performance out of Charlton Heston).

Beyond any of that, I believe that William Wyler made more good movies than any other director, ever, living or dead.. His consistency was exceptional. Between 1933 with *Counsellor-at-Law* (which is undoubtedly John Barrymore's best performance on film) to 1968 with *Funny Girl* (Barbra Streisand's best performance on film), Wyler did not make anything but top-notch, excellent films. In fact, in those thirty-five years he almost never even made a mediocre film (with the exceptions of *The Gay Deception*, in 1935; *The Children's Hour* in 1961,although he had already made a first-rate film version in 1936, called *These Three*; and the unfunny *How to Steal a Million* in 1966).

William Wyler was not a writer, yet he was most definitely an *auteur*. From 1946 onward he chose his own stories and completely controlled the writing process, bringing in the writers he wanted, having scripts worked on for years, and finally deciding when it was time to shoot or abandon them.

Wyler began his directorial career in 1925 churning out innumerable cheap westerns for Universal. In 1929 he managed to make one cheap western, *Hell's Heroes* (the first sound version of the oft-filmed story, *The Three Godfathers*), into an honest-to-goodness hit, resulting in his promotion to directing A-films. For ten years Wyler was independent producer Sam Goldwyn's number one director and is responsible for most of Goldwyn's classic films, such as: *These Three, Dodsworth, Dead End,, Wuthering Heights, The Little Foxes, The Westerner,* and *The Best Years of Our Lives.* During that time Goldwyn lent Wyler out to Warner Brothers (this is back in the days of exclusive contracts), where he made the classic films, *Jezebel* and *The Letter.* Goldwyn also leant Wyler to MGM, where he made the exquisite film, *Mrs. Miniver,* winner of the 1942 Oscar for "Best Picture" and got Wyler his first of three "Best Director" Oscars—the only director with more was John Ford with four.

Even though Wyler is my favorite director, I do not try to emulate him in my own directorial technique and never will. He was renowned for shooting many, many takes, and being very hard on actors. He made Henry Fonda do forty takes in *Jezebel* and Wyler's only direction between takes was, "Again." Fonda finally broke down, demanding to know what the problem was. Wyler casually replied, "It stinks. Do it again." And they kept right on going. Wyler was also known for frequently going over schedule and over budget. I think it's very important to get along with the actors, come in on time, and stick to the budget. If this means I'll never be as good as Wyler, so be it. I love Wyler's films, but I can't work his way.

Wyler had a theory that after about thirty-five takes actors get so angry and exasperated that they shed all of their preconceived notions about acting and the part they're playing, moving to a truer, higher level. The real problem with this approach is that, once you push an actor that far, you'd better be prepared to go to those lengths on every shot just for the sake of consistency. This approach made for a lot of hard feelings on his sets. Bette Davis, who considered Wyler the best director she had ever worked with, walked off the set of *Jezebel* and didn't return for two weeks. Nevertheless, any time he offered her a part she immediately took it. When she worked for Wyler she was always nominated for an Oscar (Bette Davis won "Best Actress" twice, the first for the non-Wyler film, *Dangerous*, in 1935; the second for Wyler's film, *Jezebel*, in 1938). On the set of *The Big Country*, after thirty or forty takes of a shot, Carroll Baker broke down and screamed, "Why are you doing this to me?" Wyler casually replied, "That's easy. They pay me to get you to do what I want you to do. Now do it again."

I believe that we've reached a point in time when *entertainment* is synonymous with *thoughtlessness*. William Wyler *always* made entertaining films that were *never* thoughtless. He never pandered to a wider audience. From early on in his career he was intent on making thoughtful adult films and never went back on that idea. And his films were very, very popular.

William Wyler came to prominence in 1936 when he had three films out: *Dodsworth*, *These Three*, and a co-directing credit (with Howard Hawks) on *Come and Get It*. The last film was done as a favor to producer Sam Goldwyn and, in my opinion, is not legitimately part of Wyler's *ouevre*. "Best Picture" in 1936 went to *The Great Ziegfeld*, a dreadfully overlong bio-pic loaded with painfully dated, overblown musical numbers. "Best Director" went to Frank Capra for *Mr. Deeds Goes to Town*, the first of Capra's average-man Capra-corn movies, and the film that introduced the word *doodle* into the American lexicon. Frank Capra began pandering to public tastes with this film and didn't stop for the rest of his career. Pandering begins with the question, "What do *they* want?" "They" being the simple-minded, unwashed masses. To avoid pandering, in my opinion, one begins with the question, "What do *I* honestly think is good?"

I have always viewed the "Best Director" Oscar this way (I will use 1980 for my example)—could Robert Redford, who won "Best Director" that year for *Ordinary People*, have directed *Raging Bull*? (which was nominated and lost, but should have won). Could Martin Scorsese have directed *Ordinary People*? I think he could have done it without much trouble and would have made as good a film (different, certainly, but no doubt as good). Could Redford have directed *Raging Bull*? Not in a million years.

Could William Wyler have directed *Mr. Deeds Goes to Town*? Certainly, no problem. Could Frank Capra have directed either *Dodsworth* or *These Three*? Never. None of Capra's films are nearly as sophisticated and intelligent as these two by Wyler (the only film that comes close for Capra is *American Madness* in 1932). Wyler, on the other hand, had just made *The Good Fairy* in 1935, which, though somewhat zanier than Capra's stuff, is still a great example of that same sort of goofy, populist, the-average-person-comes-out-on-top kind of storytelling (with a wonderful script by Preston Sturges). Wyler and Capra were in business together for a short while right after World War II. Their company, Liberty Films, produced one film, *It's a Wonderful Life* (that they forgot to copyright). Wyler took the script *Roman Holiday* with him when he left the company, a film that Frank Capra wanted to do and probably would have done well. But Wyler did *Roman Holiday* as well as humanly possible, and discovered Audrey Hepburn at the same time.

Incidentally, Wyler directed the early career-launching films of a number of big actors: Audrey Hepburn, Barbra Streisand in *Funny Girl*, Anthony Perkins in *Friendly Persuasion*, Henry Fonda in *Jezebel*, and both the Dead End Kids (later known as The Bowery Boys) and Humphrey Bogart in *Dead End*, Laurence Olivier in *Wuthering Heights*, Montgomery Clift in *The Heiress*, and Lee Grant in *Detective Story*.

Another admirable aspect of William Wyler's career is that he changed subjects all the time. You say John Ford, and you think western (which is a bit unfair); you say Frank Capra, and it's those populist pictures; you say Howard Hawks, and it's men's stories; Hitchcock, suspense; Scorsese, tough guys, etc. You say William Wyler, and all that comes to my mind is "terrific movies." What his films have in common is that they're all good and they're all different.

Can anyone tell that the same guy who made *Wuthering Heights* also made *Roman Holiday, Detective Story, Ben-Hur, The Collector* and *Funny Girl*?

When I was ten or eleven years old I stayed up after everyone had gone to sleep to watch *Dead End* on TV. I think that I was expecting to see a film like *Angels With Dirty Faces*, also with the Dead End Kids and Bogart, but made two years later in 1939. After the film was over, I remember turning off the TV and actually having to sit there and think about what I had just seen, deeply upset by the realistic depiction of poverty and violence. But this was an old Hollywood movie with the Bowery Boys and Humphrey Bogart shot entirely on a set (although, admittedly, it's a terrific set). What the heck was going on? I can't say that at that moment I became aware of William Wyler, because I didn't. I just felt *really* bad for those characters and the plight of the human species which could cause such squalor and awful behavior. I also recall attempting to discuss this feeling with my parents and having absolutely no idea where to begin.

What Wyler, with the author Sidney Kingsley, did to the eleven-year-old me is what I think movies can do best. I was completely transported to the grim, dirty, poverty-ridden New York streets of 1937 in the middle of the Depression, and I was totally empathetic. Just like my relief when Walter Huston decides to stay with Mary Astor in *Dodsworth* is completely real. My shock at Bette Davis in *Jezebel* arriving at the big ball in a red dress is real. My horror at seeing beams of light coming through bullet holes in the roof of the car in *Mrs. Miniver* is real, too. Harold Russell arriving home after the war with hooks instead of hands is as real as movies have ever gotten. Montgomery Clift pounding on the door at the end of *The Heiress*. Audrey Hepburn asleep on a bench in Rome. Laurence Olivier turning on the gas at the end of *Carrie*. Kirk Douglas going into a complete meltdown when he hears his wife, played by Eleanor Parker, has had an abortion (in 1951!). Feeling the helplessness of Fredric March and his family being held hostage by escaped prisoner Humphrey Bogart in *The Desperate Hours*. Feeling the overwhelming horror of having taken the life of another human being as young Anthony Perkins touches the body of the southern boy he just killed during the Civil War. These are many of the best moments in movies ever.

William Wyler's mission was to get me to care about these characters in this situation, whatever it may be. That's what I think the primary job of a film director is—getting the audience to empathize with the characters. This is what William Wyler did best, and, in my opinion (as well as that of the Academy of Motion Pictures Arts and Sciences), he did it better than any other film director so far. That's why William Wyler is my favorite director.

31-year-old Josh on location in downtown Pontiac, Michigan, shooting *Lunatics: A Love Story,* 1989.

The Making of
Lunatics: A Love Story

February, 1988, was truly the winter of my discontent.

I was sitting on the back step of the bungalow that I shared with two other guys vainly attempting to figure out a way to save my own life. I hadn't paid my rent in two months, I had no food, my parents weren't interested in my problems anymore, and I absolutely hated where I was living. My former friend and writing partner, but still my roommate, Scott Spiegel, and I had already come within an hair's breath of getting into a fist fight. He pushed me on the chest and I backed him into a corner with my fist raised. It was getting ugly.

So I sat on the back step, that wasn't even close to being a porch, just a step, squinting in the bright sunlight at the fence that was two feet in front of my face blocking my view of an alley, desperately attempting to figure out a plan so that I wouldn't starve to death or die from exposure, both of which seemed like imminent possibilities.

I thought to myself, "If I can just get a good idea then I'll have something to sell. A good idea, that's all I need." I sat there for hours, my face twisted into a knot, the muscles in my neck as tense as taut steel bridge cables, thinking: *What's a good idea? What's a good idea? What's a good idea?*

I couldn't get one.

So then I began to think, what's a good title? Maybe if I can get a good title, the idea will follow. Then I began to run down the terms for insanity that had been used as titles: *Psycho, Madman, Maniac, Nuts, Crazies, It's a Mad, Mad, Mad, Mad World, Dementia 13.* And then it hit me, no one had ever used *Lunatic.* I dashed for my Leonard Maltin book and found: *Luna, Lunatics & Lovers, Lunch Wagon.* No plain old *Lunatic.* All right, now what do I do with this title? Hmmmm? What if, instead of singular, it was plural and was about *two* lunatics? A boy and a girl, and it was a love story? Hmmmm? I sat there running it back and forth in my mind waiting for it to sound stupid—*Lunatics*, the story of two crazy people falling in love. After a half an hour I could sort of see the story. The boy is an agoraphobic who hates to go out; the girl is stuck outside and can't go in. It was all there. Why she couldn't go in I didn't know, but otherwise it was all there.

I called my friends at Renaissance Pictures, then located in a trailer on the Universal lot, and set up a meeting with Rob Tapert and Sam Raimi. They were developing *Darkman* at that time, but weren't shooting anything. I got Sam and Rob into Sam's office, closed the door, got them to both shut up at the same time (no mean feat), and pitched them what I had: *Lunatics*, a crazy boy and a crazy girl fall in love. He can't go out, she can't go in. I added for their benefit, "It could be done *very* cheaply. At least half the movie would take place in his apartment." Then I added in desperation, spitballing, "With a lot of hot, crazy sex."

Sam and Rob looked at each other in silence, making serious faces of consideration. Finally, Rob said, "I like it." Sam nodded, "Me, too." And I had a deal. I got $2,500 in advance for the first draft, then I'd subsequently get five hundred dollars a draft thereafter. I wasn't going to starve to death, at least not then.

I rented an apartment on Bronson Ave. in Hollywood from a very creepy Armenian man, collected my meager amount of stuff together and moved out of the bungalow on McCadden. As I carried boxes out to my car Scott yelled after me, "My new film [*Intruder*] is going to come out nationwide with three hundred prints, and have a million dollars in advertising! It's going to be ten times of a bigger hit than *Thou Shalt Not Kill . . . Except* ever was, just wait and see!"

I hauled away my boxes without taking the bait. I took the color TV that had been leant to me and left my little black and white so that Scott and Mike would not be without a TV (I tried to get it back from Scott several years later and he had given it away). When I carried out my last box I said to Scott, "We've been friends a lot longer than we've been enemies. This, too, shall pass."

I think he told me to fuck myself, but I can't exactly recall.

Intruder never did get released theatrically. Strangely enough, I still haven't seen it.

I moved into my new apartment, above a carriage house and behind an abandoned, boarded-up house, and began work on the script for *Lunatics*. In four weeks I knocked out a first draft. This version would probably have been rated 'R' or 'NC-17', which did not exist at that time. Rob and Sam seemed to like what I had delivered, but wanted changes. As they both said frequently, "Make it better." They also decided to tone it down, remove all the sex and the drug references, and go for a PG-13. I was completely against this, but got soundly shot down. I decided to go with the flow and to not get too stubborn about anything. I would give them exactly what they asked for, with a smile, since I not only needed the money, but I sincerely wanted to get this film made, and this seemed like how it was done. Hell, it was exactly what Sam was being put through on *Darkman* by Universal at the same time—draft after draft after draft. Well, if Sam could handle it, so could I (as a little historical note: *Darkman* ended up being written by three sets of brothers, the Raimi brothers, the Goldin brothers, and the Coen brothers [who went uncredited], as well as Chuck Pferrar (the guy who wrote *Hard Target*).

I delivered a draft a month for the next five months. The first draft was included in the $2,500 first payment and the other four were $500 each. I had spent a good deal of the initial payment getting out of debt and the remainder on the first, last, and security for the new place. My rent was $400 a month and I paid my own utilities. I covered all of this with my $500 payments leaving me thirty or forty dollars a month to live on.

One day while pounding away on one of the drafts of *Lunatics* on my little Apple 2-C computer, having written all morning without saving to disk (sorry, no hard drives back then), suddenly the power went out. I lost four hours of work in a micro-blink. I ran to the door and saw the Department of Water and Power man screwing around in my fuse box.

"Hey!" I called down. "What's the deal?"

The DWP man barely glanced my way. "You didn't pay your bill."

"Yes I did."

"No you didn't."

I went and got the bill and my checkbook and showed them to the guy. He looked at the bill then at his work order, then grinned sheepishly.

"I'm at the wrong address. Sorry."

He turned my power back on.

Sam was very involved in the development of *Darkman* and wasn't really paying much attention to my frequent drafts of *Lunatics*. Rob was the one who dealt with the script development of *Lunatics*. He really got into it, too, and spent a great deal of time at my place discussing it. (The skull emblem on Debbie Foreman's black leather jacket in the movie was something Rob and I saw a cute girl wearing at a movie theater in Hollywood). But with each new draft Rob kept pushing this "tone it down to PG-13" approach harder and harder, causing me to finally ask, "Aren't we making a an edgy, low-budget, independent movie?" The response I got still puzzles me. Rob said, "Pap-a-size it," meaning turn it into "pap," which is mushy, semi-liquid, infant food, or undemanding reading material. Why anyone would want to intentionally turn their work into mush was, and still is, entirely beyond me.

But I have no doubt that that's what Universal was doing to them, so they turned right around and did it to me. Moe slaps Larry, Larry slaps Curly, and Curly doesn't get anyone to slap. I knew what we were doing to my good idea was wrong, but I did it anyway—I *needed* to get another movie made.

At this point I realized that Ted Raimi, who had previously been in every movie I had ever made, would be perfect for the lead character of Hank. Both Sam and Rob enthusiastically agreed. This also added a guilt factor on Sam's part regarding helping his little brother's career, and that was just fine with me. Anything to get the picture made.

However, after I delivered the fifth draft, that Sam and Rob both agreed was an improvement over the fourth (that they said had been an improvement over the third, etc.), they now felt that they could not put anymore money into this project. *Lunatics* was about to drop dead, just like most film projects do.

This was a crossroad for me. I liked a lot of what I had done so far with the script of *Lunatics* and wasn't willing to let their present money problems deter me. I was not about to let this project die. So I declared that they didn't need to pay me anymore, I'd keep rewriting it for free until I got it right, meaning to *their* satisfaction. Sam and Rob were both flabbergasted by this extremely un-Hollywood-like response, and readily agreed since there was nothing for them to lose.

To finance this enterprise I moved back to my parents' house in Detroit, that just happened to be sitting empty at the time due to my parents' impending divorce.

For the next six months I knocked out a draft a month. I'd mail them off to Hollywood and get them back with Rob's notes. Back and forth, back and forth . . .

By the eleventh draft I finally wore the poor sons of a bitches down. The story had gone off in strange directions, but Rob felt that it was nearly ready to shoot. He contacted Bruce Campbell and David ("Goody") Goodman who signed on respectively as producer and co-producer.

Bruce and David read the eleventh draft and were both utterly confused since it seemed to bear very little resemblance to the idea and story that they had been told. I explained to them that I thought the script had started going wrong after the fifth draft, but since that was clearly the process, I had just run with it. They asked to read the fifth draft, and they both liked it *much* better, as did I. They told Rob that they would produce the fifth draft, not the eleventh, and Rob immediately said yes. So why did I write drafts six through eleven? Just to keep the project alive, I guess. Luckily for me, the voices of reason got us back to draft five (which was still "pap-a-sized" from drafts one and two), or this movie would have really been a piece of crap.

Bruce and Goody then made their notes that brought on two more rewrites addressing their problems. There was also another rewrite, entirely of my own doing, that strictly addressed the dialog, and this was brought on by hearing live human beings speak the lines.

Bruce had the legal work started, then he and David and I began the arduous task of raising money.

Many, many meetings and several months later we had $300,000 of the $600,000 we said we needed and we decided to go ahead and make the movie anyway.

Bruce had recently starred in a film called *Sundown: The Vampire in Retreat* with Deborah Foreman, with whom I was familiar from *Valley Girl* and *My Chauffeur*. Bruce suggested her for the female lead, Nancy, and I wholeheartedly agreed. I thought Debbie was very cute and sexy, and seemed to be able to act, too. Bruce said that we might actually have a good chance at getting her because she had had so little dialog in her past several pictures, and her short career already seemed to be in eclipse (her part in *Sundown* was exclusively to look sexy in a mini-skirt and carry a machinegun, something she could do effortlessly). Whereas, my script for *Lunatics*, as a complete change of pace, was pretty darn talky (all of Act II was the girl and the boy in his apartment talking for 30 minutes straight), and Bruce was sure that would interest her. Debbie in fact read the script promptly took the part.

With these two actors in the leads, I now thought I potentially had something special going on with this film. There suddenly seemed like the real possibility that the movie could actually work, and maybe even be a hit of some sort, a thought I'd never seriously entertained before. That's if I didn't fuck it up in the direction, of course.

We rented an abandoned elementary school in Auburn Hills, Michigan, not far from both The Palace, where the Detroit Pistons play, and The Pontiac Silverdome, where the Detroit Lions used to play. Although we were never able to put *all* the different rooms in the school to use, we did put quite a lot of them to use. There was: the production office (with Bruce and John Cameron, the 1st A.D./ Unit production manager); Mr. Goodman's office; the other production office (where both I, the associate producer, Ruth, and the copier, were); the art department/ special effects office (formerly a large art room, with tiny little toilets, which was particularly amusing in that all the effects guys were big dudes, led by the three burly Jones brothers); the loading room; camera storage; then upstairs there was costume and make-up; the actor's dressing rooms; and the rehearsal room.

I actually got a week of rehearsal, a truly unique thing to get on a low-budget movie (and something I've never had since). We ran the whole script, and had all of the actors come in at least once, but for the most part it was just Ted, Debbie and I working on Act II, which was basically a one-act play: 30 minutes all in one place, and in real time. Because we had that rehearsal we were able to fly right through the shooting of that entire act in three days, equaling third of the movie.

The school's gymnasium was our soundstage. Under the supervision of our production designer, Peter Gurski, we built all of Hank's apartment interior, with every room connecting to every other. This allowed me to follow the character all the way through every room, something I actually did.

Rob flew in a few weeks before we started shooting. He made one good decision and one bad decision, then left. The good decision was that he saw the layout of the set and stated, "Make it bigger." Peter Gurski, a very friendly and amenable guy, said that the set was already awfully close to the gym walls, barely leaving space to get around it. Rob nodded, "Make it bigger anyway. You'll thank me later." He was right on that one. The bad decision was that we were having difficulty making the schedule work out between day and night shoots. Rob said, "That's easy. Instead of it becoming night at *that* scene, have it become night a scene later and there you go, your schedule works." Except that I had big plans for the sunset scene that got scrapped for no real good reason. I had planned on having it become sunset during Hank's long phone conversation with his mother, that not only never cuts to the mother, but never cuts at all, nor does the camera move, for about five minutes—a *very* long time in a movie. What was going to make this scene spectacular was that during the course of that five-minute conversation the sunlight coming through the window would constantly be moving down, casting longer and longer shadows, until it finally changed from day to night, leaving the depressed Hank in a bluish twilight. It would have been great, but it was now not to be. The executive producer had made the change in the schedule and that was that. Well, without that lighting effect the scene is just too damn long and not covered properly. I ended up having to get a shot of Hank's feet later so that I was able to cut into the scene and delete some of the dialog, that now went on too long, but it could have been beautiful.

Deborah Foreman, Ted Raimi, Josh Becker making
Lunatics: A Love Story, 1989

While the sets were finished being built, we began shooting on the streets of Pontiac, Michigan (standing in for the streets of Los Angeles. Sam and Rob's company, Renaissance Pictures, was also shooting *Darkman* at the same time, that took place in Detroit, but was shot in L.A.). Pontiac is known for two things: it's where they make Pontiac automobiles, and it also has an inordinate amount of mental hospitals and halfway houses (when my older sister and I were little and acted crazy around my Hungarian Grandmother she'd say, "You should go to *Poontiac!*"), so it was the appropriate place to shoot a film called *Lunatics*. During shooting one night an African-American man walked past yelling, "*You got white stars! You got black stars! You got polka dot stars! Hollywood in Pontiac!*" But I must say truthfully that the city of Pontiac could not have been nicer or more helpful. We were given free office space while we shot on the streets. It was like having our own backlot, with free crazy extras.

Lunatics was shot in 35mm in twenty-four days of principal photography, with three days of 2nd unit pick-up (the 2nd unit was the stripped-down main unit, which is a good way of doing things). The film began shooting on Sept. 11, 1989, and wrapped on Oct. 13.

At the exact stroke of twelve hours of shooting on the first day, when I was very nearly set up to shoot my final shot, Bruce came out and pulled the plug. "That's a wrap." I couldn't believe it. I was within five minutes of shooting, and it would have taken perhaps another ten minutes to get the shot. When I asked why, Bruce stated flatly, "Twelve hours is twelve hours. Take that into consideration next time." And you can bet I did, too, and always have since then.

Bruce hired the whole camera crew as a package, without discussing it with me. I'd have a agreed anyway, but still. The young DP/operator, who was a reasonably nice guy, tried hard, and did some cool lighting, occasionally had a weird sort of dyslexia regarding camera placement. When shooting inserts—the tight close-ups of items in people's hands or people's hands doing things—he would frequently set up the camera in some place other than where I had requested him to set it up, and it was always in the wrong place, meaning over the 180-degree line. And then he stubbornly wouldn't move the camera, stating emphatically, "Inserts don't have screen direction," which is flatly incorrect, inserts most certainly do have a screen direction. This caused almost daily confrontations between the DP and I, most of which I won, but some I didn't. These over-the-line inserts always make me wince whenever I see the film.

The 2nd AD got fired within a week, having nothing to do with me. She didn't seem to have a clue what she was doing, that really angered John Cameron, the 1st AD, and he fired her. That was okay with me because all through the first week, every time we were just about ready to shoot and I went to find my seat underneath the camera's lens—this was in the days before video assist, when the director always sat directly under the lens—I'd find the 2nd AD already sitting there. I'd ask her, "May I sit there?" and she'd reply, "I was here first."

Otherwise, it was a lovely shoot. This was the first time I'd ever had anything close to a real crew, with a gaffer and grips and people to haul everything around instead of me. I kind of felt guilty at the end of the day not helping to coil all the cables and carry in the equipment, but I got over it.

The gaffer, George Lieber, who was very good at his job and a pleasure to work with, was consistently ten or fifteen minutes late every morning. One morning standing around the craft service table, George picked up a bagel and complained, "The bagels are always stale." John Cameron remarked offhandedly, though quite loud, "Huh, that's funny, they were fresh at call time."

There was a scene that got cut out of Hank banging his head on the floor. I stressed to Ted, who was young and full of piss and vinegar then, how important it was that he fake it and not really pound his head on the floor. All he needed to do was to just bring his head quickly to somewhere near the floor, and with the aid of a thudding sound effect it would sell and be fine. Although I honestly didn't want him to hurt himself, more importantly, I had a lot more scenes to shoot that went before and after this scene and I didn't want any continuity problems (as a little note, there was no script supervisor/continuity person on this film, so all continuity issues were my own). Anyway, I called "Action," and Ted began pounding his head on the stage floor for real, hard. I quickly called "Cut." Ted looked up and blood was pouring down into his eyes. There was a gash at the center of his forehead, that was followed promptly by a big red lump. Exactly what I was hoping wouldn't happen. The make-up department went to work using spackle and putty, and we continued shooting, but there are several shots where Ted's forehead is slightly distended and discolored in a Frankenstein sort of way.

Sam Raimi showed up on set one day and appears as an extra in the hotel lobby. Many of the investors appeared as dressy extras for the wedding scene at the end. My mom and Rob Tapert's parents are both in the scene, too.

In that four weeks of shooting I managed to ruin three brand new button-down shirts by putting my pen back into my shirt pocket upside down.

Bruce got mad at me on the day we shot the battle with the evil doctors in the hallway (one of whom Bruce plays, so he was there watching me instead of being in his office). Bruce looked at my storyboards at the beginning of the day and said, "You've got too many storyboards." I brushed him off and said, "No, no, I'll be fine." I had 75-100 drawings of all the various individual punches and parries, broken into various sized inserts, as Hank battles five or six masked doctors each with variety of implements, like syringes and gas masks and X-ray machines, and I didn't have one whole day scheduled to shoot the scene. I also still had other scenes to shoot that day. Well, there was no way on earth I could shoot 75-100 tricky inserts in ¾ of a day, it's not possible, and that became plainly evident one shot into the process. I stood there with Bruce in his doctor's mask and gown costume, Bruce pointing at his wristwatch, as we both watched the crew very quickly light the set, bring in and set up the dolly, assemble everything that was needed, get the actors, touch them up, then we rehearsed the scene, then we shot it a few times and guess what? Over an hour had gone by.

Bruce took me aside and said very seriously, "Okay, what are you going to do? It took an hour to get the first shot, and you have ninety-nine more to go."

During that hour my mind had just been whirring, as I got hotter and hotter under the collar. This was the exact moment I realized the difference between drawing little pictures, and actually envisioning the scene in advance and anticipating what was humanly possible in the time allotted, which is quite a different thing. So I said, "I've got a plan." And indeed I did have a plan, one I've used many times since, although I certainly didn't know it would work then. I said, "We'll shoot the whole fight with all six doctors going one way down the hall, all hand-held; then we'll relight and shoot all the fights going the other way." And that's what we did, and I got that day, and the scenes that needed to be shot after it, too.

Unfortunately, once we finished shooting the whole process came to a grinding halt due to lack of funds. Money-raising efforts continued, but progress was slow. So as to not let the momentum completely die yet again, I moved to California, installed myself in the editing room where Kaye Davis, editor of *Evil Dead 2*, would eventually cut the film, if and when we could afford to rent a flatbed editor and pay her, and I began to log all of the footage by edge-numbers (the little tiny numbers near the sprocket holes)—a long, arduous job, usually performed by several 2nd assistant editors. Sam and Rob were kind enough to pay me $250 a week for my services as a 2nd assistant editor. I came in everyday for months and logged all the footage myself.

Finally, a KEM flatbed editing machine arrived one day and Kaye went to work. My buddy Paul Harris from Michigan (who had been the assistant editor on *Thou Shalt Not Kill . . . Except* and *Evil Dead 2*) came in to be 1st assistant editor. I stayed on as 2nd assistant because I needed the money, plus I was in a perfect position to watch everything Kaye did to the movie.

Once our first cut was done we promptly ran out of money again.

We had an old friend from Michigan, Dan Nelson, hastily edit a very rough 10-minute show reel on ¾ inch video, then Renaissance Pictures got an overseas sales agent to shop the film around. Warner Bros. was interested for a while, then Columbia Tristar saw the reel at Cannes and showed real interest.

A deal was made with Columbia and on July 9, 1990 a check for a quarter of a million dollars marked "1st payment" arrived at Renaissance Pictures. We were back in business.

At the end of July we had four days of pick-up shooting with both Ted and Debbie. Sadly, Debbie had cut her hair very short, so she had to wear a wig in all the pick-up shots. It looks okay in most of the shots, but completely shitty in a couple of other shots. There's a crane shot that moves up from Ted walking one way below to Debbie walking the other way above, and the wig is crooked. I'm still horrified whenever I see it.

Ted and Debbie were a pleasure to work with, and both of them were totally dedicated to their parts and the movie. I think Debbie's scene in the phone booth talking to her uncle is very well-performed. I also think the scene on the couch with the two of them, leading up to and through him punching her in the mouth, is really terrific stuff, if I do say so myself.

For a low-budget movie there were a lot of various kinds of special effects: a stop-motion animated spider that was supposed to appear to be 10-feet tall; a giant brain set with many animated spiders crawling all over it; a miniature of the entire block around Hank's building for the earthquake and fiery fissure hallucination scene; a camera-move through a keyhole, into an eyeball and then into Hank's brain; rear-screen projection with stop-motion animation on the screen (a technique used in the 1933 *King Kong*). We hired all of our low-budget special-effects wizards in Michigan and installed them in the elementary school. Gary Jones was the special effects supervisor, Dave Hettmer created the animation, Ed Wolman did the optical effects, Jeff Ginyard supervised the construction of the miniatures. Gary's two brothers worked on the FX, too.

Here are two cool aspects of the miniatures: the front of the lead character's building is covered with posters. Jones, Ginyard & Co. photographed the posters, then made color Xerox reductions that were perfect little posters. Also, when the street is cracking open on the miniature set, the little foil-covered Hank is one of those spring-loaded toys where you push the bottom and the guy's arms and back sag, then you let go and he straightens up. By using the mechanism in the toy Hank is waving his arms and moving his upper torso while the street cracks below his feet. Very clever.

The only scenes that I was forced to cut out of the film that I miss are both in Act I—and I readily admit that Act I is too long—and both were little bits of Hank's contentious relationship with the electricity in his apartment. At one point he turned on the TV and got a shock. At another point he looked over at the electric socket, it pushed into a close-up of Hank while simultaneously pushing into a close-up of the electric socket, then it cut to the electric socket's point-of-view of Hank, while buzzing angrily. What these scenes set up, that's still in the movie, is when Nancy leaves, Hank reaches for the doorknob and gets an electrical shock, and that's why he can't leave. Also, during the rap song it still goes to a POV from inside the stereo, and was also part of this whole electrical thing. Anyway, it's about a minute's worth of footage, and since Act I was already inordinately long, at 45 minutes, another minute didn't seem like a big deal to me. La!

Bruce and I did all of the post-production sound at a place in Detroit called Joseph Productions, run by a very nice guy named

Sheldon Neuman (Sheldon had done all of the sound transfers for *Torro, Torro, Torro!* and *Cleveland Smith* for me). We worked on the first digital sound system and, from what Sheldon told us, we were the very first feature film to be entirely sound edited and mixed digitally. Sheldon was on the phone to George Lucas a few times during this two-month process who was apparently the co-owner of the company that made the digital sound system we were using. [All sound is edited and mixed this way now].

At this point in stepped Joe LoDuca with his usually grace and aplomb, composing a brilliant, jazzy, bepop/hip-hop music score, making *Lunatics* seem far hipper than it really is. Once again, Joe came through with a top-notch score. I also had the great pleasure of writing a song with Joe, the rap tune in the film called "The Reynolds Rap." I wrote the lyrics, submitted them to Joe, who funked-up my white man's wording, then composed the music to my stolen beat (thank you Run DMC). Bruce and I both thought it would be a good idea to hire a real, local rap band to sing the song and appear in the film. We auditioned eight or ten rap bands, chose one, and gave them the song. They called back the next day and said that they really didn't like my song, and that they would write another song based on my song that would be much better, and much hipper. Bruce and I thought, okay, let's give them a chance. But since there also wasn't much time, we only gave them one week. They stalled us for another week, then finally cut to Bruce and I in a little lawyer's office in some funky part of Detroit meeting with the whole band—there were five of them—as well as their lawyer, their manager, and their agent (a big posse for a small band). We went through a lot of introductions and explanations, that began bordering on excuses that were quickly becoming apologies. Finally, Bruce cut in and said, "Could we just hear the song. Whatever you've got of it." One of the guys hesitantly pushed a button on a tape player, a rap song started, played for a minute without any lyrics, then the guy shut it off. He said sheepishly, "We haven't had much time to work on it." I said, "Apparently." Bruce and I excused ourselves as quickly as was polite. As soon as we got outside we both said, "Fuck these guys." We immediately contacted the next-best rap band we'd auditioned, Detroit's Most Wanted. As I handed them my song I said, "This is the song we're doing. It will be produced by the film's composer, Joe LoDuca. Have you got a problem with that?" The three of them all shook their heads no, and everything went swimmingly from there on out. The song turned out fine, and I think it's kind of funny.

Lunatics ends with the song "Strangers in the Night." Since we could only afford the lyric rights, not the rights to Frank Sinatra's original recording, Joe hired a Sinatra sound-alike who does a terrific job fakin' Old Blue Eyes. When choosing the Sinatra sound-alike, Joe sent me a tape entitled, "Dueling Sinatras."

Bruce and I got into our single worst fight of the entire production during the sound mix. Bruce knows a lot about sound and has supervised sound editing on several features (including *Evil Dead* and *Thou Shalt Not Kill . . . Except*), and I still understand where he was coming from, but since I'm the one writing this history, I get to tell it my way. Since over half of the film takes place in Hank's apartment, located in downtown Los Angeles, I wanted a symphony of sounds going on outside his windows: car alarms, sirens, snatches of operas, arguments in Spanish, car brakes, the multitudinous sounds of a city. Bruce, as Producer, got rid of most of these sounds, explaining, "They get in the way of the dialog." Well, there's a lot of Goddamn dialog and I wrote it so I certainly didn't want to drown it out, I simply wanted all of these sounds behind it. Bruce, as Producer, overrode me. A friend of mine who is now a director, but was formerly a top sound editor (*Terminator 2* and *Bugsy,* among others), watched *Lunatics* and said that she liked the film, " . . . but there just weren't enough background city sounds." *D'oh!*

Once the film was completed and printed, (and, at my insistence, the title was officially changed to *Lunatics: A Love Story*) we had a screening for Columbia Tristar, who still had the right to back out of the deal if they didn't like the film. In which case we would then owe them a quarter of a million dollars. Well, they watched the film, liked it, and the deal was consummated. It wouldn't have been a bad of a deal, either, if there hadn't of been a sales agent involved skimming 33% right off the top. The agent did set the deal up, however, and for his couple of weeks work he made more money on *Lunatics* than everyone else combined. The investors (and Renaissance Pictures) all got their investments back, plus about 3% profit, which is better than losing your money, but that's about it.

The deal was also for "in perpetuity," meaning forever, and that seemed incredibly unwise to me, and I said so. I also wasn't happy about there being no theatrical release, and therefore the film would get no reviews or any recognition of any kind. I'd been working on this project for years, and it now felt like I was being sold down the river. So I was the one and only person against taking the deal, at least as it was initially presented. I tried reasoning with Sam and Rob, saying, "Would you have taken this deal for *Evil Dead*? I don't think so. Since Columbia clearly wants the film, can't we come back with a counter-proposal?" I was told flatly, "No." I was also told by Rob, speaking for he and Sam, that they both felt that I had "fucked up my own good idea." Rob added, "I might even remake it some point in the future." Of course, that would now be impossible, too, since they were selling off all the rights in perpetuity, including the remake and sequel rights.

To my consternation, that was the deal. The investors got all of their money back, plus about a 3% profit, a year earlier than anticipated. I was informed over and over again that this was "miraculous for a low-budget, independent film," but I really felt abused; like it had somehow all been for nothing. I was, of course, also burning inside that my friends, and producers, felt that I had "fucked up my own good idea" (Bruce never said that). So now I had to be vindicated.

With the help of the co-producer, David Goodman, we coerced Renaissance Pictures into spending the money to book *Lunatics* into Laemmle's Royal Theater in Los Angeles for two midnight Saturday screenings. We then had a press screening and the film was sub-sequently reviewed in every major publication in town, receiving unanimously positive write-ups. Kevin Thomas in the *Los Angeles Times* gave the film a glowing, half-page review ("Josh Becker's funny and beguiling *Lunatics: A Love Story*, is smart and outrageous. High in imagination, low in budget"). *Variety, The Hollywood Reporter, The LA Weekly, The LA Reader* all praised it. It would also receive good reviews in: *The Boston Herald, The Boston Globe, The Detroit News, The Detroit Free Press, The Ann Arbor News, The Oakland Press, The Detroit Metro Times, The Austin Chronicle, The Daily Texan,* as well as on American Movie Classics. *Lunatics* received two-and-a-half stars (out of four) in Leonard Maltin's "Movie & Video Guide," and it got three stars (out of five) in the Mick Martin & Marsha Porter's "Video Movie Guide." I felt somewhat vindicated, but it didn't change the in perpetuity deal, nor did it inspire Columbia to release the film theatrically.

As fate would have it, that same week that *Lunatics: A Love Story* opened in L.A. a Jamaican film called *The Lunatic* opened. The

Royal Theater put a handwritten sign in the ticket window saying, "This is not a Jamaican film."

For one week my phone would not stop ringing, everybody in town wanting a video tape of the film—agents from every agency, production executives, even the head of production at Universal, for goodness sake. By the next week, though, I was entirely forgotten and no one would return my calls. Ah, Hollywood!

The single best thing that happened with *Lunatics* was that I got it booked into the Magic Bag Theater in Ferndale, Michigan (right near where our offices used to be), and the film showed twice a night for a week. Every single screening had more people than the one before. I honestly believed I was watching the beginning of a hit as it was occurring. Unfortunately, though, it only had a one-week run and another film (*Apocalypse Now*, as a matter of fact) was already booked to replace it the next Friday. So, no matter how well it did, it couldn't keep going. I showed up at quite a few of these screenings and just sat in the lobby and listened. Every laugh I meant to get or even hoped to get, I got. It seemed funnier than I even thought it was. I'd leave before the film ended so as not to look like too big of a loser, skulking around the one theater where the one print of my movie was showing, hoping someone recognized me.

Meanwhile, Columbia Tristar released *Lunatics: A Love Story* directly to cable TV and video tape. It showed quite a few times (possibly fifty) on the premium cable channels in 1993. It was then released to video at a cost of $99.95, and it sold rather poorly, about 5,000 copies, if I heard correctly.

Then the film disappeared off the face of the Earth.

In 1995 I was visiting a friend in Gore, New Zealand, which is down at the very bottom of the country, fifteen hundred miles from Antarctica. We went into his local video shop and there on the "new releases" shelf was *Lunatics: A Love Story* with brand-new and much-improved artwork on the video box. My friend had already seen it so we didn't rent it.

At some point in the year 2000, inexplicably *Lunatics: A Love Story* began popping up on cable television again. It has since seemingly found a home on the Starz Encore Love Story Channel, where it has shown at least a hundred times.

For whatever reason, *Lunatics: A Love Story* has never been released on DVD.

What Do the Oscars *Really* Mean?

(Originally published in the April, 1992 issue of *Film Threat Magazine*)

"We've all participated in two rituals: one is the watching of the Academy Awards and the other is the putting down of the Academy Awards. Both are very sacred and traditional American events."
—*Richard Dreyfuss* , Best Actor 1977

"The Academy is the Supreme Court of the screen."
—*Lewis Milestone,* Best Director 1927-28, 1929-30

What do the Academy Awards mean and who cares? "Best Picture" is rarely the most popular or biggest grosser of the year, with the exception of fourteen times in the last sixty-three years: *Wings* (1927-28), *Broadway Melody* (1928-29), *Gone With the Wind* (1939), *Going My Way* (1944), *The Best Years of Our Lives* (1946), *The Greatest Show on Earth* (1952), *The Bridge on the River Kwai* (1957), *Ben-Hur* (1959), *West Side Story* (1961), *Lawrence of Arabia* (1962), *The Sound of Music* (1965), *The Godfather* (1972), *Rocky* (1976), and *Kramer Vs. Kramer* (1979). [That's now fifteen times, with the addition of *Titanic* (1997)]. Thus, over 75% of the time the Academy has somehow decided that the film people spent the most money to see was not the "Best Picture." Why? As an Academy official told me, "If a film makes too much money its artistic merits are in question."

"Awards for any of the arts have always struck me as unavoidably capricious and, more often than not, given for reasons other than genuine talent. Time is going to be the final judge of merit regardless of what the contemporary awards say."
—*George Roy Hill*, Best Director 1973

Initially, in 1927 when the Academy Awards began, there were conceptually two "Best Pictures:" that which was called "Best Picture" (*Wings*), representing the most popular film of the year, and

"Artistic Quality Of Production" (*Sunrise*), which represented the best produced movie. Best produced? Artistic quality? What does this mean? As the Academy official put it, "This is the inescapable and unanswerable conundrum."

"Why all the fuss? Is it really worthwhile? How important is an Oscar anyway? Besides, who needs it? Well, I suppose no one really needs it; but, believe me, it's awfully nice to have."
—*Grace Kelly*, Best Actress 1954

Just exactly who are these people who decide who gets the Academy Awards? There are approximately 5,000 Academy members, all of whom are supposed to be active in the film business (it's an Academy bylaw). However, since the greater percentage of Academy members are older than sixty-five years of age, we might assume most of them are retired or nearing retirement. Thus, there are at least two distinct factions of Academy members—the old and the young. This is what undoubtedly caused *Midnight Cowboy* to win Best Picture in 1969 and John Wayne to win Best Actor in the same year (the younger faction must have cancelled each other out by splitting their votes between Dustin Hoffman and Jon Voight). The way in which these factions of employed and retired editors, grips, production designers, make-up artists, directors, etc. make their decisions and agree, disagree, settle on, or cancel each other out, has been of great interest to the world for the past sixty-four years. This is substantiated by the Academy Awards annual television broadcast consistently being one of the highest rated shows of the year, as well as the TV show simulcast to the most countries and viewed by the largest single audience each year.

My friend, Oscar expert Rick Sandford, and I went through the entire list of Best Picture winners and cast our own votes among the nominees (as well as all the eligible films; see the accompanying list). He and I agreed with (coincidentally) fourteen of them. Once again, less than 25% (although not the same fourteen films as the money-makers).

Therefore, if the "Best Picture" each year generally isn't the biggest grosser and more often than not isn't the best produced film of the year, then what is it? The same unnamed Academy official put it as, "An attempt to acknowledge outstanding achievement."

Apparently, Academy officials are so nervous that they don't want to be named when even when they state the party line.

Frequently the "Best Picture" seems to be the "Most Important" film of the year, not in a cinematic way, but in a thematic way. If the story is about an issue that seems "important" that year, is reasonably well-handled and makes money (no "Best Picture" has ever been a box office dog), then it has a very good chance of winning. These films are: *Wings* (1927-28: men in war), *All Quiet on the Western Front* (29-30: the horror of war), *The Life of Emile Zola* (1937: judicial injustice), *Mrs. Miniver* (1942: civilians in war), *Casablanca* (1943: refugees of war), *The Lost Weekend* (1945: alcoholism), *The Best Years of Our Lives* (1946: soldiers readjusting after the war), *Gentlemen's Agreement* (1947: anti-Semitism), *All the King's Men* (1949: demagogue politicians), *From Here to Eternity* (1953: the events leading up to war), *On the Waterfront* (1954: labor relations), *The Bridge on the River Kwai* (1957: prisoners of war), *Lawrence of Arabia* (1962: one soldier's mission during war), *In the Heat of the Night* (1967: civil rights), *Patton* (1970: war), *The Deer Hunter* (1978: war), *Kramer Vs. Kramer* (1979: divorce), *Gandhi* (1982: injustice to Indians), *Platoon* (1986: the horrors of war), and *Dances With Wolves* (1990: injustice to Indians). The hot topics appear to be anything to do with war, bigotry, and injustice to all kinds of Indians. This accounts for nineteen of the sixty-three winners (five of which are crossovers to the biggest grosser list). That still leaves over half of the "Best Pictures" unaccounted for.

Of this group there are five comedies, nine musicals, and then the other twenty-five films that could be categorized as: spectacles, adaptations of best-selling books, family dramas, and warm human dramas. Even still you end up with a couple of oddballs that defy categorization like *The French Connection* and *The Sting*.

Two other factions of Academy members, as the Academy official put it, are the "conservative and the sentimental." Sentimentality has always been a pervasive and important factor in winning Academy Awards. From Mary Pickford receiving Best Actress in 1928-29—a child star having grown up, soon to retire, but also cofounder of United Artists and one of the richest women in America—she deserved it no matter what her performance in *Coquette* was, and George Arliss winning in 1929-30 for *Disreali*, partly because he was old and partly because he was an "important" stage actor, all the way up to Don Ameche getting it for *Cocoon* in 1985 for being old and acting young, or Paul Newman getting Best Actor for *The Color of Money* 1986 for having been passed over six times before, or Jessica Tandy winning Best Actress for *Driving Miss Daisy* 1989 because she was old and might not have another chance.

In several other categories beside "Best Picture" there are pretty good, well- precedented, ways of predicting the winners.

"Best Cinematography" could easily be retitled "Best Location With The Most Sunsets."

"Best Editing" frequently goes to whatever won "Best Picture" even if it's an hour too long (*Gandhi, The Last Emperor* or *Dances With Wolves*). The really excitingly edited films like *The Road Warrior* or *The Terminator* don't win because movies of this nature generally contain violence. The geriatric Academy members don't like violence. I personally sat through an Academy screening of *Robocop* and witnessed many older folks fleeing during the show. As the anonymous Academy official said, "Academy members prefer editing and direction to be invisible." This explains why neither Joseph Von Sternberg nor Martin Scorsese have ever won. Of course, if something's invisible how do you know that it's good? (Martin Scorsese finally won an Oscar for *The Departed* in 2006

In the field of "Best Documentary," both short subject and feature, if the subject is illness or infirmity it's a shoo-in to be the winner. This attitude has recently crept into the "Best Actor" category as well (*Rain Man* and *My Left Foot*).

Then there is the idea that the "Best Picture" is really just the longest picture of the year. If a filmmaker has the nerve to produce a film over two hours long then he must be saying something important. Of the sixty-three winners there are only twenty films under two hours and merely three films under 100 minutes: *Marty* (91 minutes), *Annie Hall* (94 minutes) and *Driving Miss Daisy* (99 minutes). There are actually twenty-two films that are over 150 minutes and four films that are 200 minutes or more: *Gone With the Wind* (222 minutes), *Lawrence of Arabia* (216 minutes), *Ben-Hur* (212 minutes) and *The Godfather Part II* (200 minutes).

So, what have we learned so far? That if your intention is to make a movie that has a good chance of winning "Best Picture," it ought to be about war and be over 120 minutes.

[The Academy Award is] "... The most valuable, but least expensive, item of worldwide public relations ever invented by any industry."
—*Frank Capra*, Best Director 1934, 1936, 1938

On some level an Academy Award simply means more money. A Best Picture Oscar will cause a film to remain in the theaters for several extra months, or, if it has already left the theaters, to be re-released. *Annie Hall* is far and away Woody Allen's biggest grosser because the Oscars caused it to move beyond his core audience who had all seen it on its original release. He has not had a film that's made as much money before or since.

On the other hand, the Academy Award has ended a few film careers, the most notable being both George Chakiris and Rita Moreno for their supporting parts in *West Side Story*. This could be due to the actor's agents then asking for inordinate fees for actors who were difficult to cast in the first place. It may have also made the actors feel that they were above the parts being offered to them. A few others who haven't worked very much since winning their Oscars are: Miyoshi Umeki (Best Supporting Actress for *Sayonara*) who finally got the part of Mrs. Livingston on the TV show *The Courtship of Eddie's Father* and Haing S. Ngor (Best Supporting Actor for *The Killing Fields*) who is really a doctor and has an alternate means of support.

Actually, the way it appears is that a Best Supporting award is a bad omen for performers of foreign extraction. It doesn't seem to have done much good for F. Murray Abraham either, although his Oscar was in the Best Actor category (or Peter Finch for that matter, but then he was already dead when he got it).

It is common practice for studios, and individuals, to run advertisements for their films in the industry trade papers attempting to influence (or, more politely, to remind) Academy members of their work. It has not yet been proven that the more advertising you do the better your chances of winning. In some instances the overwhelming barrage of "For Your Consideration" ads might even have caused Academy members to not vote for someone because they considered their tactics crass.

One thing we do know for a fact is that movies released in the beginning of the year do not win Academy Awards. The earliest the film can come out and still be considered is June, and then it had better play all summer. The last two movies to win best picture and be released early in the year were *Annie Hall* in 1977 and *The Sound of Music* in 1965.

My personal disillusionment with the Academy Awards began in 1978 when *The Deer Hunter* won "Best Picture." This was the first film to win that I actively disliked. Admittedly, 1978 is one of the worst years for motion pictures on record, but even still this film seems to have won strictly on a ruse. It was not even in release when it was nominated. It had played one week in L.A. on one screen. It was still not in general release when it won the award. But the word on the street was that it was "serious and important" and, of course, it was 183 minutes long (56 minutes longer than the next longest nominee).

Universal Pictures, fearing that they had a very expensive bomb on their hands, hired producer Allan Carr to devise a method of selling this thematically unfocused behemoth of a film. Carr's assumption was that with the serious topic of war and a long running time the film was bound to win Academy Awards just so long as too many people didn't see it and bad-mouth it. He was right and the film won "Best Picture" (as well as four other Oscars). Since 1978 there is only one film that I agree with as "Best Picture", *Platoon*, and I've gotten into many arguments over this.

My personal interest in the Academy Awards stems from the fact that I would like to win one, or several actually. When I saw Mark Lester portray the lead role in *Oliver!* when I was ten years old I thought to myself, "Hey! He's no older than me. I can do that." I have spent the better part of my life struggling to be in the movie business.

I believe that most of the people in the film business struggled long and hard to be in it. When someone asked Warren Beatty whether he would show up at the 1978 awards, and would he accept if he won, he replied, "If people want to get together to tell me that they like me, you bet I'll show up." Beatty didn't win that year, but he did win in 1981, he did show up and he did accept.

So, I think Oscars are meaningful to help people keep going in a heartless industry. There's something to hope for. I might have given up long ago if it had not been for the hope of hitting big, which is inextricably tied up with winning an Oscar. Sure many people who deserve it never got it, sure there's a slight smell of corruption, sure it's the industry patting itself on the back, sure it's all egotism, but who cares? It's not real anyway, it's movies.

"However maddening, infuriating, embarrassing and seemingly artificial these occasions are. However drummed up. The truth of the matter is still pure. The Academy Awards are in good faith. An attempt to honor a person or a product of our industry. And they have maintained in essence a purity a simple—well, truth."
—*Kathrine Hepburn*, Best Actress 1932-33, 1967, 1968, 1981

"It is no small comfort to know in advance that the lead line in one's obituary will read, 'Academy Award winner, etc., etc., etc.'"
—*Gregory Peck*, Best Actor 1962

THE ACADEMY'S BIGGEST BLUNDERS:

* The first six years of the Academy Awards consisted of half of one year and half of another. A letter from the Academy to its members in 1928 states, "The ruling of the committee confines the nominations to achievements in pictures first publicly exhibited in Los Angeles Metropolitan district (previews excepted) from August 1, 1927, to August 1, 1928." Janet Gaynor won the first Best Actress Oscar for three films: *Sunrise, Street Angel* and *Seventh Heaven*, while Emil Jannings won the first Best Actor Oscar for two films: *The Last Command* and *The Way of All Flesh*. It was simply expected back then that an actor would make several pictures a year and the more good performances they gave in that year the better their chances of winning the award. In the *Los Angeles Daily Times* dated May 6, 1927 there is an advertisement for the premiere of *Seventh Heaven* and in the July 8, 1927 *LA Daily Times* there is an advertisement for the premiere of *The Way of All Flesh*. That means that both *The Way of All Flesh* and *Seventh Heaven* were not eligible for awards. *Seventh Heaven* also won Best Screenplay and Best Director. Also that same year, *Chang* was nominated for "Artistic Quality Of Production" but is advertised in the *LA Daily Times* as premiering on June 24, 1927 and is thus not eligible, either. Their own rules just didn't seem to mean anything to the Academy in that first year. (Note: The 1927-28 Academy Award ceremony was held on May 16, 1929, nine months after the calendar year had ended, so it's no wonder they couldn't remember what was eligible).

* At the 1934 Oscar ceremony (for the films of 1933), MC Will Rogers announced the winner of the Best Director award by saying, "Come on up and get it, Frank." Unfortunately, there were two men named Frank nominated, Frank Capra and Frank Lloyd. Both stood and went to the podium. It was established there that in fact the winner was Frank Lloyd. Frank Capra had to go sit down. This may well have inspired him because the next year he won for *It Happened One Night*.

* In 1956 there were two films released that were entitled *High Society*, one with Frank Sinatra, Grace Kelly, and Bing Crosby that was a musical remake of *The Philadelphia Story*, and one with The Bowery Boys. As fate would have it *High Society* got nominated for Best Motion Picture Story, meaning original story. A remake is not eligible for this award, so the nomination went to the Bowery Boys movie. The nominated writers, Edward Bernds and Elwood Ullman (frequent writers for The Three Stooges), knowing that it was an embarrassing mistake, had their names removed from the final ballot. But that wasn't the end of the controversy with this specific award. The winner was one Robert Rich for *The Brave One* which was in fact a pseudonym for blacklisted writer Dalton Trumbo. Since he had left the country and no one knew that this was his pseudonym there was no one to pick up the Oscar. It sat on the podium for the remainder of the ceremony. Trumbo finally received the award in 1975.

* Barry Fitzgerald is the only actor to be nominated for both Best Actor and Best Supporting actor for the same role, in *Going My Way*. He lost Best Actor to his co-star, Bing Crosby, but won Best Supporting Actor.

THE WINNERS OF THE MOST OSCARS (Updated):

* Walt Disney won 31 Academy Awards: 12 for Best Cartoon (this category was called "Best Cartoon" from 1931-32 until 1971 when it was changed to "Best Animated Film"), 7 Live-Action Short Subjects, 4 Feature Documentaries, 3 Short Subject Documentaries, 3 Special Honoraries, 1 Special Effects, and an Irving G. Thalberg Memorial award (Walt Disney did not personally direct or produce any of those films, but the custom at Walt Disney Pictures was that he collected all of the awards for everyone at the studio).

* Gordon Hollingshead won 12 awards: 10 Live-action Short Subjects, 1 Documentary Short Subject, and 1 Assistant Director award (This award was only given from 1932-33 to 1937).
* Cedric Gibbons won 11 times for Art Direction.
* Billy Wilder won 9 awards: 6 for Writing, 2 for Director, 1 for producing the Best Picture.
* Alfred Newman won 9 for Music Scoring (Alfred's brother, Lionel Newman, was nominated 12 times for music awards and finally won his one and only award in 1969. Lionel's son, Randy Newman, was nominated for Music Scoring and Best Song in 1981, but didn't win.).
* Edith Head won 8 for Costume Design.
* Edwin B. Willis won 8 for Art Direction.
* Fredrick Quimby won 7 for Best Cartoon.
* Richard Day won 7 for Art Direction.
* Dennis Muren won 6 for Special Effects.
* Walter M. Scott and Thomas Little both won 6 for Art Direction.
* Francis Ford Coppola won 5 awards: 3 for Writing, 1 for Director, 1 for producing the Best Picture.
* Douglas Shearer and Fred Hines both won 5 for Sound.
* John Barry won 5: 4 for Original Score, 1 for Best Song.
* Irene Sharaff won 5 for Costume Design.
* Richard Taylor has won 5: for Best Visual Effects, Best Costume, and Best Make-up.
* Charles Brackett won 5: 3 for Writing, 1 for producing the Best Picture, and one Honorary.
* Katherine Hepburn won 4 for Best Actress (the most ever won in the acting categories. Katherine Hepburn also holds the record for the longest gap between Oscars—35 years, from 1932-33 to 1967).
* John Ford won 4 for Direction (the most for any director. The two runners-up are: William Wyler with 3 and Frank Capra with 3).
* Frederico Fellini won 4 Best Foreign Film awards (although the producers Carlo Ponti and Dino De Laurentiis probably retain two of them).
* Joseph Ruttenberg, Leon Shamroy and Vittorio Storaro have all won 4 for Cinematography.
* John Box, George James Hopkins, Keogh Gleason, and Sam Comer all won 4 for Art Direction.

* Joseph L. Mankiewicz won 4: 2 for Writing, 2 for Direction.
* Richard Edlund, L. B. Abbott, and Glen Robinson all won 4 for Special Effects.
* Henry Mancini, John Williams, John Green, Andre Previn, Johnny Mercer, and Dimitri Tiomkin all won 4 for Music.
* Ben Burtt won 4 for Sound Effects Editing.
* Oliver Stone won 4: 2 for Direction, 2 for Writing
* Ingrid Bergman won 3: 2 for Best Actress, 1 for Best Supporting Actress.
* Jack Nicholson won 3: 2 for Best Actor, 1 for Best Supporting Actor.
* Walter Brennan won 3 for Best Supporting Actor (he is the biggest winner in the supporting field).
* Steven Spielberg won 3: 2 for Best Director, 1 for Producing the Best Picture.
* Max Steiner won 3 for Music.
* Marvin Hamlisch won 3 for music (all in the same year, 1973).
* Ralph Dawson won 3 for Best Editing.
* Daniel Mandell won 3 for Best Editing.
* Spencer Tracy, Fredric March, Gary Cooper, Marlon Brando, Dustin Hoffman, and Tom Hanks have all won 2 awards for Best Actor.
* Luise Rainer, Bette Davis, Vivien Leigh, Olivia De Havilland, Elizabeth Taylor, Sally Field, Jodie Foster, and Hillary Swank all have won 2 Best Actress Oscars.
* Jack Lemmon, Robert DeNiro, Gene Hackman Denzel Washington, and Kevin Spacey all won 2: 1 for Best Actor, 1 for Best Supporting Actor.
* Helen Hayes, Maggie Smith and Meryl Streep all won 2: 1 for Best Actress, 1 for Best Supporting Actress.
* Shelley Winters is the only one to win 2 Best Supporting Actress Awards.
* Anthony Quinn, Peter Ustinov, and Jason Robards all won 2 Best Supporting Actor Oscars.
* Barbra Streisand has won 2: 1 for Best Actress, 1 for Best Song.
* Clint Eastwood has 2 Best Director Oscars.
* The films to win the most Oscars in total are *Ben-Hur* and *Titanic*, both with 11.

* The films to get the most nominations are *All About Eve* and *Titanic*, both with 14.

* There have only been two ties: Frederic March and Wallace Beery in 1931-32, and Katherine Hepburn and Barbra Streisand in 1968.

FAMILY MEMBERS TO WIN OSCARS:

* The Coppolas, Francis Coppola, Carmine Coppola and Sofia Coppola, are the only family to have won Oscars over the course of three generations.

* The only two fathers and sons are: Francis and Carmine Coppola, and John Huston and Walter Huston (Michael Douglas won Best Actor and his father, Kirk Douglas, won an honorary, but that doesn't really count).

* The only sisters to win Oscars were Olivia DeHavilland and Joan Fontaine.

* The two sets of brothers and sisters to win were: Lionel and Ethel Barrymore, and Shirley MacLaine and Warren Beatty (Best Director for *Reds*).

"My memories of that night [winning the Academy Award] include someone saying, 'Don't scratch it. There may be chocolate underneath.'"

—*Martin Balsam,* Best Supporting Actor 1965

Writing and Selling a Screenplay

I am one of the very few people I know of who's sold a spec screenplay. I know a number of people who have made a lot more money than me writing screenplays, but they were all commissioned or developed. The script that I am referring to is called *Cycles* and it was purchased by Beacon Communications (producers of *Air Force One*). Although I have recently heard that *Cycles* is on the development "fast-track," it has not been produced, nor do there seem to be any immediate plans to do so. Nevertheless, I did sell it. [As of ten years later *Cycles* still hasn't been produced].

This essay is in response to all of these WRITE A SCREENPLAY THAT SELLS books in the bookstores written by all these people who have never sold a script. I've written 28 full-length feature scripts [that's 35 now]. I've written many scripts with the explicit idea of selling them and none of those sold. I wrote *Cycles* strictly because I thought it was a good idea that would make a cool movie. I dismissed all concessions to what anyone else might like, writing the script entirely for myself. This was (and is) a movie that I would very much like to see.

Since that time I have tried to write all of my scripts with exactly the same attitude. I think it's the way to go. Write what matters to you; write the movies that you would really like to see. Ignore the trends. If you can see that there is a trend, you missed it. You, and numerous others who are much further along than you, are all too late. It's only the first two or three films that caused there to be a trend (sci-fi movies in 1997, for instance) that are any good and make all of the money. Everything that comes out thereafter will suck and bomb. Then every script in that same genre, in all their various stages of development, all get shit-canned.

Take westerns in the 1990s as an example. Two good westerns came out in a row (admittedly a year apart, but no one had been making any westerns for a long time), *Dances With Wolves* then *Unforgiven*, both of which made a lot of money and each won the

Oscar for "Best Picture." All of the westerns that followed in the next year or so sucked and bombed (*Bad Girls, Tombstone, Wyatt Earp, Geronimo, Wild Bill,* et al). And of all the films that failed in the wake of the two hits, at least one hundred times that many western scripts were in development. By 1995 nobody in Hollywood would bother to read a western script, let alone consider buying it or producing it. That's until somebody else makes a good western because they love westerns, not because it is or ever was a trend.

In 1983 or '84 I saw a documentary called *Hell's Angels Forever.* In the film a fat, bearded biker in his late 30s or 40s (it was hard to tell) told the story of how he became a biker, which was because his dad was a biker. He then went on to quickly explain the history of motorcycle gangs, that had begun right after World War II by disenfranchised veterans, among whom was this biker's father. I thought to myself, "That's fascinating. I didn't know that."

For the next eight or nine years this idea rattled around in my head.

In 1992, for no known reason, the idea resurfaced in my mind. I pitched it to a couple of different friends who each responded exactly the same way I did when I heard the idea: it seemed like a great idea on an interesting subject that no one knew anything about.

Meanwhile, I was on a flight from L.A. to Boston to attend the Boston Film Festival, where my film *Lunatics: A Love Story* was showing. The guy seated next to me, wearing hand-painted blue jeans and a black leather jacket, was cracking his chewing gum so loudly I couldn't read. This kept up for inordinately long time, with me throwing him annoyed sidelong glances from behind my book, and him ignoring me.

Finally, unable to bear anymore, I said, "Excuse me—"

He cut me off, "—Are you going to the film festival?"

"Yes, I am."

"So am I." He put out his hand, "My name's Bill Fishman."

I shook his hand, "Josh Becker."

It turned out that Bill had written and directed *Tapeheads* with John Cusack and Tim Robbins, which I had seen and gotten a few laughs out of. I was mildly impressed.

I met Bruce Campbell, Ted Raimi and David (Goody) Goodman in Boston, and we all ended up hanging around a bit with Bill, as well Bobcat Goldthwait, who was there with his film, *Shakes the Clown.*

When we got back to L.A. David Goodman began playing basketball with Bill Fishman. One day on the court, Goody told my *Cycles* story to Bill, who has a small production company with his brother, Jim. They liked what they'd heard of the idea from Goody and asked me to come in and pitch it to them, which I did. Afterward, they nodded saying they did indeed like the idea, then they said exactly what every other producer in Hollywood will say under the circumstances, and that is, "We'd love to read it when it's written."

So I wrote the script. Since half the story takes place in Texas, I began studying the dialect and made a glossary of "Texas-isms:" ("Do you reckon?" and "I don't cotton to that," etc.). Since the story also took place in 1946, I began to study the period dialog, mainly through watching old movies, and made another glossary of "40s-isms:" ("Was it rugged?" and "Are you hep?" etc.). I stuck both glossaries on the wall in front of my face while writing.

It took me a couple of months to knock out the first draft of *Cycles,* and it seemed pretty good, but not exceptional. This puzzled me, and I mused about it for a few weeks. How do I improve this? It's a good idea, it all makes sense, it all goes together logically, the characters are reasonably well-motivated, what's the problem?

Then it struck me, everything happened exactly as you expected it to happen. The good guys were good, the bad guys were bad, the good guys beat out the bad guys and everything worked out fine. There was nothing surprising about it because the story was happening to these characters, as opposed to coming out of them. Who they were wasn't effecting the outcome. Also, people aren't really just good or bad, most folks are caught in the gray area in the middle. This was big breakthrough moment for me in my development as a writer.

With the next draft I muddied everyone's motivations, giving good traits to the bad guys, and bad traits to the good guys. Suddenly, the whole story and all of the characters really seemed to come to life to me. There was now a sense of the unexpected, which is much more intriguing than feeling like you know exactly where the story is going. I liked the results so much that I did it again, going through yet another draft of trying to push everything into the gray area. By the time the third draft was done, after about four or five months, I was quite pleased with the results.

I gave it to the Fishman brothers and they promptly optioned it for, I am ashamed to say, three years.

The Fishmans then turned right around and optioned *Cycles* to Beacon Communications, who, at that point, had produced: *The Road to Wellville*, *Princess Caraboo*, and *Sugar Hill*. I didn't even know that you could re-option a script to a third party. You can.

Then the sands of time blew over the giant stone pyramids, wearing them slowly to tiny nubs.

Two years and ten months later, having never once actually communicated with Beacon Communications, nor with the Fishman brothers in over a year, I figured I was getting my script back, which was fine with me since I happened to like it.

Then Beacon contacted my lawyer and subsequently bought the script. I blush now in recalling that I actually went to some difficulty getting a "best effort" clause so that they would have to use me to do the rewrites. I've always imagined that the dialog at Beacon (if indeed there was any) went something like this:

EXEC#1: Okay, let's get this new project, *Cycles*, rewritten, pronto.

EXEC#2: Hey, C.B. There's a "best effort" clause in the contract saying we have to use the kid that wrote the original script to rewrite it.

EXEC#1: Oh, yeah? *Fuck him!* That's my best effort, now get a *real* writer.

I heard that the script went through eight or nine different writers and god knows how many drafts. I also heard that Phillip Kaufman (*The Right Stuff*, *The Unbearable Lightness of Being*) was attached for a while, but he subsequently moved on to bigger and better things. I also heard that the title has been changed to *Griffen*. There was no one named Griffen in the script when I wrote it.

This brings up an interesting question should the film ever get made. Who gets the credit? It will certainly go to Writer's Guild arbitration and they will ultimately decide. I don't think it's possible to ever entirely remove the original author, but who knows? They may make it into a science-fiction musical, for all I know. Even with the aid of my lawyer I haven't been able to get anyone at Beacon to ever talk to me.

And even though I sold a script to a Writer's Guild signatory company, using Writer's Guild contracts, and following Writer's Guild rules—which, to my limited understanding, is sufficient for getting into the Writer's Guild—I did not get into the Writer's Guild. This was based exclusively on the fact that I did not sell the option to Beacon. Of course, when Beacon finally wanted to purchase the script they had to deal with me, since I was the copyright owner. However, in the eyes of the Writer's Guild, I never did business with Beacon. The fact that they wrote a check to me to purchase the rights from me did not cut it with the Writer's Guild. And then they made me feel bad about it, too, like I was trying to pull the wool over their eyes.

I received Writer's Guild minimum for a high-budget movie, which at the time was like $68,000. I then spent most of the money financing my film *Running Time*. Should they ever make *Cycles,* and I get screen credit, I'll make more money and be able to shoot another low-budget movie.

Hercules in the Maze of the Minotaur, 1994,
Josh Becker directing Anthony Quinn.
(photo by Pierre Vinet)

Hercules in the Maze of the Minotaur, 1994, crew shot. Front
row, L to R: Kevin Sorbo, Eric Gruendemann (producer), Chloe
Smith (NZ producer), Josh Becker.
(photo by Pierre Vinet)

Directing Anthony Quinn

I first met Anthony Quinn down in New Zealand where he was playing Zeus in five Hercules TV movies. I initially saw him on the set of the first of the five films, *Hercules and the Amazon Women*. Mr. Quinn, as we all called him, was sitting in a director's chair in his Zeus outfit seated beside his wife, Iolanda. He was speaking to the film's director, Bill, and the writers, Andy and Dan, all of whom were paying close attention. I sidled up and listened.

Quinn was holding forth on who he thought Zeus was. Every point he made was a good one, not that he was pausing for validation. His insights were the keenest observations I'd heard regarding any character in the series. It was fascinating and informative, and I truly wish I'd had a tape recorder. I could only think that this was the best actor I'd ever been near in my whole life.

Finally, after I had stood there listening for about ten minutes, Bill, the director, introduced me, bless his heart.

"If I'm Boy Number One," Bill poked his own chest, then pointed at me, "this is Boy Number Five." Meaning, Bill was director of the first film (and the third), and I was the director of the fifth film. Mr. Quinn had already begun calling Bill "Boy," and Bill was about fifty.

I shook hands with Mr. and Mrs. Quinn.

I said, "I'm also the second-unit director on this film."

Quinn nodded politely and walked over to shoot a scene. I followed after to watch.

* * * * *

I knew Anthony Quinn was staying in the same hotel as me, the Pan Pacific, but I never saw him. A cab driver told me he'd seen him in front of the Pan Pacific right after having just seen him in a World War II movie and he thought he was losing his mind for a second. The employees of the restaurant had all seen Quinn and his wife numerous times. They told me a story of Mrs. Quinn ordering some-

thing that was not on the menu and making them run out and get it.
If she could get the New Zealanders to run for anything, I admired
her. I found them to be a rather mellow, non-running society.

I did finally see Mr. Quinn and his wife in that restaurant.

I didn't bother him, nor did anyone else that night.

* * * * *

Then word came down that I was to direct Mr. Quinn's intro-
ductory shot in the show's main titles. What an honor. "What's he
supposed to be doing?" I asked. Nobody knew. Since Zeus is a lech-
erous character, I thought it would be appropriate to track behind
him while a pretty, scantily-clad girl walked past coming toward us.
Zeus would stop, turn directly into tight close-up and react to her,
superimpose title, "And Anthony Quinn as Zeus." Everyone seemed
to think it was a fine idea.

The second-unit set up three lengths of dolly track right near
where the main unit was shooting and waited . . . and waited. I
had the pretty girl clothed in a sheer, diaphanous dress, and ide-
ally I wanted her back-lit so that we could see her lovely form right
through the dress. Well, backlight time came and went and still no
Quinn. When he finally did arrive the light was reasonably flat, but
still acceptable. I explained the shot to him.

"You walk along the dolly track going that way. You see Sarah,
who is portraying the pretty girl—"

"—I'd have known that," Quinn cut in.

We all smiled. I went on, "You see her, turn left, and react to her
fine female form. You'll be in a tight close-up. That's it. I'd like it all
to happen pretty quickly."

Then, as always, the DP decided that the light was better ten feet
back, so the crew flew into action and quickly moved the dolly and
track and reset the shot we'd been sitting on for three hours.

Someone brought a chair for Mr. Quinn, and Eric the producer
showed up.

"How's it going?" (Eric's perennial question).

"Great. It'll be a great intro. Stay and watch."

He nodded. Maybe he would stay, and maybe he wouldn't. He
was like a phantom the way he appeared and disappeared. I liked
him very much.

As we waited I stepped up to Mr. Quinn and said, "You might very well think I've wasted my life, and perhaps I have, but I've seen *Lawrence Of Arabia* about a hundred times. I know your entire speech in the tent at Wadi Rumm. May I do it for you?"

He chuckled, "Go ahead."

I launched into my imitation of him as the hook-nosed Bedouin leader, Auda Abu Tayi. "'I'm Auda Abu Tayi! Auda Abu Tayi! Auda serves the Turks? Auda serves? I carry over twenty-five great wounds, all gotten in battle. I have killed eighty-five men with my own hands in battle. I burn their tents, I scatter their flocks. I receive 50 golden guineas from the Turks every month, but I am poor. Why? Because I am a river to my people!'"

Mr. Quinn seemed honestly amused.

Meanwhile, we did three takes of the intro shot, and Quinn was hysterically funny in all three. I thought it went brilliantly, and it is the single thing I miss most that did not make it into the films.

Eric suggested that we shoot Quinn against the blue sky as a possible plate (with a blue background they could, if they cared to, superimpose Mr. Quinn on top of something else, like exploding volcanoes or a star field).

While the camera and silk (a big piece of parachute silk to diffuse the sunlight) were being set up, I asked Mr. Quinn, "Why did you only direct the one picture, *The Buccaneer?*"

His amusement faded. I'd gone directly to a sore spot—a knack I have.

Quinn said, "At it's first preview people said, 'It's the best picture C.B. [DeMille, Quinn's former father-in-law] ever made.' Since he was only the producer, he took it into the editing room and made sure it was no longer his best picture. It was also his last film."

"What was Yul Brynner like to work with?" I asked.

"He was a *poseur*. But Charles Boyer was wonderful."

I said to Mr. Quinn. "Now I need you to stand against the sky, posing."

As the camera was about to roll, I said, "Survey the lands that you've created, then sigh in satisfaction . . ."

". . . And smile," requested Eric from behind me.

Quinn's face went stony. "Do you want me to sigh, or do you want me to smile?"

I grinned and pointed at Eric. "He's the producer. Smile."

Quinn both sighed and smiled.
This shot wasn't used, either.

* * * * *

I was sitting alone at one of my two usual spots in the hotel restaurant, and Anthony Quinn came in and sat down by himself two
tables away. He wore a dark sport coat, no tie, and ordered a bottle
of wine. He then donned thick reading glasses, removed folded script
pages from his pocket, and began to study his lines. I found this very
ingratiating—not only do the great end up eating alone; they had to
study their lines, too.

Over the course of the next half an hour three people came up and
asked for autographs. In all instances, Quinn put down the pages,
took off his glasses, smiled, shook hands and signed the autograph.
He seemed like he was in a fairly amiable mood, so I walked over to
his table. He looked at me with a totally blank expression, as though
he'd never laid eyes on me before.

I said, "Excuse me, Mr. Quinn, but since everyone else in the room
feels they can bother you, so do I. My name's Josh Becker, and I'm
directing the fifth Hercules film."

He was very cordial. "Oh, really? Nice to meet you." He shook
my hand.

I didn't mention that we'd not only already met, but had spent
several hours working together.

"Would I be disturbing you if I sat down?"

"No, please"

I sat. We discussed the Hercules films, and his character, Zeus, and
finally I said: "So, what's Kazan like?" (Elia Kazan directed *Viva Zapata* for which Quinn won his first "Best Supporting Actor" Oscar).

"He's evil," replied Quinn. He explained that during the making of *Viva Zapata* Kazan came to Quinn's trailer before they were
about to shoot an argument scene between Marlon Brando and
Quinn. Kazan said Brando had told him he thought Quinn was terrible as Stanley Kowalski, a part Anthony Quinn had taken over
from Marlon Brando on Broadway in 1949, when Brando went to
Hollywood to make his first movie, *The Men*. Quinn said he didn't
believe it for a second. Why? He'd never heard anything before,
and this was five years later. So, as he was walking to the set he saw

Brando, who said, "Kazan says you didn't like my interpretation of Kowalski." Quinn replied: "He said the same thing to me, that you didn't like *my* Kowalski. I thought yours was the best performance of the 20th century." Brando said, "Well, I liked yours, too. Kazan is just trying to get us mad at each other to make the scene better. Why don't we just do our jobs and go act?"

Mr. Quinn then told me how, when he was making *Attila* for Dino De Laurentiis in Italy, Federico Fellini brought him the script for *La Strada*. Quinn took the script to Dino, who said there wasn't any time to make it. Quinn suggested that since they were shooting *Attila* with a French crew, who didn't start shooting until noon, they should shoot *La Strada* with an Italian crew in the mornings, which he said they did. My research says that *La Strada* is 1954, and *Attila* is 1958, but who knows? He's lived a long time and made a lot of movies.

I asked, "What was Vincent Minnelli like to work with?" (Minnelli directed *Lust for Life* for which Quinn won his second Oscar).

"He was a joy."

"I suppose you know," I said, "that your performance in that film was the shortest ever to win an Oscar."

"No, I didn't," Quinn answered, looking surprised.

"Yes, it's seven minutes long. Since then, however, Beatrice Straight has also won a supporting Oscar for a seven-minute performance in *Network*."

I began to talk movies in general and wasn't *really* showing off, although I guess it must have sounded like it. Mr. Quinn looked a bit surprised and said, "I don't see that many movies. I don't like movies that much."

* * * * *

When I got him to sign my *Barabbas* poster on his last day of shooting on *Hercules in the Maze of the Minotaur*, Therese, one of the coordinators, said, "Who is that woman you're kissing on the poster?"

Quinn replied, "Oh, that's a very young Sophia Loren."

I couldn't help myself. "No, that's Silvana Mangano," as it plainly said on the poster.

Quinn looked up, "Oh, yes, it was."

* * * * *

Another time, Quinn was talking about *The Savage Innocents*, an Eskimo picture he'd made with Peter O'Toole (this is where Bob Dylan got the idea for his song, "Quinn the Eskimo). I asked him, "What was Nicholas Ray [the director] like?"

"He was cracking up," said Quinn. "About to have a nervous breakdown."

"That would have been about 1960, right?" I proffered.

Quinn became outraged. "No! It was the mid-seventies!" He dismissed me as though I were an utter fool, and walked away.

My books say *The Savage Innocents* is 1959.

He also related how, on this film, when they got into the studio in London, out of nowhere the dogs went crazy. It seems they were using salt for snow (as had been done on the Hercules film immediately prior to this one we were shooting, on the same stage). "There was salt all over everything, you've never seen anything like it," stated Quinn, although everyone within earshot had seen nothing but salt for the past several weeks. Well, as it turned out, the salt was getting on the dog's testicles. Mr. Quinn said that they had pouches made for the dog's balls by a tailor on Savile Row.

* * * * *

The first day that Quinn worked on my film *Hercules in the Maze of the Minotaur*, the first scene, I wanted him to sit on a log and deliver all his dialog. He decided that he wanted to stand up near the end.

All right.

In the next scene I wanted him to stand up at a certain point, and he decided on a different point.

Fine.

During this scene, at night beside a campfire with Hercules, his pal, Iolaus, and Zeus, the lighting was being set up and Quinn was sitting by himself. I stepped up and asked, "In *Lawrence of Arabia*—"

Quinn looked up sharply and snapped, "—*Fuck off!*"

"I'll just sit over here by the monitor," I mumbled, quickly walking away.

I stepped up beside Eric, the producer, and said, "Quinn just told me to fuck off."

"I've got *five* on you," replied Eric. "He's told me to fuck off *six* times already."

* * * * *

For a long dialog scene in a barn between Hercules and Zeus I had conceived a long "dolly-edit" also known as a "sequence shot." It's where one shot will cover the entire scene, but not by itself. It's intended to be cut into, at specific points when the camera isn't moving. Such as, going to a close-up of one character, thus needing the other close-up, or the other over-the-shoulder shot.

It's nice to want.

The day began with a meeting with Mr. Quinn, Eric, and Kevin Sorbo, who played Hercules, in Mr. Quinn's trailer.

Quinn absolutely hated his reveal entrance in this scene, that he had already done numerous times in the previous four films. He wouldn't do it again, and that was that. He then raged on and on against his dialog, which he'd rewritten, waving around yellow pages he wasn't offering to anyone else, and referring to the two young writers as "Shakespeare and Homer."

Eric and Kevin were nodding in a placating fashion, agreeing wholeheartedly.

I asked, "And how do you see yourself entering instead of the reveal?"

"I'll just be there already," Mr. Quinn explained. "He'll hear me laugh."

"And where will you be?" I inquired further.

"I'll be up on a platform, like boxes and barrels, or what have you, with steps so I can climb down, and I'll need a rail up near the ceiling so that I have something to hold onto while I climb down from the platform. So I don't fall."

The look on Eric's face was priceless. This was a scene that was supposedly shooting within the next hour. Suddenly he was looking at the construction of a platform and a rail. How long would that take?

Since my dolly-edit scheme had gone into the crapper, I was curious as to what it was I was about to shoot.

"Do you suppose that you and Kevin will ever get close enough to one another so that I can get you both in a two-shot?" I asked.

Quinn, suddenly filling the small trailer with his dramatic, overbearing presence, proclaimed, *"How the fuck should I know?"*

That was the conclusion of the meeting.

Mr. Quinn then showed us where he wanted his platform and railing and, basically, what he had in mind. Oddly, it was all about what he would be doing; he didn't care what Kevin or the camera would be doing. I suppose my face showed some slight trace of skepticism that this was an improvement over what I'd had in mind, that he'd never given me a chance to explain.

Quinn pointed into my face. "David Lean moved two thousand horses when he realized my idea was better than his."

As it turns out we were shooting with one horse that day.

"I only have one horse, Mr. Quinn, but I'll move it anywhere you'd like."

He smiled, turned and went to his trailer.

I quickly revised my dolly-edit idea, and we shot the scene.

It turned out that Quinn had taken a couple of paragraphs and turned them into a several-page speech, including a very silly imitation of a talking bird. I thought, Sure, why not? Let him do what he wants. I'll just use what I want and cut out the rest (and that's what I did).

The scene was going along, and long was the word—it was just going on and on. I was wondering if we had enough film in the camera. Somehow, we got through it.

"That's great, " I said. "Let's do another one."

"Going again," bellowed George, the 1st A.D.

"Wait a minute," said Quinn. "What was wrong with that?"

All work stopped. He was flatly confronting me in front of everyone, which isn't done all that often on a movie set. All right, who *was* the director of this picture, anyway?

I chose my words carefully. "There were a lot of great parts in that last take, but I'd like to get a whole take that's great."

Mr. Quinn, who's a big man, stepped right up to me and put his incredibly lined, leathery, old face directly into mine and yelled, "I want some *fucking direction!* What was wrong with it?"

I replied calmly, "You were reaching for some of your lines."

Anthony Quinn stated in a steely tone, "Human beings have to think about what they're going to say next. That's what I was doing."

In a clear, unexcited manner, I explained, "There is a difference between thinking about what you're going to say next and reaching for your lines. You were reaching."

Now Quinn was furious. "Then we'll stay here 'til *fucking* midnight 'til you think it's *fucking* excellent!"

I said: "Exactly. Let's do it again."

And we did. And when the next take was done I said, "That was excellent. Let's move on."

* * * * *

Later, after we were through with that scene and onto something else without Mr. Quinn, he stepped up to me in his sweat-suit and sneakers and put his hand on my shoulder. "Look, son, I'm sorry about the way I acted back there."

I smiled. "That's perfectly all right. You are the best actor I've ever worked with. I'm happy to go through whatever it takes."

He shook my hand and smiled. "That's very nice, son. Thank you."

All of the other directors were "Boy," but I had just graduated to "Son."

* * * * *

I had a dialog scene between Mr. Quinn and the minotaur. Since I did not want to reveal what the minotaur looked like this early in the picture, I had a wall of vines and cobwebs built that would be between them, so that all of Zeus' point of view shots of the minotaur would be obscured.

As we rehearsed the scene, Quinn said, "I'm going to walk right through this stuff and confront the monster face to face."

I was confused. "How are you going to get through? It's pretty thick."

"I'm not going to *really* go through it, I'll just come around, and you'll do some kind of special effect that makes it look like I'm walking right through it. I am Zeus after all, king of the Gods. Some sticks aren't going to stop me."

I turned and looked at the cinematographer who had as puzzled of an expression as I did. Suddenly we were doing a special effect that (A). we didn't know if we had the money for, and (B). since no one had ever thought about it, we couldn't be sure it would work.

As it turns out, it worked quite well.

* * * * *

My next scene with Mr. Quinn was in a wonderful, green, mossy woods. It was night, and it was cold. I had scenes to shoot *after* this scene with Quinn, so it was imperative that I get him in and out. I could not allow his scene to take a long time because we would never return to this location, so everything that had to be shot there had to be done that night.

I lay in bed the night before this shoot wondering how I could best deal with Anthony Quinn. I really needed him to hit *my* marks, as opposed to coming up with his own blocking. Then it occurred to me: wide shots of Quinn don't matter, he's a hundred times more interesting in close-up, so screw the wide shots. Therefore, I started shooting the scene with Quinn's close-up, thus pinning him to my mark, then I backed my way out of the scene. Now, as we shot the wide shot, if he didn't hit the mark I'd set for him in the close-up, it wouldn't match with the footage we'd already shot, so we'd then have to shoot it again, and since Quinn was not about to reshoot anything, he just hit my mark because it was easier and quicker.

I had him do half the dialog in one close-up, then step out of that and into a tighter close-up. I blasted through the scene in no time and it was good. And I got Mr. Quinn out of there before midnight. He was happy, Eric was happy, I was happy, and I was just sorry I hadn't thought of this approach earlier.

* * * * *

My last scene with Mr. Quinn was in the studio, on the set of the underground lair of the minotaur, full of stalagmites and fog. Rain was crashing down on the tin roof of the warehouse we used as a soundstage so hard that day it was deafening. Since there's no way to record usable sound under those circumstances, that meant all of the dialog for these scenes would eventually have to be replaced. Since his whole scene was being played down to the dying minotaur who was impaled on a stalagmite on the floor, I knew there weren't too many ways to block the scene. Mr. Quinn would just have to do it my way, since it was the simplest way—and, in fact, he did. Besides, I had gotten good at dealing with him, and I started with his close-up again. He really only wanted to make the scenes better, but he was old, and impatient, and wanted to get done as fast as possible. Once he knew that I understood this, he was my friend.

I have three photographs of Quinn and myself. One is a group shot of Quinn, me, Eric, Kevin, George, and Therese. But what I *really* wanted was a shot of me directing Mr. Quinn. I conveyed my request to Pierre, the French-Canadian still photographer. He said that he couldn't get a decent photo because I always stood facing Mr. Quinn when I was directing, with my back to the camera. If I wanted a good shot I'd have to stand beside Mr. Quinn, facing Pierre and his camera. However, since Mr. Quinn had gotten mad at me several times when I'd gotten close to him while he was running his lines to himself, I was leery of getting too near him unless I really, really had to. I just didn't want him yelling at me and slowing things down.

So, Mr. Quinn was standing in the middle of the set running his lines to himself for his last shot. I glanced over at Pierre, and he pointed, indicating that now was the time. I discreetly sidled up beside Mr. Quinn. I got to where I thought that I was close enough, and Quinn still hadn't noticed me, so I looked up and posed. Pierre took the shot then indicated that I should get closer still. I edged a couple of feet closer, and Pierre shot another one and nodded. He'd gotten it. I quickly stepped away from Mr. Quinn. One might even think that I'm directing him in the photo, but in fact he is entirely unaware of my presence.

Mr. Quinn completed his last shot, and I called, "Print it."

George, the 1ˢᵗ A.D., stated, "Ladies and gentlemen, that is a wrap on Anthony Quinn in all five Hercules movies."

The crew applauded heartily.

Anthony Quinn stood up, raised his hands, tears in his eyes, and said, "The only language that will express what I'm feeling at this moment is *Italian* . . ." then launched into a whole speech in Italian, which, unfortunately, no one in the crew understood. When he was done with that he segued into English and said he loved New Zealand and would love to have a house there. Everybody clapped again.

Mr. Quinn never once referred to me by name. As I said, he never called me "boy," either. He called me "son."

After the completion of his last shot, I handed him a *Barabbas* poster for him to sign that I had purchased just for this moment. He looked at me, looked at the poster (the top half of it had three pictures of Quinn, from *Lawrence of Arabia*, *The Guns of Navarone*, and *Zorba the Greek*), he looked at me again, his face a study in blankness, the pen poised in his hand, and he obviously had no name to put with my face, so he wrote:

"Fondest Regards—
Of all the pictures I've made, these are the ones I love,
Anthony Quinn."

The Making of *Running Time*

I conceived the idea for *Running Time* at about midnight on New Year's Eve, 1995-96.

I was sitting in my apartment in Santa Monica considering going to one or more of several parties that I had been invited to, but did not feel like attending. Instead, I sat on my couch and asked myself, as I've asked 10,000 times before, "What's a good idea?"

After some length of time, my internal response was, "Hitchcock's *Rope* is a great visual concept— theoretically no cuts; all in real time—so why isn't it a very good movie?"

So I sat there and thought about it. Well, first of all *Rope* is a play, all stuck in one apartment, so it's not great movie material to begin with (nor is it a very good play, either). Second, if one is going to go to the trouble of shooting in real time with no cuts, shouldn't time be the issue, which it's not in *Rope*? "Therefore," I continued to think, "what plot has an inherent time issue?"

A heist. I'll buy that for a dollar.

Okay. Now, what are the technical problems? A roll of film is only ten minutes long, so, just like *Rope*, there must be a hidden cut every ten minutes or so. Most of the "hidden cuts" in *Rope*, however, aren't really hidden at all. In fact, there are two straight cuts that no one ever discusses, and several of the other cuts are so awkward that I can easily imagine hearing the deleted soundtrack with Hitchcock's voice calling out in concern, "Jimmy, don't move. We're almost out of film and we must now dolly into your back. Just freeze." Then the camera bouncily rolls into Jimmy Stewart's back to cover the "hidden" cut. So, where else can cuts be hidden? Going past dark objects (Hitchcock uses the lid of the trunk containing the dead body, which is okay, but it's not really moving and the camera's not moving, so it's not a great choice). Going past pillars or other foreground objects is always effective, which Hitchcock *never* does in *Rope*.

Then I really thought about it and realized that cuts can also be hidden in the blur of fast camera moves, commonly known as whip pans. Hitchcock didn't do any of those, either.

Then I thought, instead of just running each roll of film out to the very end and letting the hidden cuts fall where they may, which is what *Rope* does, it would be a *much* better idea to put the cuts in the best possible places—where you'd naturally pass a foreground object or need a whip pan for story purposes—and integrate the cuts into the story. Also, it would be best to do the hidden cuts somewhere between 4 and 4 ½ minutes, that way I'd get two shots a roll, and make better use of the film stock. If your shot is 7 minutes long, you're wasting 3 minutes of film.

Also, if I wasn't going to shoot entirely on a set with controlled lighting, but was in fact going to go from inside to outside in the same shot on location, there would subsequently be color problems: different filters are needed for sunlight or incandescent light. A very simple solution immediately presented itself—shoot in black and white. No color problems and it stylistically fit the idea of a heist film; crime; noir, etc.

That was my revelation on New Years 1995-96.

For two weeks I mused, "A real time heist in black and white. Hmmmmm?" I came up with several entire plots that I didn't like and summarily rejected.

I called my friend Peter Choi, pitched him what I had, and suggested that we get together and kick the idea around. He didn't sound terribly enthused, but said sure. So, we got together and to my surprise and delight, instead of kicking it around, Peter pitched me Act I of a story, and I was astounded; it was perfect—a guy gets out of prison, meets his buddy, there's a hooker waiting for him in the van, then they go on a heist. It was exactly what I was looking for, but it was only Act I. I had to work out just what the heist was, who these people were, and where this all lead, which was Acts II and III. But that all fell into place pretty quickly over the next few weeks.

Now that I had a story, I spent the next three months writing the script. It was a very difficult script to write, too. After my first draft I never added another scene; all of the ongoing work was in the scenes that were already there, expanding them from within. The number of pages had to account for the number of minutes the film would run, give or take. It also had to be physically possible to do everything I was describing without a cut and a reset. There is a sequence when the truck has a flat tire, that is then fixed during the course of single take. It seemed like a cool idea, but could it be done? Could squibs (blood hits) be set off during the course of very long takes, because that's certainly not how it's usually done.

And since I intended to keep the camera moving as much as possible, where would the lights and the boom go? And the crew, for that matter?

All good questions. Every time I brought the idea of actually making this movie up to anyone they would display interest in the idea, and complete disbelief that it could be pulled off.

I've done some pretty long takes before in other films—one minute, two minutes, even three minutes—but to do a 4 to 4 ½ minute take, which is longer than I'd ever done before, one after another after another did seem kind of daunting. Nevertheless, I continued on . . .

I wrote the lead part with my good buddy, Bruce Campbell, in mind. If I could actually convince Bruce that I was making this movie—considering that I hadn't made a film in seven years—then I would be a long way toward honestly making it. Bruce is a busy actor and generally booked on a lot projects long before they're made, and these are all well-paying projects. So if I booked him for this and asked him to hold open that time, a project where he wasn't being paid, I'd better mean it.

Well, I somehow not only convinced Bruce to star in the film, but to invest in it as well (now that's my kind of actor, and a friend).

I then offered the second-lead to Jeremy Roberts, an actor I had worked with on *Xena: Warrior Princess*, who was terrific, and basically stole the show (on the 1st season episode, "A Fistful of Dinars"). Jeremy read the script and accepted. My two leads were cast.

I ran into an actress, Anita Barone, whom I knew slightly from Detroit, at a party in L.A. I'd seen her in several plays so I knew that she was a first-rate actor. Without thinking twice I offered her the part. She subsequently read the script and also accepted. Now I had my entire lead cast, and they were all my first choices. That was the moment I thought, "This movie might be *really* good."

Since Bruce, Jeremy, and Anita work all the time, the next thing I had to do was to choose shooting dates that would accommodate all three of their schedules. I chose my birthday, August 17, five months hence. Bruce informed me upon my declaration of the "locked-down, absolutely-no-chance-of-changing" shoot dates, that if I didn't shoot the film then, he'd "kill me." We finally ended up pushing the date back two weeks, but this was partially at Bruce's request, so there was no need to kill me.

My good friend Jane had just broken up with her mate of twelve years, and had also quit her job of ten years with Steven Spielberg (she was his comptroller). I asked her if she'd like to produce my film with me and she agreed. I would entirely handle the legal and monetary end of things, she and I together would handle the actual producing.

I must digress again. My optimism about having the money to make the movie was based primarily on the recent sale of my script, *Cycles*, to Beacon Entertainment, thus giving me some disposable income to squander. I was hoping to put up about half the money myself and raise the other half from friends and loved ones. I ended up putting up more like three-quarters. The final production budget, by the way, was $135,000, $15,000 over the predicted final cost.

In March of 1996, Jane and I began scouting locations. Although the story is very limited in its scope, it still has numerous locations, many of which had to co-exist directly next to other locations because we couldn't cut between them. In the succeeding months, Jane and I drove up and down every side-street and alley in Santa Monica, Venice, West L.A., West Hollywood, Burbank, Northridge, Van Nuys, Glendale, and downtown L.A. We also looked at warehouses and abandoned factories all over the city. Our locations finally ended up being: downtown L.A., Glendale, Santa Monica, and the prison location was in Lancaster, 90 minutes north of L.A. (and where Judy Garland grew up).

After Jane came aboard, the next person to join up was the casting director, Donise Hardy. She put out the call for all of the other actors we needed on the internet, and within a week we had a pile of headshots over five feet tall, literally 1,000 of them. We culled it down and culled it down until we finally auditioned 60 actors for the five remaining parts. Donise made the casting a joy, and her taste was always right on the mark.

I then made two important decisions: I chose 16mm, Kodak, ASA 64, black and white stock; and I decided to shoot full-frame at a screen ratio of 1.33:1.

First of all, ASA 64 is a particularly slow-speed film stock, meaning it's thicker and has more chemicals on it, but needs more light to penetrate those chemicals and expose properly. The result of using slow film stock is finer grain and a sharper image. I personally just like the look of a fine grain image, which isn't used very much anymore in movies even in color, but hardly at all in black and white (I had to special order the stock). Beyond that, if I ever needed to do a 35mm blow-up—which I did—the image quality would theoretically hold up better. More on that later.

The second decision was choosing to shoot at a screen ratio of 1.33:1. The average movie right now is shot at 1.85:1, meaning the picture is 1.85 times as wide as it is tall, almost 2 to 1. At 1.33:1 the picture is nearly square—very similar to the size of an average TV screen. With only a few experimental exceptions, all movies were shot at 1.33:1 from the beginning of motion pictures until 1953 when Cinemascope (which is 2.35:1) was introduced. That's why all old black and white movies from the 30's and 40's look fine on TV. Until the advent of letterboxing, all the wide-screen movies of the 50's and 60's just look wrong on TV with half the image cut off. The average movie shot at 1.85:1 is losing more than 25% of the image when shown on TV, unless it's letterboxed.

One popular method now of bypassing this problem is to shoot Super-16mm, which has a screen ratio of just about 1.85:1, thus blowing-up almost perfectly to the present 35mm theatrical standards. The way that Super-16 achieves this wide-screen format is that instead of running double-perf film stock, meaning there are sprocket holes on both sides of the film, it runs single-perf, which is in fact print stock. 16mm print stock only has perforations on one side so that the optical soundtrack can go on the other side. Since there is no optical soundtrack while shooting (sound is recorded on a sound recorder and transferred to optical in post), that allows extra space for the image to cover, thus giving you the 1.85:1 screen ratio. Here's the big problem: you can't make a 16mm print—you've used up the area where the soundtrack goes—so now you *must* blow-up to 35mm to show the film theatrically. Since 16mm prints are less than half as much money as 35mm prints, not to mention the cost of the blow-up, I decided that I wanted to make 16mm prints to send out to the film festivals. Also, Super-16 camera equipment is considerably more expensive to rent than regular 16mm. Beyond that, aesthetically, wide-screen didn't seem appropriate for the subject matter of the film nor the technical problems that I knew I would be facing trying to hide light stands, booms, and the crew with such long takes. So I chose 1.33:1. Hey! *Citizen Kane* and *Gone With the Wind* both look terrific at 1.33:1.

Jane and I then put together our small, young, mostly inexperienced, college student crew. The first thing we did was to hire Ida Gearon, Bruce Campbell's wife, as associate producer. She and Jane would be a team during production, when I would no longer be co-producing, but from then on just directing. Also, Ida had just completed taking classes at Cal State Northridge (one of her instructors was a 90-year-old Abraham Polonsky, who wrote *Body and Soul* in 1947), and this is where we wrangled most of our crew.

I had already been a 2nd unit director on two TV movies, and my 14-person 2nd unit crew could do anything the 75-person main unit crew could do, but way faster. Having this invaluable knowledge, I now put together an exceptionally small, lean crew.

On *Running Time* the entire camera/lighting department consisted of: the Director of Photography, Kurt Rauf; the Steadi-Cam and camera operator (the same person), Bill Gearhart; a 1st Assistant Cameraman, a key grip/gaffer, and a loader, and that was the biggest department by far.

There were no assistant directors, however the production coordinator, my buddy Paul Harris, took over the 1ˢᵗ A.D. position on set by sheer attrition (I was usually stationed in another room with the wireless monitor). Bruce Campbell also did his bit as 1st A.D. He'd regularly get fed up with what he considered too much dithering around and would suddenly launch into a perfect impersonation of a crabby, impatient 1st A.D., clapping his hands, *"All right, that's it! We're done! Off the set! Now! Move it!"* And before I knew it we were shooting, which was lovely. I encouraged Bruce to do this anytime he felt like it.

We shot for ten days—two five-day weeks—and wrapped early every single day. On the sixth day of shooting we got so far ahead of schedule (we shot 14 pages instead of just 8), that on the seventh day we ended up wrapping at 10:30 A.M. because I couldn't reschedule the pyro-technician who was coming the next day to come any earlier. Jane and I ate our catered lunch for 20 by ourselves. We kept saying to each other, "Eat! Eat!"

(As an amusing sidelight, a mutual friend of Bruce's and mine from Detroit, John Cameron, was working as 1st A.D. on *Men in Black* simultaneous to our shoot. Each day he and Bruce would speak on their cell phones from the sets and compare notes about how much got shot — *Running Time*: 8 pages; *Men in Black*: an 1/8 of a page; *Running Time*: 14 pages; *Men in Black*: a 1/4 of a page, etc.).

On location in downtown L.A. shooting *Running Time*, 1996. L to R: Jeremy Roberts, Stan Davis, Bruce Campbell, Gordon Jennison.

A big portion of Act I of *Running Time* takes place in the aforementioned truck. The way this sort of sequence is generally shot is either: (A) pure fakery, meaning people are shaking the truck to make it look like it's moving while other people are swiveling lights past the truck to give the impression of movement, or (B) using rear-screen or blue screen projection, having a section of the truck set up on a soundstage and projecting a moving image of the passing road behind the actors, or (C) towing the truck behind another truck that is also towing a generator to power the lights illuminating the actors inside the truck. For the sense of both realism and practicality (remember, I can't cut), I wanted to shoot in an actual moving truck driving through city streets. Since we could not afford a real, quiet, movie generator, or another truck big enough to haul our picture truck, the answer, in my mind, was to create a portable lighting grid in the truck powered by DC current from a car battery. Also, since our space was very limited inside the truck, there was a reasonable chance that whatever lights I used would be seen, so they had to be of a nature that might actually be in a truck. I purchased ten standard, black, clamp lights, tore out their guts and replaced them with low-wattage, DC, movie-projector lamps and bulbs, then wired them all into an extra-large car battery. The lights were all clamped to strips of wood attached to the truck's ceiling so that they could be slid back and forth or side to side. It all worked brilliantly, I'm both happy and proud to say. Kurt was able to achieve some very specific and impressive lighting effects inside the truck with these lights.

Squibs are usually wired into an actor's costume, the wires or "tail" running out their pant leg, then detonated by a pyro-technician sitting out of frame. This would not be practical with long, extended takes. I asked my good buddy, Gary Jones, who had done special effects on my first two films, how I should handle the squibs? Gary's sharp response was to have the actors set off their own squibs—the detonator switch running down their shirt sleeve into their own hand. Since there would be blanks in the guns, when the actor heard the blank fire, they'd push their button—Pow!—and die. Once again, it worked great.

Shooting the very long takes quickly turned out to be difficult, but a real time-saver. Once you get it, you've got it; there's no close-ups, reverse-shots or inserts to pick up. What we also realized pretty fast was that after two or three rehearsals, even if it hadn't come together, which it generally hadn't yet, it was time to shoot it. Basically, you don't get a 100% from anyone—nor do you even want it—until you run film through the camera.

Actors remembering their lines was not a problem. Before shooting we had four rehearsals of a couple of hours each where we worked out a lot of blocking and line-changes. The actors knew which 7-10 page hunks we'd be shooting everyday, and 7-8 pages is what any actor in a leading part will have to learn for any given day of shooting on a TV show anyway, so it was no big deal. Plus, of course, I used good SAG actors, the single largest cost on the film (one-third of the budget), and they were worth every cent. You can't put your money in a better place on a low-budget movie, in my opinion. I'd rather have no effects and good actors then a lot of effects (be they good or bad) and bad actors. But that's just me.

For the first and only time in my life on *Running Time* I shot entirely in order (something that is very rarely, if ever, done), moving from scene #1 to scene #2 to scene #3, onward to the end. It was wonderful. Showing up to work everyday was like going to see a serial unfold. When we shot the last scene we were done and the movie was over. It caused some scheduling problems, but was well worth it, particularly when shooting this type of film, in real time, one thing leading directly in to the next.

When shooting most things, even if there's a line-flub or the boom drops in or a light flares or whatever, you can just keep going because some part of it may be usable, and if you really want it you can just cut in and out to get it. When shooting in long takes, if something goes wrong, it's now all wrong and you can just stop. Our biggest ongoing problem was at some point or other catching the poor boom man. Still, this was far preferable to using wireless microphones (that we did revert to a couple of times), just because the boomed mike sounds better. This also allowed me to use a few old-time Hollywood lines that amuse me. When, four minutes into a take, suddenly the camera pans and there is the boom man crawling on the floor looking sheepishly into the lens, pretending to suddenly be invisible, I would happily yell: "If you join SAG you'll get residuals!" which the boom man wasn't terribly amused by, but it always got a laugh. Nevertheless, our boom man was excellent and it wasn't really a big problem. He ultimately did a lot of crawling on the floor, below frame, without the boom, just holding the mike by hand.

I did another odd thing that worked out wonderfully well. At the end of every shot I would have all of the actors group together under the microphone and run the entire sequence again, without a camera motor buzzing or clothes rustling or a cameraman's footsteps or anything else. This allowed me to eliminate thousands of dollars of voice-replacement in post-production. I did do one hour of looping with Bruce adding some huffing and puffing to all of his running, and that's it.

Our ten day shoot, wrapping early every single day, went by so fast it's like it happened in a dream. There were various other moviemaking shenanigans with police and vehicle permits and a creep who rented us a stage, then made us pull our set down, then rebuild it the next day. Movies are just like that, and I love that about them; as hard as you try to plan and scout and prepare, there's always the unexpected that you must contend with as well.

Jane and I had found the perfect alley we had been searching for and searching for in downtown L.A. It was very long, with a dead end, and a door into a building right near the end. We spoke with the owner of the building and got permission to use the backdoor. That was one of the days with the pyro-technician and also an L.A. fire marshal. I had everybody and everything I needed to shoot the scene. We went to open the door into the building, the one we had gotten written permission to use, *but had never actually tried to open*, and nobody in this large factory could find the key to open the door. I stood there with my whole cast and crew waiting, at about $10,000 a day, whether I rolled film or not, as these schnooks slowly went through a key ring of 500 rusty old keys, none of which even came close to fitting the rusty old lock. Jane and I kept suggesting that we get a locksmith in and we'd pay for it, and the manager kept saying, "No, no, we'll find it." After an hour of this, at about key one hundred, they just gave up, meaning "You can't shoot here today." But the movie gods were smiling down on me that day because I had a real, honest-to-god, L.A. Fire Marshal with me, an officious, 75-year-old man in his uniform, who calmly informed the factory's manager, "You can't run a factory in this city where you have one fire exit, and it won't open. Would you like me to shut you down now?" The manager was utterly horrified, and gasped, "No." The Fire Marshall said, "Then let them get a locksmith in here right now, before I write you up." Jane quickly added, with a smile, "And we'll pay for it." The manager said, "Get the locksmith." And so I was able to shoot that day. But a lesson was also learned that day: if you're going to go through a door, don't just assume that the door opens, check it.

Meanwhile, I purchased 15,000 feet of film and ended up shooting just over 10,000 feet. The final film in 16mm is 2,800 feet long, so my shooting ratio was 3 ½ to 1. I immediately sold my unused film stock to Steadi-Systems (which, like Studio Film & Tape, buys unused film stock and short-ends). A few weeks later I decided to shoot two more scenes, and when I set up my pickup shoot I ended up buying my own damn film stock back from Steadi-Systems, at $20 extra a roll. The moral of this story is: don't get rid of your extra film until you're absolutely sure that you're done shooting.

This one-day pickup shoot didn't replace anything in the movie, but added two new scenes: one scene was the shot of Bruce having just run away from the heist, standing at the end of the street holding his bloody arm, just about to pass out and the camera begins circling him until he drops to his knees, he sees a car coming, stands and runs away; the other scene was Bruce running into a tunnel, the camera spinning 360 degrees, him freaking out and flashing back (without a cut) to several different things, then coming out of the tunnel, another 360 degree spin on the camera, then pulling back down an alley and finding the junkie/getaway driver who wasn't there when he was supposed to be, Bruce beats the crap out of him then runs away. This last shot, by the way, was suggested by my good buddy, Jack Perez, and I'm still both incredibly thankful, yet still utterly aghast that I didn't think of it myself.

Every exterior shot had to be planned with the time of day and the position of the sun in mind so as to avoid camera shadows—and even still I got a couple.

To keep the camera mobile on the interiors I decided to circle the actors on many occasions. To achieve this an entire conga line of technicians was always following the camera. In the girl's apartment at the end of the film (that was in fact my apartment), to get the camera fully around the actors sitting on the bed (a camera move I did several times), I first had to make sure that the headboard was sturdy enough to support a guy wearing a Steadi-Cam and an Arriflex SR camera. Next, for the cameraman to step up onto the headboard a person had to set a box under his foot as a step, then about ten stuffed animals had to be cleared away from around the cameraman's feet, then another box was put in so he could step down from the headboard, then all of the stuffed animals were re-placed so that as the camera continued around everything looked normal. Quite frankly, it's all unnoticeable in the film itself, exactly as it ought to be.

There are 30 cuts in the film, 32 with the front and end titles at-tached. Since, unlike any other movie but *Rope*, no more cuts could be made under any circumstances, the editor, Kaye Davis, and I spent a lot of time experimenting with those 30 cuts, a frame this way, a frame that way, two frames this way, two frames that way, etc. I'd say 20 of the 30 cuts are perfectly hidden. 10 of the cuts are somewhat dodgy.

Having now worked in this style of filmmaking I would not only happily do it again, but I'd do a much better job the next time. I got caught in several of the same traps as did Mr. Hitchcock—movement straight into the lens makes for a clumsy cut; movement *across* the lens makes for a much better cut.

Running Time was cut on a non-linear editing system, the D-Vi-sion, that is already obsolete. I have cut on both Avid and Light-works, the other non-linear editing systems, and they're all great. It is definitely the way to go if you can afford it. In my case, my friend and editor, Kaye, owns this D-Vision machine, and she not only edited the film for free, but threw in the use of her equipment, too.

Also, my good friend, Joe LoDuca, who composed the scores for my first two films (as well as all three *Evil Dead* films, and *Hercules* and *Xena*), composed and recorded the score for *Running Time* for free.

I think both Joe and Kaye were so impressed that I actually got another movie made after so many years that they helped me out of the sheer kindness of their hearts. I gratefully thank them, too, as well as everyone else who worked on the film.

Running Time crew shot L to R: Josh Becker, Bruce Campbell, Anita Barone, Bill Gierhart, Kurt Rauf, Rob Disner, Ida Gearon, Steve Heuer, Jorenz Campo, Ana Powell, Paul Harris.

The post-production sound was done by Ideal Sound, a small company that specializes in low-budget features (many of the films they've done are parts two, three, and four of films you've never heard of). These guys were friendly and cooperative and did a good job. For one flat (and affordable) price they did everything (I won't say how much because everyone has to make their own deals). They cut all of the sound effects, background tracks, and dialog, then mixed the film very well in both stereo and mono (stereo for the video and 35mm tracks, mono for the 16mm track).

Our 16mm prints were made by Hollywood Film Lab, a small and very friendly lab right in Hollywood.

I also made a one-print 35mm blow-up of the film, at a cost of $5,500, which is significantly less than the $40,000 I paid for the negative-to-interpostive (IP) blow-up I had done on *Thou Shalt Not Kill . . . Except*. But you only get the one print, whereas with an IP blow-up you make a new negative, then make as many prints as you want. However, I wasn't expecting to get a theatrical release, I simply intended to four-wall the film at one theater for one week so that the film would be reviewed.

I contacted the friendly Laemmle family (descendants of Carl Laemmle, founder of Universal Pictures), who own many of the art-house movie theaters in L.A. (I had shown *Lunatics* at their theater, The Royal in Westwood, five years earlier). This time I rented the Laemmle Theater in Santa Monica on 2nd St., that was 26 blocks from my apartment at that time (I was just off 28th St.), for the week of Dec. 19, 1997 . . .

Meanwhile, I was on six weeks of jury duty for the entire time I was setting up this screening—and I never even ended up on a jury! That's the second time I'd had jury duty in L.A., shown up for weeks at a time and didn't get called onto a jury. Something about me is clearly objectionable. Finally, I sat in a courtroom waiting my turn to be questioned by the lawyers and the judge to possibly end up on a jury, but probably not, given my track record. When they called my name I stood up in front of the judge and explained that I had been showing up daily for six weeks, still hadn't made it onto a jury, and I had a feature-length movie opening in a theater in Los Angeles at the end of the week, at which time I was truly no longer available to serve on a jury, so please god, let my people go. The judge asked, "What's the name of the film?"

"*Running Time*, your honor," I replied. This got a chuckle from the assembly.

The judge nodded and smiled. "Good luck with your film. You're dismissed."

The cast and crew screening of *Running Time,* on Thursday, Dec. 18, went very well. The 35mm blow-up looked and sounded all right, although too grainy and contrasty for my liking, but you get what you pay for. Also, since I had chosen a very slow, high-contrast film stock in the first place, I came to realize it wasn't particularly suitable for a 35mm blow-up (my two experiences of blowing-up from 16mm to 35mm taught me that contrast is bad, but grain can be lived with).

The reviews came out and they were almost unanimously positive. Kevin Thomas in the *LA Times* gave the film a half-page review, with a photo, and said, "An amusing and highly effective example of how shooting an entire 70-minute feature in a single take can bring intense immediacy and psychological validity to a traditional caper-gone-wrong plot. Stylishly adroit, well-acted and certainly entertaining." Andy Klein in the New Times wrote, "An extraordinary technical achievement. The continuity makes the suspense almost unbearable. Observant viewers will find themselves marveling at just how the director is pulling it all off. This is both a very taut thriller . . . and an amazing accomplishment."

I guess I fooled them.

Meanwhile, the actual day *Running Time* opened, Friday, Dec. 19, also happened to be the same day that the film *Titanic* opened. Woody Allen's film, *Deconstructing Harry*, opened that day, too, right across the hall from my film at the Laemmle. Pretty much nobody came to see *Running Time* or *Deconstructing Harry*, but the line for *Titanic*, showing two blocks away, stretched off into infinity. I momentarily considered getting a sandwich board that read, "If you can't get a ticket for *Titanic*, there's more film entertainment available two blocks this way," but I didn't.

Even though I thought that I had made the perfect film festival movie, apparently it wasn't perfect enough to get into any of the major festivals. Not Sundance, Telluride, Toronto, New York or Seattle. The film did get accepted to Slamdance, though. The festival organizers called me up brimming with praise for the film, and said, "This is a *great* first film."

I said, "Thanks, but it's not my first film, it's my third."

"Oh," they said sadly, "then we can't show it. We only show first films."

Which I think is exceptionally stupid.

Running Time was shown at: The New York Underground Film

Festival, The Orlando Underground Film Festival, The Sao Paulo
Film Festival, and the Helsinki Film Festival, among others.

At the New York Underground Film Festival, I arrived at the
theater in Union Square a half an hour before the screening and
there was a large crowd of over a hundred people standing outside.
I thought, "Wow! This'll be a terrific screening." A moment later a
fellow stepped out of the theater beside where my film was showing and said, "*Tap Dogs*, now seating," and literally every single
person went in to see it, leaving me entirely by myself on the corner. However, mere minutes before showtime the 200-seat movie
theater completely filled up. The audience was comprised mainly
of hip-looking, sort of punkish, New Yorkers in their 20s and 30s,
many sporting black leather jackets. At the end of the film, when
you think Carl has left Janie forever, but instead returns, there was
a communal sigh of satisfaction from the tough-looking audience.
They may have appeared hard, but deep down they were all soft-
ies.

At the screening in Sao Paulo, Brazil, there was no sound for the
first ten minutes (nor did I have electronic subtitles that appeared on
many of the films shown there). Also, once everybody was seated,
they inexplicably locked the theater's doors so that any time someone had to go to the bathroom they then had to pound on the metal
doors until someone would come let them out. The 16mm print of
the film is in two reels so the projectionist must do a change-over
between the reels. This isn't very difficult if you're paying attention.
Reel one ended—flap, flap, flap—no reel two for at least ten minutes. When reel two finally began, no sound again. And since no one
in Brazil speaks English, and I don't speak Portuguese, there was no
Q&A. For that I flew 6,000 miles in each direction.

Subsequently, *Running Time* was picked-up for DVD/video distribution by Anchor Bay Entertainment, the folks who already had
Thou Shalt Not Kill . . . Except. That seven-year deal has already
gone its full-term, and Anchor Bay renewed for seven more years.
They also included *Running Time* as a second disc with *Evil Dead*
in the United Kingdom.

Running Time has been shown on the Independent Film Channel
about 32 times, if I'm not mistaken. This deal was made by a sales
agency called Creative Light who not only didn't return one penny
to me, but then promptly went out of business and took a number

of my film and video elements with them.

Then Anchor Bay ended being sold up, then sold again, and is now owned by Starz Entertainment. Since the new Starz/Anchor Bay no longer intended to push any of their somewhat obscure low-budget titles, including *Running Time*, they kindly gave me back the rights to the film.

I have since licensed *Running Time* to Synapse Films (who are strangely located right near me outside Detroit, just like Anchor Bay, and it's not like there are all that many film companies around here). Synapse will release the film on high-definition DVD in 2008. There will also be a second disk included with it that will contain my super-8 film, *Holding It*, as well as a documentary about the good old days of shooting super-8, with interviews with Bruce Campbell and myself.

Whatever the merits or deficiencies of *Running Time* may be, it continues to be released, and I count that as a victory.

Kids These Days

I imagine this same discussion going on between two men walking along the Appian Way two thousand years ago in ancient Rome or between two women standing on Ishtar Avenue in Babylon four thousand years ago, shaking their heads and sighing, "What's with kids these days? They're lazy, rebellious, and they don't listen." I only bring this up because it's in the news with kids shooting each other in their high schools, and it's on the cover of *Time* magazine this week. But I would like to relate it to a bigger issue, which is that our present culture is a repetitive, regurgitated bore.

When I made my film *Lunatics: A Love Story* in 1989 I had to give serious consideration to the idea of including a rap song ("The Reynolds Rap") in the movie because I thought it might quickly date the film. What if rap went out in the next year or two and I still hadn't gotten the film released? I mean, rap had already been around for five or six years at that point; why would it possibly last much longer?

Slow dissolve to now, ten years later, and rap and hip-hop are still around. Isn't there supposed to be something new? [And eight years after that there's *still* nothing new].

What's the big film right this minute? *Star Wars.* Hey, wait a minute, that's a movie from when *I* was young (or younger anyway), twenty-two years ago. It seemed kind of new then, but I've got news for you, there's nothing new about a *Star Wars* movie now. [This is like déjà vu all over again].

Let's face facts, there's inherently nothing new about *any* sequel. That's the point! The same, of course, goes for any remake, whether it's a movie remake of a movie, a movie remake of a TV show, or a TV show remake of a movie (that was easy for me to say).

It's also been the same two big TV shows for years, *ER* and *NYPD Blue.* They're both good shows, but there's nothing new about either one. There's always going to be a cop show and a medical show on the air. Nor is there anything new about any of the sit-coms. In fact,

I'm kind of surprised that there still are sit-coms after all these years because, with their insulting, inane laugh tracks and stupid, obvious jokes, they really seem like a painfully dated form.

Nothing's new.

When I was twelve years old, in 1969, *everything* seemed new because it was new. Hippies, draft dodgers, heavy metal, electronic music, drugs, riots, civil rights, women's rights, a man on the moon, Woodstock, Altamont. None of these things had ever happened before. Hollywood was in complete turmoil. An X-rated movie, *Midnight Cowboy*, won "Best Picture." They were taking off all of their clothes on Broadway in *Hair* and singing about sodomy and fellatio. One of the biggest moneymaking movies of that year, *Easy Rider*, was also one of the lowest-budget and all about buying and selling cocaine set to contemporary rock songs. I was a different person coming out of that movie than I was going in. I immediately sewed an American flag on the back of my jacket, just like Peter Fonda.

Anything was possible, and everything was new.

When I was twelve I didn't give a crap about anything meant for twelve-year-olds. If it was aimed at kids, I wasn't interested. My favorite movie at that time was, oddly, *Becket*, the story of the friendship between King Henry the 2ⁿᵈ and Thomas á Becket, the archbishop of Canterbury. It's a bright movie, and it wasn't the slightest bit over my head, and I don't think that I was all that exceptional of a twelve-year-old.

Except that maybe I was exceptional in that I was focused on wanting to know about and see as many movies as humanly possible. This was not all that easy of thing to do in Detroit in 1969-70. There was no Museum of Modern Art like in New York, nor were there all the revival theaters like in L.A. I had to stay up and watch the Late Show and the Late-Late Show or hitchhike up to the college town of Ann Arbor and see 16mm prints. By the time I got to Hollywood in 1976, however, I had seen a lot more movies than most people ever had.

Now, if you're interested in movies they're on TV twenty-four hours a day, no commercials, and in their proper formats. It seems to me that there ought to be kids running around all over the place who have seen more movies than me by the time they're fifteen. Except that there aren't.

I could grab the next one hundred people twenty-five years old and younger who walk by my front door and ask them if they've ever heard of *A Man For All Seasons*, winner of "Best Picture" in 1966, and I don't think a single one of them would know what the hell I was talking about, let alone have seen it.

By the time I was twenty-five I had seen all the Oscar winners for "Best Picture" (most in the theater) not that it's really a very big deal, there are only seventy-one one of them, for goodness sake. It's not like learning how to play an instrument well enough to be in a classical orchestra. You're just sitting through movies, but, one hopes, you're paying attention and getting something out of it.

Kids could be studying the entire history of cinema without leaving their houses, yet no kids seem to be doing it. Instead they watch the new movies that they're supposed to watch, *Star Wars 4* and *Batman 4* and *Lethal Weapon 4* and *Bullshit 4* and *Horseshit 4* and *Dogshit 4*.

Kids have nothing new to call their own. So, to prove that they're unique individuals, they end up doing exactly what the media tells them to do. They go see *Dogshit 4* the week it opens then try to kid themselves they've seen something new, which they clearly know they haven't. It's amusing to me when people are disappointed with *Star Wars 4*. It's as though they just purchased a Pet Rock, brought it home, and realized that it didn't do anything. The point is *you* spending *your* money; not you enjoying the product, or it having any value.

Were I twenty-five or younger, instead of over forty and perpetually pissed-off, I'd be angry, too.

Yet, rather than get a machine gun and shoot people at high school or just get sullen and depressed, isn't it our job to make things better? I think it is, but I sure as hell don't run into many other people with this same attitude very often. The main ambition I encounter these days among young people is of the mercenary variety, the "I-want-to-be-rich" kind, and that's a complete bore. This is the attitude behind people defending *Star Wars 4* or *Titanic* with "Sure it sucked, but look how much money it's making," as though that elevates it above the level of regurgitated shit that it is, but it doesn't. Anyone who uses this rationale, in my opinion, is a soulless zombie firmly in the grips of the giant corporations.

So why is there so much apathy, laziness, and angst among young folks? Why are kids now regularly put on antidepressants when they're five and six and seven years old? Why are kids taking weapons and shooting apart their high schools? What's to be depressed about?

Hey! We're not in a world war or a depression or the Dark Ages or the black plague. What's the big bummer?

My sister ventures that part of the problem with young people may be that there is no discipline anymore, meaning, ultimately, you can't hit kids. I'm single and have no kids, so I can't say. But this is the very first generation of kids whom it was illegal to hit for any reason. Perhaps there is no discipline, or so my sister proffers. And possibly the lack of discipline has led to apathy.

This may be the reason for all of these cases of ADD, attention deficit disorder, a malady that didn't exist when I was a kid. Actually, I hear that ADD doesn't exist anywhere else in the world except the United States. France and England don't accept it as a legitimate ailment. If anyone would have been diagnosed with ADD thirty years ago, it would have been me. I hated school, hated authority of all kinds, got lousy grades, talked back constantly, and was always in trouble. Had they put me on antidepressants (that didn't exist then, either) or Ritalin (that did) or whatever, would I have become the person who I presently am?

Something of a shameful family secret may well have also been a crucial turning point in my young life. When I was seven or eight years old my father, who was a bit of an uptight hothead as a young man, got so pissed off at me for not paying attention, that he conceived and initiated "The Awareness Game." The way this "game" worked was that my dad and I would drive down a residential street (in his Ford Falcon) and he would ask me, as an example, "How many stop signs did we pass?" If I said three and he saw four, he'd smack me and command me to "Pay attention!" These were not pats, either. Nor were they punches, but they were meant to make me cry. Then we'd drive down the next street, and he'd ask, "How many green houses did we pass?" Etc. I realized quickly that there was no way to win this game.

Once after playing the Awareness Game we stopped at a restaurant for breakfast, and my dad commanded me to write one hundred times on the back of paper placemats, "I will be more aware." I printed it out the first time, and he promptly smacked me—in a restaurant, mind you—and yelled, "*I said write it, not print it!*"

I replied in my quavering little seven- or eight-year-old voice, "But, Dad, they haven't taught us how to write yet."

He then wrote it out for me in script, and I copied it one hundred times while he smoked cigarettes and watched. I now realize that this might account for the fact that I never write anything in script and never have. I either print or type.

Although this story is generally invoked as an example of my father's volatile temper, he may well have done me a favor. I do pay attention, and I can focus my thoughts. Perhaps I would not have this ability were it not for my dear old dad smacking the importance of it into me. I sincerely hope, however, that there is some better way to achieve this result than by playing The Awareness Game.

All I know is that the young people I come into contact with in the film business, on film crews, living in my building, and through my website, seem to be, for the most part, befuddled and clueless. In a way I don't blame them, either. If one's desire is to get into the film business, for instance, there's no logical route to achieve it anymore. I've personally thrown in the towel as far as making Hollywood films go. I accept the fact that I'm an independent filmmaker, and I'm proud of it. But I didn't choose it; it chose me.

I recently spoke at a Writer's Guild weekend at Lake Arrowhead (I am not a Writer's Guild member, by the way). The two other speakers were David Milch, executive producer of *NYPD Blue*, and Ted Elliot, co-writer of *Mark of Zorro*, *Godzilla* and *Little Monsters*. I missed David Milch, but I hear he braved the twenty-two miles of hairpin turns scaling the San Bernadino Mountains to Lake Arrowhead in a stretch limousine. Ted Elliot, who was very amusing, began his presentation with, "Why does my resume suck so bad?" The reason, as he presented it, is that everything he's ever worked on was taken out of his hands and rewritten before it was shot. Mr. Elliot called the development process the "dissection" process, where the story is picked to pieces. He concluded sadly that, "Nothing comes out of the dissection process alive."

I then got up and tried to explain to all these timid, struggling writers (who seemed like if I unexpectedly yelled, they'd all piss in their pants), that, in my opinion, screenwriting is not art and never would be, even at its very best. It's a craft, like building tables, and they were all craftspeople. A script is a blueprint and there are no blueprints in the Louvre. I recommended that they try building sturdier tables. I think every single person in that room considered themselves to be an artist, and I may as well have been speaking Swedish.

I'm now dealing with a number of young writers and filmmakers mainly through the Internet, but also a few in real life, and they all seem equally as timid, but also apathetic as well. Many of them have said in their own ways, "I'll shoot some stupid story just so I can get something made."

Guess what? Shit in, shit out. Start with shit and you will most assuredly end up with shit. If you begin the process of idea exploration with, "I'm not going to put myself to any trouble here, I'll just make something that's just like something else," you'll most certainly end up with a piece of shit.

And that's where I think we are at the moment. Our art is being created by lazy, timid, undisciplined people who have nothing to say, are only in it for the money, and even still can't get their simpleminded, utterly mercenary visions up on the screen. It's a sad state of affairs.

But why bother paying attention if there's nothing new and nothing seems worth paying attention to anyway? Sadly, one thing feeds right back into the other. Ultimately, *you* are the person making shit for *you* to watch. If you won't exert yourself and try to do better, you'll never get anything better. My films may not be anything special, but I am trying to set an example—I'm attempting to make good films for the sake of making good films. Not for money, not for fame, not because I think "they" might like them, "they" being the masses or the critics or whomever. I'm simply trying to make good movies, and if I'm succeeding or failing, it's my own fault.

The key to all of this, I think, is the old adage, "The point of life is not the destination, but the journey." There is no goal out there that's good enough. Fame and money seem like nonsense. It reminds me of when I was fifteen years old and thought, "If only I had my driver's license, everything would be great." I got my license and realized that I didn't have a car. I got a car and realized I didn't really have anywhere to go.

A friend of mine cannot sit still for five seconds. He needs constant amusement. If I stand up to change the CD, he'll grab anything in sight and start reading or will pull out his pen and begin doodling or making diagrams or lists. He cannot sit for a single moment with his own thoughts. This is a variation on ADD—*amusement* deficit disorder. It's not that he can't pay attention; I think he's petrified of being bored. If he's not being amused, then he must be bored.

I think that there is a whole wonderful world between amusement and boredom. This is where all of my stories come from, that magical fugue state in the middle. I guess it takes discipline to go there, just as it takes discipline to go to the gym and work out, but neither one is *really* difficult. We're not talking about brain surgery here.

This gets back to yet another problem I've noticed among young screenwriters is that most of them sit down to write thinking that all of the writing occurs at the keyboard. Once again, afraid of not being amused, they must have their glowing monitors and clicky keyboards or they're bored. The crucial element in writing is not the computer or the software, it's your thoughts. You can use lipstick on a mirror if that facilitates the process for you. As John Irving put it, "When I finally write the first sentence, I want to know everything that happens, so that I am not inventing the story as I write it; rather, I am remembering a story that has already happened." This is a crucial bit of information.

Yet, though there are seemingly more and more amusements out there, people seem to be increasingly more bored. There may well be more and more amusements, but none of them seem new. Fifty channels can become a hundred channels, but, if there was nothing to watch on the fifty, there still won't be anything to watch on a hundred.

If you need amusement but you don't want to think, you get *Star Wars* and *Batman* and *Die Hard*. And the big problem with living on nothing but amusement is that it's like trying to sustain life on popcorn alone; there just are not enough vitamins, minerals, and protein to do the job. Eventually, you will wither up and die.

Shooting "Xena: Warrior Princess," 2001.

Lucy Lawless and Josh

Xena's Final Wrap:
The End of an Era

I received the invitation for the big, final wrap party for "Xena: Warrior Princess" being thrown down in New Zealand. I won't be going—it's a long, expensive flight just for a party—but it was nice of
them to think of me and send an invitation. This isn't just the wrap
on "Xena," though, it's a final wrap for all of Renaissance Pictures'
(known as Pacific Renaissance Pictures in New Zealand) shows that
have been shot there since 1993. That would include: "Xena: Warrior Princess," "Hercules: The Legendary Journeys," "Young Hercules," "Amazon High," "Jack of All Trades" and "Cleopatra 2525."
315 hours of television programming is what the invitation states.

Included with the invitation was a complete list of every episode
of "Xena." I am proud to be one of two directors—along with New
Zealander, Garth Maxwell—to have made it through all six seasons
of the show. Of the 135 episodes of "Xena," I directed nine, and I
co-wrote the story for two others.

I began work down in New Zealand in 1993 when Pacific Re-
naissance Pictures first opened their doors for business to make five
TV movies about Hercules. I was on the same flight down as Kevin
Sorbo, who was to play Hercules, and was going down for his first
time. These five TV movies were part of a thing called "The Action
Pack," which I thought was a clever idea. Universal TV made four
or five episodes of a number of different possible series. There was
"Hercules: The Legendary Journeys," and William Shatner's "Tek
Wars" and "Midnight Run," and "Smokey," (as in "the Bandit"),
as well as a martial arts thing. Anyway, out of "The Action Pack"
emerged not only "Hercules," but from that they spun-off "Xena,"
which still has an "Action Pack" credit on the end. And then they
never did The Action Pack again. Two hit series out of the experi-
ment seems like a success to me, but what do I know?

However, when we first got down there, it was strictly to make
those five TV movies. I began as the 2nd unit director on the very first
film, *Hercules and the Amazon Women,* and I also 2nd unit directed

the third film, *Hercules in the Underworld* (*Hercules in His Under-wear*, as we so cleverly called it). I was then main unit director on the fifth film, which ultimately became *Hercules in the Maze of the Minotaur*, but initially had no story, no script, and was a completely unknown commodity. After I wrapped *Minotaur* in June, 1994, I got the job back as 2nd unit director and I stayed on to the bitter end, cleaning up the missing bits and pieces for all five films.

For some odd reason Kevin Sorbo was still under contract and Rob Tapert, the executive producer, being the slave-driver that he is, made Kevin come out and work on 2nd unit the day before he left New Zealand. Kevin bitched a little when he showed up on the set, like why wasn't I using a double as 2nd unit generally did? I told him I didn't know, but it wasn't my problem, I was going to shoot with whichever Hercules they gave me, and if it happened to be the real one, so much the better. Kevin was perfectly cool and we shot all the stuff we had to. As he and I were walking away, I said that Rob Tapert had mentioned to me the night before that he thought Hercules would get picked up and become a series, at least for 13 episodes.

Kevin laughed disdainfully and waved his hand, "Man, I've heard that shit before. I've already been in five or six pilots and they all say that. Believe me, I've made other plans" and he walked away. Cut to him returning to New Zealand in a few weeks and staying for the next five years.

In the original Pacific Renaissance Pictures' office, in Mount Wellington (a suburb of Auckland), there was a big blackboard on the wall with the names of four of the Hercules movies written out, and they're various shooting dates. When I said to people that I was not only the 2nd unit director, but I was also the main unit director on the fifth film, everyone replied, "But, mate, there's only four films," then I'd have to explain that there was really a fifth film, but the script wasn't written yet. I have no doubt that everybody (except Eric Gruendemann, the producer, who knew there was a fifth film coming) thought I was completely insane, with delusions of grandeur. I think Rob was giving himself a backdoor escape hatch in case it didn't come together, although I was determined to make sure that it would.

Meanwhile, Rob Tapert and I have known each other for over 30 years now, since 1976 when he was going to Michigan State University and was roommates with my good buddy, Ivan Raimi, Sam's older brother. I've also worked for Rob on and off since his first feature film, *Evil Dead*, in 1979. As will be apparent in the forthcoming events, Rob and I frequently don't see eye to eye on things, and we've had many disagreements. Since Rob is the employer and I'm the employee, he generally wins the arguments, but not always. And yet, incredibly, almost inexplicably, we have somehow continued to remain friends through all of it. I tell these stories as examples of the crazy, circuitous way things get done, and certainly not as any kind of indictment or smear of Rob. As executive producer, Rob had a million issues on his mind throughout this time, and I was merely one of them. Somehow Rob managed to get five TV movies made, that spawned a hit TV series, that immediately spawned another, bigger hit TV series, as well as a bunch of other things, too. I was but one thread in the giant patchwork, and very happy to have been involved, even if it doesn't always sound like it.

Anyway, one of my first jobs as 2nd unit director was to shoot the front title sequence of the show. However, nothing had been written or storyboarded or even vaguely conceived, so I just kept going out and getting random shots of Kevin running around in different locations, at various film speeds, swinging his sword and stuff. This quickly got silly and redundant, so I suggested that Hercules be arm wrestling a huge guy, slam the guy's arm down, crush the table and flip the guy, which still seems like a pretty cool shtick to me. The casting people went out and found the biggest man they could in New Zealand, named Alistair, who was over 500 pounds. I think he said that he was actually 40 stone, which, at 14 pounds a stone, put him closer to 600 pounds. He was big. And a very nice guy, too. They put him in his costume, he took one step and literally split the pants in half.

As I was walking out the door of the office to go shoot this arm wrestling sequence, someone ran up and got me because Rob Tapert was on the phone and wanted to speak to me. Rob said that he suddenly hated the idea of arm wrestling, and I should instead make it a real fight sequence. I said, "But Rob, this guy can't fight. He's huge."

"No, no, a huge guy is good. Herc should kick the crap out of him."

"It should be a stunt man," I said.

"Naw! A stunt man looks like a stunt man. This guy's huge, right?"

"Right."

"Good. Make a good sequence out of it."

And I hesitantly agreed.

Cut to the 2nd unit crew on this grassy hill somewhere outside Auckland with Kevin Sorbo, Alistair the 600-pound man, and me attempting to shoot a believable fight scene. Alistair's arm honestly had to weigh 75 pounds. He was about as uncoordinated as it's possible for human being to be previous to becoming incapacitated. If you were casting for the exact opposite of a stunt man, Alistair was perfect for the part. If he ended up on the ground, god forbid, it took four people struggling as hard as they could to get him back on his feet.

So I had Kevin and Alistair throwing fake punches at each other, none of them looking very convincing, and within three or four punches Alistair was huffing and puffing, wheezing, verging on coronary arrest and out of control. I called cut and explained to Alistair, for the seventh time, to take it slow, that all I needed was for him to sell one punch and one hit and I'd be happy. There could be as much reset time as he need between punches.

I called, "Action," Alistair pulled his fist *way* back, launched an enormous haymaker that threw him off balance so that it continued right on through and walloped Kevin Sorbo in the mouth with a crunching *Thud!*, flattening Kevin to the ground. *Holy shit!* I ran over to find Kevin flat on his back in the grass with blood coming out of both his nose and mouth. My short TV career flashed before my eyes. Ice was quickly applied to Kevin's face. Moments later the assistant director's phone rang, and naturally Kevin was immediately needed back on main unit. He was quickly hustled into a car and driven away.

That was the end of shooting for 2nd unit that day. It was also perhaps the end of my TV directing career forever.

Apparently, when Kevin arrived back on main unit his face was so swollen and bruised and that they couldn't shoot with him anymore that day and he was sent home. Had this been my harebrained idea I'm sure I would have been fired, but luckily it wasn't. Kevin was also very good about saying he didn't think it was my fault.

Strangely, when I first started as the 2nd unit director, I was on a 6-day week, being Monday through Saturday, but the 2nd unit crew was only on a 5-day week, starting on Tuesday. So, one Monday I ended up shooting tight inserts of Amazon babes putting knives into boot scabbards and oiling their skin, all by firelight, with only myself as the entire crew. I was in a corner of the stage as main unit was shooting in the same place, which is a very odd set-up, indeed. So there I was doing everything, putting up the background, setting up and aiming the lights, controlling the propane fire bar, as well as operating an enormous 35mm Arriflex camera with a big zoom lens. I had three very attractive young girls, all models, dressed as Amazons in strips of leather, and I was actually getting some good shots—several of which were in fact used in the finished film—when someone from the office came onto the stage and got me saying the co-producer, Liz Friedman, was on the phone from the USA.

Liz said, somewhat hesitantly, "Rob would like you to get these Amazon girls to have . . . orgasms."

"Excuse me?"

"Orgasms."

"Liz, these aren't actresses, these are models. Young models."

"Rob wants orgasms."

I threw my hands in the air, as Liz obviously already had, and said, "Okay. Orgasms it is."

The look on the faces of these three pretty Kiwi girls when I came back and told them what was now being desired of them was priceless. I may as well have been asking them to wave their arms and fly. It was quickly apparent that the prettiest, blondest one of the bunch had never even heard of orgasms, let alone had one. Somewhere in a vault lies a piece of film with this poor, befuddled, very cute young girl suddenly smiling widely, as though a cute puppy has come into view, then looking forlornly directly into the lens. The next girl energetically slammed her wrists together, then jumped up with her arms raised over her head like a cheerleader and I thought for a second she was going to do the splits, but she refrained just short of it. Oddly, none of these shots ended up being used.

I think I may have shot the two most used shots in all of Hercules and Xena. One was a tight close-up of a yellow flower, that tilts up to reveal a whole field of yellow flowers; and the other was this gorgeous sunset that was occurring behind us as we were setting up the camera to shoot Anthony Quinn in *Minotaur*, so I had the camera turn around and get it. Both of these shots have been used many times in numerous episodes of all the shows that Pacific Renaissance made.

Also, way back there at the very beginning in the first film, *Amazon Women*, the lead Amazon babe was portrayed by the soon-to-be star of "Touched by an Angel," Roma Downey, and the second-lead

Amazon babe was Lucy Lawless. It shows what a terrific actress Roma is that she got and easily handled that part, given she's a tiny person, or, as she would say with her beautiful Irish brogue, a wee little person. I was going through a very serious Van Morrison phase at that time, that's never really stopped, and as we passed each other she and I would exchange lines from his songs.

Meanwhile, I set eyes on Lucy Lawless and kind of swooned—she was such a babe, with incredibly big blue eyes, that it took my breath away. 2nd unit was on a exceptionally light schedule those first few days of shooting and I did very little else except follow Lucy around and vainly attempt to be charming by saying over and over as though I were Ricky Ricardo with a Cuban accent, "Lucy, you got some 'splainin' to do." After two unrelenting days of this, Lucy finally turned to me and said, "You're doing an imitation from Lucille Ball's TV show, right?"

I nodded, smiling, "Yes."

"We never got that down here," she stated flatly and walked away.

Still undeterred, I continued dogging her heels until a day or two later she brought her husband at the time, Garth Lawless, to the set. This may well have simply been to have Garth out to the set, but it did cool my ardor a bit.

Lucy ended up marrying my old buddy Rob Tapert, which I still think is pretty amusing.

Meanwhile, nobody knew what to do with the 2nd unit on this first film. They also had made a big blunder by thinking that Rick Allander, the 2nd unit DP, could also function simultaneously as the main unit Steadi-Cam operator. In essence, he needed to be two places at once all the time, so that scheme couldn't possibly work. And in that tug-of-war, main unit always won. Also, the director of *Amazon Women* didn't like or understand 2nd unit, and given a choice, he was much happier to have a Steadi-Cam on hand on main unit, and I don't blame him. Thus, the rest of the 2nd unit crew and I were forced to sit and wait for our DP/camera operator to return, and that turned out to be a great deal of the time. I burned through two 1,000-page books, Colleen McCullough's "The First Man in Rome" and "The Grass Crown," and was ready to begin the third in the series, when I got a call from Rob Tapert himself telling me that I could no longer read on the set, it was a bad influence on those around me. So, they wouldn't let me work, and I wasn't allowed to read, either—this had to be some new rung of Dante's Hell. All that was left for me to do was smoke cigarettes and drink coffee, and I did both these things profusely.

Finally, main unit began to fall behind schedule, and here was an entire 2nd unit sitting around with their thumbs up their bums. So missing shots began to fall to us, then parts of scenes, then finally whole scenes were given to 2nd unit to shoot. After I shot my first entire scene, the Amazons attacking the men's village, the director took me aside and really let me have it, saying he just hated everything I'd shot. Needless to say, I found this very encouraging (not). 2nd unit finally ended up shooting most of the fight scenes, as it always should have. I watched the DVD recently and I think the fights still hold up pretty well.

During my couple of week hiatus while the second film was shooting, I flew back home to the USA. There was still no story and no script for the phantom fifth film, the one I was supposed to direct. There was even talk of it being canceled because none of the writers had time to work on it. Also, there would be about half as much money for this fifth film as there was for the other four films (the first four films were $2.5 million each, with five-week shooting schedules; the fifth film would ultimately be $1.5 million, with a three-week schedule), so maybe it wasn't even possible. Rob was also now convinced that the fifth film, if there was one, had to contain footage from the other films because there wouldn't be time to shoot a full 90 minutes worth of new footage (I repeatedly said that there was time, but I was ignored). Well, I wasn't about to give up my first chance at directing a TV movie, at least not without a struggle. So while I was home I sat down and read a few books on Greek mythology. When I read the story of Theseus and the Minotaur, I flashed on that sequence in *Time Bandits*, with Sean Connery as Theseus. The Minotaur was just a mechanical bull's head strapped onto a big man's shoulders, and that didn't seem insanely difficult. Also, Hercules's seventh labor had been fighting the Bull of Minos, so the story was still within the Hercules mythology, not that it really mattered. Then I came up with a story about Hercules having retired from the adventurous life and settled down, somewhat unhappily, with his wife and three kids, although he keeps daydreaming about the good old days (that would be the footage from the other films). Simultaneously, the Minotaur, who has been locked down in his maze for a thousand years, is mistakenly set free, and the beleaguered town asks Hercules for help, but he refuses, saying he's retired. Finally, Hercules's wife, Deianira (Tawny Kitaen), who sees that he's unhappy, tells him she wants him to go, so he does. Zeus (Anthony Quinn) keeps showing up and getting in Hercules's way, and finally reveals that the Mino-taur is Hercules's evil brother. Hercules ends up killing the Minotaur and returning to his family, and there you have it.

I pitched the story to Rob and he liked it. I wrote it as a treatment, knowing that they wouldn't let me write the script and that it had to be written by the writers they'd already hired. I turned it in and flew back to New Zealand to begin work as 2nd unit director on the third film.

To my consternation, *Hercules in the Underworld*, the third film in the series, had the same oblivious director as the first one. Luckily for me, though, the second film, *Hercules: The Journey Begins*, had been directed by Harley Cokliss, who had himself been a 2nd unit director (on *The Empire Strikes Back*), and therefore knew how to properly use a 2nd unit, so the whole approach to 2nd unit had thank-fully been reconfigured while I was gone. Rick Allander was now strictly the 2nd unit DP, and we didn't have to just wait for scenes to fall to us, the fights and effects scenes were assigned to us from the beginning. But the director kept fighting this and foolishly attempt-ing to take 2nd unit scenes back to main unit. And every time he'd do this he'd screw the scenes up by shooting them too fast, then 2nd unit would get them back and have to fix them.

One scene of these clearly 2nd unit scenes that was illogically taken back to main unit was all the shots of the three-headed dog, Cer-berus. This special effect was a live-action, life-size, radio-controlled puppet, created by KNB Effects (Kurtzman-Nicotero-Berger, all of whom were there, with their effects crew, to operate the dog), who had previously done the two-headed Hydra on *Amazon Women* (as well as a thousand other movies). So the KNB guys and their crew, and me and my 2nd unit crew, were all made to sit on the main unit set all day long while they shot other things. Finally, in the very last hour of the day, the director said, "Okay, let's shoot the dog." The KNB guys all sprang into action, several of them positioned behind radio-control joysticks, while several other of these big dudes with beards had to squeeze inside the 7-foot-tall, 3-headed puppet. The director called, "Action," the three heads began to move, the eyes blinking, the mouths opening and closing, except that one of the dog's eyes began blinking uncontrollably, while one of the heads came loose from it's mooring and hung there useless and incapacitated. The director called, "Cut. Print it. That was great! We're done," and turned to leave. Bob Kurtzman, who had been running one of the joysticks and could therefore see how poorly the effect had come off—and let's face it, this was a *very* complicated effect—was utterly horrified. "What'dya mean, 'that's great, we're done'?" asked Bob. "Nothing worked right. One of the RCs went nuts, and one of the heads came loose." The director smiled reassuringly and shook his head. "No, no, it was fine. That's all I need. Really," and turned to leave again. Bob promptly went ballistic. "*That's all you need?* We spent months building that dog, it cost a fortune, I've got a whole crew here that was flown down to New Zealand, and you only do one take? *Are you insane!!!???*" At which point the director just walked off the set. 2nd unit stepped in, we spent two entire days shooting the dog from every possible angle, and every part of it worked fine. I felt good, and the KNB guys left happy.

The director also tried to shoot a fight scene between Hercules and Erix the Boxer, played by the tallest man living, George Gonzales, who was 8'1", in one, long, uncut Steadi-Cam shot. Well, George and Alistair, the 600-pound man, could both vie for who was the most uncoordinated person living (and poor Kevin Sorbo got to do fight scenes with them both). Not only did the scene completely and totally not come off in this one big shot, but you never got any sense of just how tall George was, which seemed particularly crazy having gone to the trouble of casting the tallest man living. So 2nd unit had to reshoot the whole fight. I broke it down into it's smallest possible chunks, bits of action that George could handle, and I even staged a whole section of the fight off-camera—Herc and Erix (both stunt doubles) crash through a door into a house, we stay outside tracking along seeing parts of the front of the house rattle and fall off, then finally the two combatants come crashing back out a window.

2nd unit's final triumph occurred when this same nutty director decided to leave before the film was entirely finished. There were a bunch of bits and pieces missing from all over the film that included lead actors and dialog, so they certainly weren't 2nd unit, as well as a big scene—the Ghoul Trench—that had not turned out to anyone's satisfaction. So 2nd unit worked for another week finishing the film.

We not only did it on time and on schedule, but we also did it to everyone's satisfaction.

I then turned over the reigns of 2nd unit to my buddy, Jack Perez, and I began pre-production as main unit director on the last of the five films, *Hercules in the Maze of the Minotaur*. Sadly, we still didn't have a script, nor was it even yet listed on the big board.

I flew back to L.A. and met with Rob, and Andy and Dan, the two young writers who were now available to write the script, at Barney's Beanery, and I talked them all through the story. I said, "The only part of this story that I've written out exactly is the big bar fight, and as soon as I get back to New Zealand, while I'm waiting for the rest of the script pages, I'm going to work out the choreography and logistics of the fight, so please don't change it."

I flew back to New Zealand and began pre-production in earnest, or at least as much as I could without a script, that is. I met with Peter Bell, the stunt director, many times to work out all the moves of the big bar fight. Peter carried little toy people with movable arms and legs with him all the time to illustrate what he had in mind. I also met with Richard Taylor, the special effects supervisor from Peter Jackson's effects company, WETA. Richard has since gone on to win five Oscars for the *Lord of the Rings* movies and *King Kong*. Richard made two beautiful sketches of completely different Minotaur heads, and asked me to choose. I pointed at one of the sketches and said, "That one," and Richard's face drooped. "What's wrong?" I asked. Richard said, "I like the other one." I shrugged, "Well, I like the first one. I think it's much better. Go with that one." He shrugged, "Okay." When he returned a few weeks later he had built the one he liked, not the one I had chosen. I couldn't believe it. "How could you do that?" I asked incredulously. Richard, who's a terrifically nice guy, looked utterly horrified, as well as completely befuddled, and just shook his head, mumbling, "I don't know. And it's too late to change it now, y'know." I nodded my head sadly, "Yeah, I know. I'm really glad you asked me to choose." Richard left, still shaking his head in confusion. The Minotaur head, meanwhile, turned out very well, looks really cool, and has a lot of great facial movement. But it's still not the one I chose.

I've been on a fair amount of film shoots in my day, and when they start off wrong, they rarely if ever get turned back around the right way. Because no one in the crew was aware of the existence of the fifth film until after the third one was finished shooting, most everyone had made vacation plans that they now had to break (they had all been working for six months straight at that point, and that's a long time to be shooting). This put most everyone in a foul, rebellious mood before we even started. Plus, everyone was now being asked to work faster since we had a shorter schedule. From the first minute of the first day there was a palpable bad vibe on the set, with people snapping at each other and generally being snotty. The worst offenders were the camera crew. Jim, the gray-bearded, 60ish, DP, had never been nice to me throughout the first six months, and had actually been quite mean to me on a few occasions for no particular reason. But Jim was a pussycat compared to his obnoxious camera operator, Turts, and the creepy 1st AC, Cameron, both of whom were supreme assholes. All three of these shit-heads did their very best to make my first directorial effort on a TV movie the most miserable experience of my whole life.

Jim got a funny line off at my expense that I remember because it may be the stupidest thing any DP has ever said to me. In one scene, Hercules and a heavyset man walk through the maze and arrive at a spot where the rock walls are very close together, making it difficult for Hercules to get through, but impossible for the fat guy. I initially wanted to put the lens right between the tight rock walls, then dolly the camera back to reveal how close the walls were together. Except that the way the set was built we couldn't get the lens into the tight area. Being in a time crunch, as always while shooting, I suggested that we use a zoom lens and zoom back through the tight area to reveal it, which would have worked just fine.

Jim grandly announced, "I don't use zoom lenses." I was a bit shocked because, when everything is said and done, it's not his call. I was the director and I called for the zoom. End of story, as far as I'm concerned. Had I been the producer too I would have fired his snotty ass on the spot. However, since I wasn't the producer, merely just the director, and still in a time crunch, I tried to diplomatically pursue the issue, since the alternative was to call in the art department and rebuild the set, and that certainly didn't sound like a quick process.

I said, "A zoom lens is a tool in the filmmaker's toolbox. It has it's place."

"Yes," proclaimed Jim to one and all, "It has it's place—in the truck." This got a big laugh from the crew. I persisted, "So then you won't get the zoom?" Jim repeated, "I don't use zooms." I said, "But *I do.*" Jim stated categorically, "But *I* don't." So I just let it go. The art department was called in and it took and hour and half to rebuild the set, then I was in a total shit-fight for the rest of the day to shoot what had been scheduled. But now, every time I see a cool zoom shot in a film, like say in Bernardo Bertolucci's *The Conformist*, shot by the great Vittorio Storaro; or in Stanley Kubrick's *Full Metal Jacket* or *Barry Lyndon* (Oscar-winner for Best Cinematography for John Alcott, and it's loaded with zooms), I am always reminded of that fucking idiotic statement Jim made.

But my real nemesis on that crew was Turts, the camera operator. No matter what I asked him, he snapped at me or was just plain old snotty, and frequently wouldn't do what I asked. At one point, as I was speaking to an actor out in front of the camera where the scene was to be shot, Turts yelled at me, "Get out of the way."

I looked around, not sure whose way I could possibly be in, and asked, "Excuse me?" Turts repeated, "Get the fuck out of the way. I'm trying to set the focus."

Once again, were I the producer, Turts's worthless sorry ass would have been shit- canned on the spot. Since I was only a director-for-hire, though, I kept my mouth shut, walked over to George Lyle, the friendly 1st AD who had just witnessed this exchange, and asked, "What happens if I break a C-stand over the camera operator's head?"

George thought for a second, then said, "It'll definitely slow us down."

I nodded. "Good point."

And while I was firing people, I'd have gotten rid of the asshole creep 1st AC, Cameron (who will show back up later to torment me on "Xena"), as well as Axel, the snotty the boom man (who also reappeared on "Xena").

When the script pages arrived for the big bar fight, the one I had completely storyboarded, worked out all the details with Peter Bell, and all of the stuntmen had been preparing for, the fight was written out entirely different than I had written it. As we shot this 7-minute bar fight, using two whole days of shooting, I simply ignored the script and worked from my storyboards. Line by line, the script supervisor would read it and ask, "Is this what's happening now?" I'd say, "No," and then I'd show her my storyboards. She would then white-out the line and write in what was really being shot. Page after page, she'd white-out every line until she reached the bottom, then say, "I can replace that with a blank sheet of paper."

Up until this bar fight in *Minotaur*, every fight scene had been shot as a series of individual angles and inserts, that through editing and the juxtaposition of the shots would ultimately equal a fight scene. It would be like Alfred Hitchcock shooting a fight scene, breaking it all down into it's individual bits and pieces. I, on the other hand, decided to shoot big hunks of the fight all the way through. I covered the fight with two cameras at once, both hand-held, one in an over-the-shoulder shot, the other in a medium close-up, first looking at Hercules, then looking back at whoever he was fighting. This allowed everybody to actually get some momentum going, plus it was a much faster method. Anyway, that ended up being the method that was used to shoot almost every fight scene thereafter on both "Hercules" and "Xena."

I completed *Minotaur* on time and on budget, at three weeks and $1.5 million. Of the five Hercules films it received the second-highest rating next to *Amazon Women*. But the atmosphere on *Minotaur* was so awful, having absolutely nothing to do with me, at least as far as I'm concerned, that I was not hired again by Renaissance Pictures for over a year and a half, and I was never hired again on "Hercules."

When I got back to L.A. I offhandedly asked Rob, "So, do I get any money for writing the story for *Minotaur*? And I'm getting the credit, right?" Rob said he'd look into it. Soon thereafter I was informed that the writers, Andy and Dan, were disputing my story credit, and intended to take me to Writer's Guild arbitration about it. I thought, fine, I've got all of my dated notes, as well as a dated treatment that everyone in the cast and crew had seen, I'll be happy to fight it out with these guys in arbitration. Rob called me to meet him at his office on the Universal lot. I put all of my *Minotaur* notes in a manila envelope and drove over there. Rob informed me flatly that there would be no Writer's Guild arbitration, since it might potentially hold up the air date. Not only that, I wasn't getting a story credit, nor any remuneration, and if I pushed this issue one inch further, he would not only never hire me for anything ever again, he would never speak to me again, either. Well. I took my thick manila envelope of notes home and didn't do anything.

The five Hercules movies got good enough ratings to spawn an order for 13 episodes of the series, "Hercules: The Legendary Journeys," that immediately went into production (the five movies and those 13 episodes comprise the 1st season of "Hercules," whereas the next four seasons are all the standard 22-24 episodes each). Rob Tapert already had the idea for a spin-off show based on a female warrior character named Xena. He had this Xena character written into three of these 13 Hercules shows. Now all he needed was an actress to play the part. I immediately said, "You should cast Lucy Lawless as Xena."

Rob said, "She's good, but I need a star. Besides, she's a Kiwi, she can't handle it."

I scoffed, "Oh, come on, gimme a break. What kind of star are you going to get anyway?"

"I'm talking to Sandahl Bergman."

I was aghast. "Rob, Sandahl Bergman looks like a man, and she can't act. Lucy Lawless is a babe, and she *can* act."

But, as usual, he ignored me. I wasn't the only one who felt this way, either. Diana Rowan, the casting director for "Hercules" (and "Xena," and almost everything down there), also knew that Lucy was very good casting for Xena and she began bugging Rob about it, too. I brought it up enough times so that Rob finally got mad at me and told me to shut up, something I personally never appreciate.

Rob finally cast an actress named Vanessa Angel in the part. As fate would have it, however, she was on a shoot in England, got sick and couldn't make it to New Zealand in time to begin shooting the first Xena episode of "Hercules," so at the last possible second they recast Lucy Lawless in the part, mainly because she was right there in Auckland. Her being a New Zealander certainly wasn't a detriment anymore. It's funny how quickly things can change.

When the three episodes of "Hercules" that contained Xena caused the order for the first season of the show, "Xena: Warrior Princess," there were no writers, no staff, no nothing. I took advantage of this momentary anomaly and quickly reworked a Hercules story that I had written (with Jack Perez), that had been rejected out-of-hand, and made it into a Xena story. I literally used Search & Replace and changed Hercules's name with Xena's, replaced "he" with "she," then quickly turned it in. Rob thought it was terrific and bought it. This became the second "Xena" episode, "Chariots of War," (that actually started shooting first), and it doesn't even have Gabrielle, Xena's sidekick, in it.

I finally got to direct the 15th episode of the 1st season of "Xena:

Warrior Princess," entitled, "A Fistful of Dinars." It was originally titled "Three the Hard Way," yet the whole episode is following four people. I asked, "Shouldn't it be 'Four the Hard Way,' or doesn't Gabrielle count?"

My first important big contribution to the show at this early stage came during the script development stage. I suggested to Rob and Liz Friedman, the co-producer (who, incidentally, is gay), that there ought to be a gay subtext to the relationship between Xena and Gabrielle. I didn't think this up out of nowhere because already the talk about the show was, "Are these characters gay?" So I was just suggesting that we embrace this, but keep it as a subtext. I said, "Xena and Gabrielle are both straight, but yet they're attracted to each other." Rob looked horrified, and said, "This is a family show." Liz asked seriously, "What is 'straight'?"

As soon as I got down to New Zealand I brought this up to Lucy and Renee, and they were both totally into it, as any actor would be having subtext added to their characters. And so the two of them, as well as the writers, ran with this as the subtext of the show for the next six years. My other big early contribution was that I asked Lucy why she kept grimacing in the first 14 episodes, and I urged her to knock it off. I kept saying to her, "You've got a beautiful smile, show it."

"But I want to look tough," Lucy would say.

"Xena's the toughest babe on the block, she can afford to smile."

So Lucy began to smile more (see the accompanying photograph and inscription).

The co-star of this first episode was Jeremy Roberts, who would later co-star in my film *Running Time*. Jeremy is a terrific actor, and given half a chance to be funny, is a scene-stealer. Lucy and Renee O'Connor, who played Gabrielle, completely enjoyed Jeremy's performance and graciously let him steal his scenes. It was an extremely fun, enjoyable shoot, and I brought it in on time and on budget, with no overtime. Everyone was pleased.

One bit of funny stuff from that episode made it into all of the Xena gag reels from there on out. At the very end of the episode, Xena and Gabrielle are standing at the edge of a volcano and Xena is holding the Ambrosia, a prop made of hard plastic about the size of a basketball. The two cameras were both way the hell down inside the volcano's crater. Lucy was supposed to throw the Ambrosia in the crater as far as she could, past the lower camera. So, Lucy and

Renee step up, exchange a page of dialog, Lucy turns and heaves the Ambrosia into the crater, and in the world's luckiest shot, like making a full-court basket, the Ambrosia hit the cameraman right in the head. He was ultimately uninjured, but nobody knew that for a second. And meanwhile, the second camera was still running on a closer shot of Lucy and Renee, who were now supposed to finish the scene and exit, except that Lucy thought that she might possibly have just killed one of the cameramen, and the look of concern and horror on her face was, while still delivering her lines, priceless.

Who should be the camera operator on "Xena"? Cameron , the former 1st AC from *Minotaur*. Cameron didn't like me and I didn't like him, and that's all there was to it. The big difference was that I was trying as hard as I possibly could to be upbeat, pleasant and professional, and Cameron was always a downbeat, frowning, complaining creep, day in and day out. He wasn't even nice to Lucy, which seemed particularly stupid to me. But since New Zealand has a somewhat socialistic government where it's nearly impossible to fire people, a system that allows an unpleasant creep to keep his job forever and never feel compelled to get along with anyone, including those who outrank him, there was nothing that could be done. The show's DP, Donnie Duncan, a wonderfully sweet, pleasant, talented guy, always defended Cameron because he was stuck with him. I understood this and never held it against Donnie, with whom I truly enjoyed working.

I directed the first episode of the second season, "Warrior . . . Princess . . . Tramp," and this was my first episode with Ted Raimi as Joxer. He and I would eventually do seven episodes of "Xena" together. I love working with Ted, and he truly slaughters me. He and I laugh all day long when we work together, and in my opinion, that's as good as work gets. I think Lucy, Renee, Ted, myself, with a clever, funny script by "Xena's" head writer/co-executive producer, R.J. Stewart, made this an extremely funny episode (Lucy once said it was her favorite episode, but I'm not sure that she was being serious). Lucy plays three parts: Xena, the princess, and the tramp, all exact doubles, of course. There are many scenes where it's Xena dressed as the princess, pretending to be the tramp, or Xena dressed as Xena, but pretending to be the princess, etc. and Lucy kept it all straight, and made it all work, too. It's a helluva piece of comic acting, I think. The DP on this episode, Allan Guilford, a heavyset man in his early 60s, was just wonderful—smart, fast, funny, and a joy to talk to, everything I look for in a DP. Also in the second season, as I was about to do the episode, "Blind Faith," Lucy fell off a horse while shooting "The Jay Leno Show" and broke her hip (they apparently had her dressed as Xena and riding up to the Burbank Studios as a gag, but the horse slipped on the pavement). Suddenly, a week before we were to begin shooting, an entirely new script was concocted and written (a truly valiant effort by Adam Armus & Nora Kay Foster, who wrote a number of the episodes that I directed), this one entitled "For Him the Bell Tolls," and starring Joxer. In the opening and closing scenes with Xena, I shot with a double and Lucy's close-ups were shot later on after I was gone and cut in. On this same episode I asked Cameron, very nicely, to use the Steadi-Cam he was wearing at the time to do a whip pan, where the camera pans as fast as it can creating a blur. Cameron disgustedly took off the Steadi-Cam, hung it up and stated vehemently, *"You can't do a whip pan on a Steadi-Cam!"* Well, having recently made my film *Running Time*, that's literally loaded with whip pans performed on a Steadi-Cam, I knew this was blatantly untrue. In fact, a Steadi-Cam is the *perfect* piece of equipment to achieve a whip pan since the camera is almost frictionless and nearly floating. Steadi-Cam operators often whip the camera back and forth out of boredom between shots. Anyway, Cameron walked off the set and I didn't get my whip pan. Donnie looked at me with deep empathy and sighed, "I guess you *can't* do a whip pan from a Steadi-Cam, at least, not that one, anyway."

For the one and only time in one season I also did a third episode, "Blind Faith," that I think is a good, solid, both dramatic and funny, but non-slapstick, episode. This time I had a different DP, John Cavill. John had a flat-top brush-cut, was very energetic and upbeat, as well as being extremely talented, but at first he didn't listen to a word I said. Early into the first day of shooting, I asked John for the camera to be on the dolly, with dolly track going from the window to the door, on a 35mm lens set a bit below eye-level, then I went outside and had a cigarette. I came back a few minutes later to find that the camera and John were now positioned on the camera crane, and no dolly track had been set up. I asked John and Simon Ambridge, the incredibly sweet 1st AD, to please step outside. I asked John, "How, when I ask for the camera to be on a dolly, did it end up on a crane?"

John said, "I thought it would be a better shot."

"And who asked you?"

John was clearly taken aback and said, "I thought this was a collaboration."

I smiled and shook my head. "You're mistaken. *You* work for *me*. When I say the camera is on a dolly, it's on a dolly. Got it?"

John overdramatically threw his hands in the air and declared, "*Fine!*"

And for the rest of the shoot he was in fact fine, and we got along just fine, too. I think John's lighting is exceptionally good. When we were done I asked him, "How was the collaboration?"

John shrugged and smiled, "I can handle it."

In the third season I directed "Fins, Femmes & Gems." This episode contains some of the best comedy I have so far done in my career. Ted plays a character named Attis, who is a monkey man, so he and I got together and watched *2001: A Space Odyssey* to pick up good monkey moves. There's also a flashback in that episode that I'm rather proud of cinematically. Xena is remembering coming to the same place to fish in her youth and we see her younger incarnation and her little brother run past behind her, thus getting into a flashback without a cut, simply a change of focus. It then comes back to the present by morphing young Xena into present-day Xena, and it worked quite well, if I do say so myself.

"Fins, Femmes & Gems" was the most-controversial episode of the whole series, in that it was originally going to be the "coming out" episode, when we'd finally find out that Xena and Gabrielle were gay. I didn't think this was a good idea and I said so, but Rob, as usual, paid me no heed. He also said that I had to shoot a love scene between Xena and Gabrielle's shadows, exactly like a DeBeers Diamond commercial. I received a tape of every version of these DeBeers shadow commercials. The point of this was so that Rob would get a free diamond ring for Lucy, whom he was about to marry. There was also a scene in the script where Xena and Gabrielle were to be rolling in the surf kissing, just like *From Here to Eternity*. There was another scene where Xena bends down for something and Gaby looks up Xena's skirt and checks her out. This particular scene absolutely infuriated the New Zealand co-producer, Chloe Smith. Chloe, who was very good at her job, and was feared by many on the crew, simply couldn't have been nicer to me, even when I was the 2nd unit director. Anyway, Chloe stood up at the

Head of Department Meeting and strenuously objected to the looking up the skirt scene, stating, "Women don't do that!" I was 100%
with her. I asked both Lucy and Renee, "You guys are really going
to roll around in the surf French kissing?" They both shrugged and
dismissed it, meaning, whatever the script says, that's what we're
doing, which was no doubt a much healthier approach to the situation than mine, since I was starting to panic—this episode was going
to be a disaster, and it would probably get blamed on me.

Finally, just a few days before shooting started, a top executive at
Universal TV read the script and called Rob saying he didn't think
Xena and Gaby ought to be gay, either, nor should there be a De-
Beers commercial within the show. Apparently, Rob said, "But the
'coming out' episode of 'Ellen' was huge." The executive replied,
"But this isn't 'Ellen'. This is 'Xena,' and she's not coming out of
anywhere." We then received an *entirely* rewritten script the morning we began shooting. Since there was no time for the actors to
learn their lines, the dialog was fed to them by the script supervisor
line by line. Ted and I improvised entire scenes, like him talking to
all of the animals in the jungle, or him giving commands to the fish,
"Fish-brother. Go. Bring tribute." I think the scene where Attis envi-
sions Gabrielle as his dream ape girl is extremely funny.

Aside from the fact that we didn't get the script pages until right
before we shot, the weather was gorgeous, we were out at the beach,
there were a ton of laughs and it was very fun episode to shoot.

In the fourth season I directed two episodes, "In Sickness & In
Hell," where Xena and Gaby are both ill in various ways—head lice,
skin crud, etc.—and "If the Shoe Fits . . . ," a reworking of "Cinderella." Both are highly silly episodes, and I like them both a lot.

In the fifth season I did "Kindred Spirits," another troubled script
that got completely thrown away during pre-production, then entirely rewritten in a massive hurry with a brand new story by Rob
that was a huge improvement over the original. We did all of the
pre-production based on a poorly-typed, two-page outline by Rob.
The finale of the story is a big-time, WWF wrestling match between
Xena and Joxer that I completely thought up and put into the episode and was never in the script in any way. I got away with this
kind of thing because, A. I was friends with Rob, and B. I kept getting the totally fucked-up scripts that had to be bailed out.

This was the year 2000. "Hercules" went off after five seasons, and *Lord of the Rings*, that had just begun shooting down in Welling-ton, absorbed the entire "Hercules" crew. A few members of the Xena crew defected as well, among them, to my utter delight, was the miser-able camera operator, Cameron. He was replaced by an exceptionally nice guy named Dana, who couldn't have been sweeter, and did a much better job, too. At one point I asked for a whip pan from the wrestling ring to Xena, and Dana said, "Oh, I'll do it on the Steadi-Cam." Donnie, the D.P., turned to me, grinned and said, "Huh, and I thought you couldn't do a whip pan on a Steadi-Cam." At the Christ-mas party, as a gag gift, the crew gave me a framed photograph of Cameron, signed, "Merry Christmas, Love, Cameron, XXX."

In the sixth season I did "Soul Possession," another problem script that I was only able to somewhat bail out. It does have a few funny moments, though. This was the third to last episode of the entire show. Donnie Duncan was also gone by then, and this time I worked with another funny, upbeat, knowledgeable, talented, young, British DP named Simon Riara, who slightly reminded me of Terry Thomas ("But *surely* you'll want to use the crane on this shot. *Surely*."). This was also the last episode for the actor Kevin Smith, who portrayed the god Ares in "Hercules," "Xena" and "Young Hercules." But this was the first episode where he and I had worked together, and we had a terrific time. Not only was Kevin tall, dark and handsome, and in perfect shape, but he was ridiculously funny and a complete joy to be around. Not long after that, Kevin was making a film in China, fell off a set and died. That was a severe shock. When some-one that joyous and full of life suddenly dies so young, it seems like life for everyone on the planet is slightly diminished.

Meanwhile, I also have a co-story credit on another episode, "Locked Up & Tied Down," that Rob and I wrote together, but I didn't direct. I believe it turned out to be a solid, worthy dramatic episode in the series.

Then there was the ill-fated show, "Jack of All Trades," for which I directed the first two episodes. Rob and Sam had the novel idea of making two half-hour shows combined as one hour-long show, containing: "Jack of All Trades," a zany 18th century swashbuckling comedy; and "Cleopatra 2525," a trashy sci-fi show.

"Cleo" began it's unfortunate little life with me when I was about fifteen years old, in the early 1970s, when I was a major sci-fi fan, which at that time meant reading sci-fi books (as opposed to just seeing movies and TV shows). My favorite sci-fi author was Isaac Asimov, who had just edited a trilogy of books called "Before the Golden Age," a collection of his favorite sci-fi stories when he was a kid, from 1931 to 1938. A story in the collection that I just loved was "Tumithak of the Corridors" from 1931 by Charles S. Tanner. Martians surround Earth with spaceships and begin bombing us. We fight back while digging bomb shelters and moving underground. The war lasts over 100 years, and eventually we lose. The Martians, who look like spiders with clawed thumbs for legs, and humanoid heads with only one eye, take over the surface of the Earth, and all humans now live underground, having dug deeper and deeper corridors. The story picks up thousands of years in the future, when the humans at the deepest levels have died out, and the ones at the next deepest level that are still alive have reverted to barbarism. The lead character, Tumithak, is a strong, burly, 18-year-old, barbarian warrior (written before Robert E. Howard's Conan stories), who decides that he is going to make his way through the unknown corridors above him, all the way to the surface, and kill a Martian. My good buddy, Jim Rose (who died in 2004), also loved this story, he and I often discussed how good of a movie to would make, and cheap, too, because you could keep reusing the same corridors for each different level and just redress them.

We do a slow dissolve to the mid-1980s when Sam, Rob, Bruce, Scott and I had offices in Ferndale, Michigan, where we made *Evil Dead* and *Thou Shalt Not Kill . . . Except*, and Rob blurted out the apocryphal statement, "Everything good that's ever been written has already been filmed." I shut my eyes so as not to swoon, then replied, "Only someone who doesn't read books could make such a statement." I pulled out Book #1 of "Before the Golden Age," opened it to "Tumithak of the Corridors" and said, "Here, read this. It would make a great movie, it hasn't been filmed yet, it's been sitting around for about 50 years and it's probably in the public domain." Rob read it and readily agreed that it was a good story that would make a cool movie.

Slow dissolve to the early 1990s when we now all lived in L.A. and Rob was over my bungalow, located right off Sunset Blvd. near the Cinerama Dome. Rob asked, "Whatever happened to that story, 'Thumbelina in the Hallways'?"

"'Tumithak of the Corridors'," I corrected. "It's still collecting dust, ever since 1931." Rob asked if I'd make him a copy and send it to his office, and I said sure, and I did. Rob called a few days later and said, "Hey, that's a good story." I sighed and said, "Yeah, it is."

Slow dissolve to the late 1990s, and Rob called and asked if I'd send him another copy of "Thumbelina," so I did. Rob called and said, "Okay, I'm actually going to do something with 'Tumithak' now, what do you want?" I was really thrown for a loop. "I can't ask for anything, I didn't write it. But what you can do for me is to not fuck it up." There was an exceptionally long pregnant pause, which, after a point, clearly meant, "It's too late, I've already fucked it up."

And boy oh boy, had he. Tumithak the young warrior had become three dimwitted busty babes, the lead babe, Cleopatra, had gone into the hospital in the present-day for a boob-job, then wakes up in 2525 (ala Woody Allen's *Sleeper*), where she finds that humans live underground, aliens have taken over the surface, robots fly around, blah, blah, blah. It was an astoundingly bad show, and Rob never hired me to work on it, either.

"Jack of All Trades," on the other hand, I would say was a near-miss. Although, when I got the script, Jack was British, Amelia (Angela Dotchin) was supposed to be French, it took place in no specific time period, but was specifically set in Pulau-Pulau in the Dutch East Indies, mysteriously controlled by the French. Since I was directing the pilot episode, (as well as another episode at the same time, a method called "block-shooting") it was my job to establish everything in the series. Well, I already knew that Bruce Campbell was going to play Jack, and that Angela Dotchin, who's from New Zealand, was going to play Amelia. So I immediately suggested that Jack be American, that way Bruce wouldn't have to be putting on a phony accent all the time, and that Amelia be British, so that neither would Ang (yes, British and New Zealand accents are not the same, but they're close, and Ang had zero difficulty doing British, whereas if she'd had to do a French accent the whole time, that would have been a whole other can of worms. Ang actually thanked me from saving her from that horror). I also suggested that it be set specifically in the very early 1800s, when Thomas Jefferson was president. I also suggested that it be set on the island of Ibiza in the Mediterranean so that the bad guys could be the pirate countries of the Barbary coast—Morocco, Algiers, Tunis, and Tripoli—who were in fact America's foremost enemies at that time (and is why we formed the U.S. Navy and the U.S. Marine Corps. That's where the line, "To the shores of Tripoli" comes from in "The Marine Corps Hymn"). The Barbary pirates kept specifically taking U.S. sailors as hostages, over a hundred of them, and would then sell them into slavery, never to be seen again. This was because America would not pay a yearly tribute to these pirates for use of the Straits of Gibraltar to enter the Mediterranean, as did most of the Europeans countries at the time. As far as Bruce and I were concerned, this was a perfect setting and enemy, with many interesting contemporary allusions, and numerous, colorful villains.

Rob bought that Jack was American, that Amelia was British, and that it was set during Thomas Jefferson's presidency, but refused to change the setting of Pulau-Pulau, in the Dutch East Indies, inexplicably run by the French. I said, "But it was the *Dutch* East Indies, Rob, the French had nothing to do with it."

Rob replied, "Yeah, but everyone hates the French."

"But why the East Indies?" I persisted.

"Because that's what I told the production designer."

"Rob, it's just a superimposed title. If we say it's 'Ibiza,' it's Ibiza, if we say 'Pulau-Pulau,' it's Pulau-Pulau. There's a ton of inherent drama on the Barbary coast at that time; there's no drama whatsoever in Pulau-Pulau."

Rob, as usual, got mad at me and told me to shut up.

Rob's next brainstorm was, "It should be just like 'Moonlighting'. Everything they say is sexual innuendo."

Bruce and I were both dumbstruck. "Isn't this show for kids on Saturday afternoons?"

So "Jack of All Trades" became the adventures of an American secret agent in Pulau-Pulau, during the presidency of Thomas Jefferson, working with a British female agent, and contained a lot of sexual innuendo, while Jack and Amelia constantly befuddled the bumbling local French authorities. The show now had such a thankless premise that there was no hope of it ever succeeding, not to mention it was attached to the even more thankless "Cleopatra 2525."

Nevertheless, Bruce, Angela Dotchin and I and the whole cast and crew had a swell time shooting the first two episodes, even though it didn't make any sense to anyone. Kevin Riley, yet another terrific young New Zealand DP, did a wonderful job shooting it, and I think the show looks really good. It's got an enjoyable, funny flavor, too.

I'm proud of all of the episodes I worked on in New Zealand (even *Minotaur*, that still remains the single worst experience of my professional life, but the film itself functioned dramatically, got good ratings, and allowed me to work with the late, great Anthony Quinn, so it wasn't a total loss). "Xena" was the best, long-running experience of my professional life so far, and I'd sincerely like to thank everyone involved: Rob, Lucy, Renee, Ted, Eric Gruendemann, Chloe Smith, Liz Friedman, R.J. Stewart, Steven Sears, Simon Ambridge, Paul Grinder, Donny Duncan, John Cavill, Allan Guilford, Robert Gillies, Di Rowan, Nigla Dickenson, Bernie Joyce, Rob Fields, Jim Pryor, Tim Batt, Alex Tydings, the late Kevin Smith, Karl Urban, Peter Bell (and all of the stunties), Edith, Sue, Dave, Moira, Phee, Sally, Jane, Tracy, George (Lyle & Port), Luke, Keith, Linda, Charlie Haskell, Rick Allender, Joe, Splash, and all the other terrific crew and cast members who all did a wonderful job.

Thank you so much.

Lucy Lawless

The inscription from Lucy reads: "Joshua, To my favourite director of all time! With great love & fondest regards, Lucy Lawless. P.S. You taught me everything I know. I just wish I could smile more. 11/95."

March, 1992

The Oscars:
What Could Have Won and
What Should Have Won

by Josh Becker and Rick Sandford

The authors of this list both work in varying capacities in the film industry and have both been fascinated by the Academy Awards since they were young children. Rick can recall the awards of 1957 (for the films of 1956) where Ingrid Bergman won Best Actress, but had Cary Grant accept the award for her since she had left the country in shame nine years earlier bearing Roberto Rosellini's illegitimate child (Isabella's older brother). Josh, being eight years younger than Rick, can only remember back to 1969 (for the films of 1968), with Barbra Streisand saying to her Best Actress award (in a tie with Katherine Hepburn), "Hello gorgeous." Rick has in fact made it a life goal to see all of the Academy Award nominated films. The winners would be approximately twenty-two categories multiplied by sixty-three years. That's thirteen hundred and eighty-six movies. The nominees, however, makes it twenty-two times sixty-three times five! That's six thousand nine hundred and thirty films! And he's over three-quarters of the way there (he's actually over four-fifths of the way there in the feature categories, it's the short subjects that are messing up his average). In the course of the past fifteen years Rick has dragged Josh to innumerable dull, Oscar-nominated films. The authors speculate constantly about the Academy Awards even though they are both no longer interested in either what's nominated or what wins. Old habits apparently do die hard.

Here is a list of all the Best Picture winners, the films that the authors would have chosen of the nominees, and the films they would have chosen of the eligible films released that year. Rick happens to have all of the Academy Award reminder lists, the lists of all the eligible films in each given year going all the way back to 1927. Quite handy, really.

YEAR	WINNER	NOMINATED	ELIGIBLE
27/28	Wings	The Last Command	Sunrise
28/29	Broadway Melody	The Patriot (The Patriot is the most famous)	The Docks Of New York
29/30	All Quiet On The Western Front	All Quiet On The Western Front	All Quiet On The Western Front
30/31	Cimarron	Skippy	Morocco
31/32	Grand Hotel	Shanghai Express	Shanghai Express
32/33	Cavalcade	I Am A Fugitive From A Chain Gang	Love Me Tonight
1934	It Happened One One Night	It Happened One One Night	The Scarlet Empress
1935	Mutiny On The Bounty	The Informer	The Devil Is A Woman
1936	The Great Ziegfeld	Dodsworth	J: Dodsworth R: Swing Time
1937	The Life Of Emile Zola	Dead End	Dead End
1938	You Can't Take It With You	The Adventures Of Robin Hood	J: The Adventures Of Robin Hood R: Bringing Up Baby
1939	Gone With The Wind	Gone With The Wind	Gone With The Wind
1940	Rebecca	The Grapes Of Wrath	The Grapes Of Wrath
1941	How Green Was My Valley	Citizen Kane	Citizen Kane
1942	Mrs. Miniver	The Magnificent Ambersons	The Magnificent Ambersons
1943	Casablanca	Casablanca	Casablanca
1944	Going My Way	Meet Me In St. Louis	J: Meet Me In St. Louis R: Since You Went Away
1945	The Lost Weekend	The Lost Weekend	The Lost Weekend
1946	The Best Years Of Our Lives	The Best Years Of Our Lives	The Best Years Of Our Lives
1947	Gentleman's Agreement	Great Expectations	Black Narcissus
1948	Hamlet	The Red Shoes	The Red Shoes
1949	All The King's Men	Letter To Three Wives	The Bicycle Thief
1950	All About Eve	All About Eve	All About Eve
1951	An American In Paris	A Place In The Sun	A Place In The Sun
1952	The Greatest Show On Earth	The Quiet Man	J: The Quiet Man R: Los Olvidados
1953	From Here To Eternity	R: Shane J: From Here To Eternity	R: Band Wagon J: From Here To Eternity
1954	On The Waterfront	On The Waterfront	On The Waterfront
1955	Marty	Marty	J: Marty R: East of Eden
1956	Around The World In Eighty Days	Friendly Persuaslon	J: Friendly Persuaslon R: Seven Samurai
1957	The Bridge The River Kwai	The Bridge The River Kwai	The Bridge The River Kwai
1958	Gigi	Gigi	Gigi
1959	Ben-Hur	The Nun's Story	J: The Nun's Story R: The 400 Blows
1960	The Apartment	The Apartment	J: The Apartment R: Ikiru
1961	West Side Story	West Side Story	West Side Story
1962	Lawrence Of Arabia	Lawrence Of Arabia	Lawrence Of Arabia
1963	Tom Jones	Tom Jones	Fellini's 8 1/2
1964	My Fair Lady	Dr. Strangelove	Dr. Strangelove
1965	The Sound Of Music	The Sound Of Music	J: Sound Of Music R: Tokyo Olympiad
1966	A Man For All Seasons	Who's Afraid Of Virginia Woolf	Who's Afraid Of Virginia Woolf
1967	In The Heat Of The Night	Bonnie And Clyde	J: Bonnie And Clyde R: Persona
1968	Oliver!	Romeo & Juliet	2001: A Space Odyssey
1969	Midnight Cowboy	J: Midnight Cowboy R: Z	The Wild Bunch
1970	Patton	Patton	Woodstock
1971	The French Connection	The Last Picture Show	The Last Picture Show
1972	The Godfather	The Godfather	The Godfather
1973	The Sting	Cries And Whispers	Cries And Whispers
1974	The Godfather Part Two	The Godfather Part Two	The Godfather Part Two
1975	One Flew Over The Cuckoo's Nest	Jaws	J: Jaws R: Nashville
1976	Rocky	Taxi Driver	Taxi Driver
1977	Annie Hall	Annie Hall	Annie Hall
1978	The Deer Hunter	Abstain (The 1st Totally Bad Year)	The Fury
1979	Kramer Vs. Kramer	Apocalypse Now	Hair
1980	Ordinary People	Raging Bull	Raging Bull
1981	Chariots Of Fire	Atlantic City	J: Atlantic City R: Gallipoli
1982	Gandhi	Tootsie	The Road Warrior
1983	Terms Of Endearment	Tender Mercies	Tender Mercies
1984	Amadeus	Places In The Heart	Stranger Than Paradise
1985	Out Of Africa	Witness	J: Witness R: Brazil
1986	Platoon	Platoon	Platoon
1987	The Last Emperor	Hope & Glory	Hightide
1988	Rain Man	Abstain (The 2nd Totally Bad Year)	A World Apart
1989	Driving Miss Daisy	Born On The 4th Of July	Born On The 4th Of July
1990	Dances With Wolves	Goodfellas	J: Goodfellas R: Last Exit To Brooklyn

Postscript:

When I got the assignment to write the lead article for Film Threat's Oscar issue, the first thing that I did was get together with Rick Sandford, my friend the Oscar expert. We sat around for an afternoon discussing the Academy Awards and pretty quickly I knew what my article would be about. Since Rick was unemployed at the time and had a particular ax to grind with the Academy (the fact that young attractive males don't win Oscars), I suggested that he write his own article which I would see if I could get published as a side-piece to my article (Film Threat regularly included short articles printed along side of the main article). Then, since we were on a roll, I suggested that we make the "what could've won, what should've won" list. By 1936 we were already in a disagreement: Rick thought *Swing Time* was a much better movie than *Dodsworth*, and I adamantly disagree. 1938 we disagreed again, then 1944, then 1953, then 1955 . . . By the end we were sick of making the list, sick of the Academy Awards and sick of each other. I wrote my article, Rick wrote his, and I turned them both in.

Later . . .

Rick: So, what did you think of my article?

Josh: It was great. I turned in mine and yours.

Rick: You did what?!! But it wasn't done!

Josh: It wasn't? It sure seemed done.

Rick: Well it wasn't! I would have gone back and double-checked some of the facts again.

Josh: Do it. If there's any changes, I'll phone them in.

Rick: I can't believe you just went and turned them both in without talking to me. I'm so insulted I don't even know what to say.

Josh: Insulted? Didn't you write it for the explicit purpose of giving it to me so I could give it to them?

Rick: I'm talking about your article.

Josh: My article? You've got nothing to do with my article.

Rick: I would have proof-read it for you.

Josh: I didn't need you to proof-read it for me. It met my standards which are much higher than Film Threat's standards, and that's enough for me.

Rick: But it may not have met my standards.

Josh: It probably didn't, but there's only one of you.

At which point he hung up on me.

A couple of weeks later, when all seemed to have settled down on this front (Rick double-checked his statistics and they were all correct), the Oscar issue of the magazine came out. I snagged two early copies (that they don't like to give out) and left one in Rick's mailbox. Later that evening, I called him and asked what he thought of seeing his article in print?

"I'm too busy making my notes on your article."

"Who asked for notes?"

"You should've had me proof-read this before it was published."

"Well, it's published, so I don't need your notes."

"I'll do them anyway."

I received his notes—five, single-spaced typed pages—in the mail a few days later. He used every uncomplimentary adjective he could come up with: "Stupid, lazy, ridiculous, etc."

I thought of many witty retorts, then finally settled for, "Rick, you are my friend. This gives you the ability to hurt me if you want. Please don't take advantage of that ability. Your friend, Josh."

I then received yet another five-page, single-spaced salvo taking on my whole life in the same terms he took on my article. "Now," I said to myself, "all bets are off." I wrote back to him being as snotty and insulting as he had been to me.

That was that. Rick and I did not speak for over a year.

A mutual friend informed me that Rick has been diagnosed HIV positive. I dropped over his place and we picked our friendship right back up like nothing had happened and only a week had gone by. After a couple of pleasant visits, Rick said he wanted to discuss our fight, just to settle a single point.

"When did you get mad at me?" he asked.

"A year ago."

"No, I mean the specific moment?"

"Well," I thought, "when I got your first letter."

"Ah-ha!" he proclaimed. "I was mad at you before you were mad at me!" He had gotten mad at me when I wouldn't let him proof-read my article.

And so I acquiesced. "Fine."

Rick and I became very good friends again.

As I held his hand on the way to his radiation and chemo therapy treatments, very soon before he lapsed into a coma that he never came out of, he asked through tears:

"Have we left any of our personal problems unresolved?"

"No, I don't think so."

"Good."

Rick died soon thereafter.

On location in Tujunga, CA, shooting If I Had a Hammer, 1999.

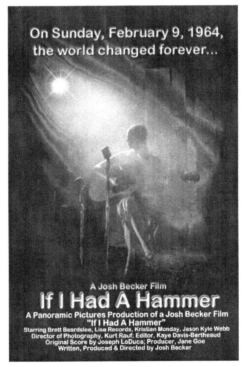

(Photo by Josh Becker, Artwork by Renee Cooper)

The Making of
If I Had a Hammer

As I have spent much of my life, I spent the first half of 1998 searching for a new idea to write. I was reading Peter Bogdanovich's wonderful book "Who the Devil Made It," a collection of interviews
with old-time Hollywood directors, and in it Allan Dwan mentions
his film, *I Dream of Jeanie*, which was a 5-day production of a musical biography of Stephen Foster. He chose Foster because he'd been
dead so long that all of his well-known songs, like "Oh, Susanna,"
were now in the public domain, meaning the songs are so old that
the copyright has expired and they're free to use.

This got me thinking about a public domain folk musical. Part of
the whole folk music zeitgeist was about finding and digging out old
songs. Therefore, if I just stuck with old songs, I could make a folk
musical with entirely public domain songs, and not have to pay anything for any of them. Well, only half of the songs that I ended up
using are actually P.D. I used nine different songs and four of them
are still under copyright, including, of course, "If I Had a Hammer"
(as a little historical note, the original version of the song by the
Weavers, who wrote it, is not actually called "If I Had a Hammer,"
it's called "The Hammer Song," although all subsequent versions
since the Weavers have used the title "If I Had a Hammer"). Nevertheless, that's where the idea began (and this is where I made my first
mistake by not sticking to the P.D. concept).

I went back through my journal yesterday trying to pinpoint the
moment I got the idea for this story, but I wasn't able to find it. I
did, however, find the moment when the whole story coalesced for
me, which was June 17, 1998. *If I Had a Hammer* is the doomed
love story between a committed folkie girl and apathetic rock & roll
boy, and takes place over the course of the weekend of February 8-9,
1964, culminating with The Beatles first appearance on the "Ed Sullivan Show." My supposition is that the folk movement died at that
exact moment, and that's when the rock & roll era really began.

I was then out to lunch with my friend John Walter (director of
the documentary *How to Draw a Bunny*), and I pitched him this

P.D. folk musical idea, and to my surprise, he really liked it. The next thing you know, by June 17th, I had already conceived the entire story, as I noted in my journal.

So, from conception of the actual story to completion of shooting took 14 months. The film was budgeted at $250,00 and has actually cost $275,000 so far, about $80,000 of which I put on my credit cards. I shot twice as much film as I anticipated, about 100,000 feet, which correspondingly sent up processing and telecine costs (synching up and transfer to tape).

If I may say so, I think it all went incredibly well, too.

Once I had written the script and was convinced that this was the story I needed to shoot, I enlisted the help of Jane Goe, who had co-produced *Running Time* with me. Jane wasn't actually very eager to get back into the film business, but I pursued her relentlessly. I finally made her this deal: you can back out at any time you want, up to and including the first day of shooting, without the slightest reproach or any ill will from me. She didn't back out—thank goodness—but she did seem to need to know there was an escape hatch.

Since the story takes place in a mythical American city over the weekend of February 8-9, 1964, I knew that I would need at least one block of generic storefronts that I could dress to the time period. Years ago I used to go to the dentist in San Fernando, up in the northeastern part of the San Fernando Valley in L.A., and this became lodged in my head as the appropriate location. Jane and I drove extensively around the valley and found exactly what was needed in a small community just east of San Fernando called Tujunga.

Tujunga had just what I needed: an entire block of storefronts, situated on a side street, most of them were out of business. I immediately rented a storefront in the middle of the block that I ended up using for not only two different locations, but as a production office during the first half of the shoot, then as an the editing suite at the end (as fate would have it, my editor, Kaye Davis-Berthaud, who had already cut *Lunatics* and *Running Time* for me, lived nine minutes from Tujunga). So, then the idea was to dress the entire block back to 1964. This meant finding old cars—an entire city block's worth.

Jane and I began our old car search at Cinema Vehicles, where we

had rented the main picture truck for *Running Time.* Cinema Vehicles' selection of old cars is very impressive, but they're also $250-
400 a day each, so an entire block's worth would be prohibitive.

Using my new Industry Flip Book (that's just like the 411 book,
but with a metal, spiral binding on top [and has since gone out of
business]), I began calling everyone listed under "Picture Vehicles."
Also, through the production designer, Jane and I met a man who
rented vehicles for movies, ironically named Van, who had recently
purchased one of the old movie ranches, Iverson Ranch, where the
Manson Family had lived for a short time. Van had about 40 or 50
old cars, but every single one was a convertible. He had a cherry
1957 Chevy in every factory color, meaning like 22 combinations—
all convertibles. And even though Van seemed like a very nice guy
who really wanted to make a deal, I could not rationalize a community where *everyone* drove a convertible.

I kept calling and calling and finally found Sy Mogel at Classic
Auto Rentals by Sy. Sy had over a hundred old cars located in the
large backyards of ten houses in Pomona. Sy had supplied all the
old cars for the *Back to the Future* movies, and that's when Jane
had been Steven Spielberg's production controller, so Jane and Sy
had obviously met before, although neither could remember doing
so. Sy, who was also a very nice guy, immediately liked the story of
If I Had a Hammer and said he'd supply the cars for the picture for
whatever I had to spend, taking a big load off my mind. Every night
that the old cars had to be in place on the street, or actually drive,
Sy had two driver/mechanics there to keep the cars running. The
old cars in the film, by the way, were: a '56 Packard Patrician, a '54
Kaiser, a '64 Corvair, a '63 Plymouth Valiant, a '58 Dodge Pioneer,
a '63 Rambler wagon, a '64 Chrysler 300, and Jane's and my friend,
Shalini Waran's, '63 Ford Falcon Futura convertible. I really got my
money's worth out of that Kaiser, and I put it in the background or
foreground of a lot of scenes.

Generally, what you see and hear in movies when someone sings
or plays an instrument is called "playback," meaning the song was
recorded earlier by someone else and the actor is just miming singing or playing. I immediately flash on Paul Newman and Sidney
Poitier as hip jazz musicians in *Paris Blues,* or Kirk Douglas as Bix
Beiderbecke in *Young Man With a Horn,* or Jimmy Stewart as Glenn
Miller, or Robert DeNiro in *New York, New York,* and, as far as I'm

concerned, every musical number is embarrassing—they're not play-ing, I know it, you know it, everybody knows it. I therefore decided to shoot all of the songs in the movie in synch, meaning that the ac-tor who you see singing and playing is in fact singing and playing. When I first proposed this to the casting director, Donise Hardy, she said, "Don't you think you're setting the bar kind of high?" I thought about it for a second, then replied, "No, I don't think so. If you got to Hollywood in 1947 you'd have better known how to act, sing, *and* dance. I'm sure there are actors out there who can do it." And you know what? There were plenty of them. Most actors have a lot more talent then they're ever called on to use these days.

The most difficult part to cast was Bobby Lee Baker, the angry young Bob Dylan-like character, who sings "In My Time of Dyin'." The character enters, has an angry speech, sings a song, then walks out of the club. What screwed me right away was that one of the early auditions for the part, by Brett Beardslee, was just great. One of the best auditions I've ever seen. So I asked Brett to come back and read for the lead part, and when he did, I gave him the lead part. But now there was a standard set for the Bobby Lee Baker character since Brett can act, sing and play. I then saw over 30 people for this part, many of whom could play the song, but very few who could get mad convincingly, or at all, really. Since I only had the casting facility for a few days, I had these seemingly pissed-off guys with their guitars traipsing in and out of my apartment for the next sev-eral weeks. This one kid who was 22 or 23 and a fine musician, re-ally had an terrific angry-young-Dylan look happening, but couldn't dredge up the slightest shred of anger—he was simply a pleasant, nice guy and that's it. The fellow who got the part, David Zink, is a terrific musician, but not necessarily an actor. However, he *really* wanted the part and tried as hard as he could, including, and I'm still impressed by this, while he was auditioning in my apartment, he pulled the cigarette out of his mouth, dropped it on my carpet and ground it out. It was such an audacious move and so entirely in character, not to mention he played the song terrifically, I gave him the part. He did a darn good job, too. (And there was still a burn mark on the carpet three years later when I moved).

We shot the film for three weeks during the summer of 1999. I was actually able to squeeze 19 days of shooting out of three weeks, by having two six-day weeks, and one seven-day week. I went into overtime once, the last day we were on the stage and we knew we'd never be back there again. Otherwise, we worked 12-hour days.

It was also ridiculously hot. It was averaging 100 or more degrees up there in the Valley in August. Since I was shooting 100 ASA film stock, that's rather slow and needs extra light to illuminate, we had a lot of lights on the set and it was easily 110-120 degrees at all times on the stage, even with the assistance of a big industrial air conditioner. Also, since it was a club set and needed to look smoky, we had to keep the stage fogged-out all the time since it took 15-20 minutes to get it fogged back up if we let it diminish. The combination of the heat and fog made it nearly unbearable on the set. At one point, Kurt (the D.P.) and I were so hot we began discussing winter shoots in Michigan (where we're both from) where we had gotten so cold that it hurt. This at least amused us for a moment, thus taking our minds off the unbearable heat.

Shooting all of the musical numbers over a couple of days was terrific fun. One of the acts is a folk quartet called The Four Feathers, who were supposed to be like The Weavers, meaning they're three guys and a girl, and a little older than everybody else because they're from the earlier folk movement after WWII. None of these four musicians had ever performed together before, and it was thrilling creating a band.

Just by the way, the film is dedicated to The Weavers and Leadbelly. The Weavers because they're just my favorite folk band, and I always liked what they, and particularly Pete Seeger, stood for, which was liberal left-wing activism. The reason I also included Huddie "Leadbelly" Ledbetter, was because I used so many of his songs in the film, like: "Rock Island Line," "Bourgeois Blues," and "Goodnight Irene." Leadbelly was a bluesman, not a folkie, but he was a big inspiration to the folkies.

All of the songs performed in the movie were songs that I had chosen and specifically written into the script for each of those characters.

The most difficult day of shooting was attempting to get enough appropriate reaction shots of the audience to cover the eight songs performed in the club over the course of Act 2, which is an hour long. I was initially going to have a 2nd unit come in at night to shoot these many shots, but ultimately couldn't afford it and had to do it myself (and that's why I added the seventh day of shooting onto the third week). This is strictly an issue of numbers: eight songs times 30 extras equals 240 close-ups, that's not feasible in a day of shooting, nor is 120 two-shots, for that matter. Nor did I really have time to take each one of these extras through the eight songs and various other reactions that I needed.

What to do?

I got together with my 1ˢᵗ assistant director, Edith, on Sunday and we worked out all of the beats that were needed from each person or group. We quickly realized that all explanations of why they were reacting as they were was wasted time. All the extras needed to know was what to do: look right, smile, laugh, talk to each other, look left, sing these lyrics, "Oh, when the saints, go marching in . . ." applaud, etc. The sound man had playback set up for the appropriate songs, that we'd play for 30-seconds, then move on. Edith and I got the whole routine down to two and half minutes. When we shot, Edith had all the beats boiled down into a rap song, "Now we're lookin' left, now we're lookin' right, now we're havin' fun drinkin' with our mates . . . " Edith is from New Zealand and says things like "mates."

I think that I got just minimally enough reaction shots for my purposes.

One interesting aspect of the *Hammer* shoot was that we fired six people in three weeks, the most on any film I've ever made. First came a very cute production assistant who seemingly couldn't do anything but gab with the male crew members. Given any job, she would return without having done it. Finally, Edith thought and thought what job can one give to someone who can't do anything? Ah, set security! This P.A. could sit on the set while the rest of us went to lunch for an hour. Ten minutes into lunch the P.A. contacted Edith on the walkie-talkie and said that she was just too tired and couldn't stay awake. Edith told her to stay awake anyway. The P.A. called back five minutes later saying that she was *really* tired. Edith told her to drink a Coke. The P.A. called four more times in the next 40 minutes, so Edith got her first taste of what it was like firing someone. The cute P.A. burst into tears and begged to be allowed to stay, but that was not granted. Edith found the experience quite disconcerting. It doesn't particularly bother me, but then I generally have someone else as my hatchet-person.

Next came the production designer and his two sons. This production designer had done at least a hundred super low-budget movies, yet all of his initial sketches were clearly set in the wrong time period, three or four years *after* the story took place (he seemingly couldn't escape the psychedelic late-sixties, and all of his drawings looked like set for the "Sonny & Cher Show"). When I would point this out to him he would then try to convince me that it was possible for these designs to exist at that time, which I wasn't buying. During pre-production he kept bragging that he would bring in his department for half the money we had budgeted. He finally turned in an art department budget that was in fact about half of what we had allotted—except that it had no labor costs included. Once those were put in it was over what we had budgeted. Nevertheless, he continued his low-budget bragging even when his mistake had been pointed out to him. He was also intent on using left-over materials from other productions, including some really boring rub-on letters that he used for every sign he made, as well as some ¾ inch thick particle board, that's simply too thick and heavy for most uses.

As we moved into the fourth day of the shoot, the Production Designer and his offspring had not yet been ready for one scene when it was time to shoot, and I found this entirely unacceptable. And I just knew I was going to have troubles that day regarding the big, illuminated sign that was to be installed above the front door of our club location. Since all of our scenes in front of the club played directly under this sign, plus it would have to be put up, taken down, then put back up the next day, I had heartily recommended that the sign be as light as possible. The day before it was to be installed Jane and I both saw it for the very first time and it was made out of, surprise, surprise, ¾ inch particle board, and weighed hundreds of pounds. Jane expressed her concern about playing scenes under this monstrosity to me and I wholeheartedly agreed. I called up the production designer and said that the sign was too big and heavy and was not at all what had been discussed. I was told repeatedly it would be fine. This went on for a half an hour until I got it through to him that it would not be fine, that it had to be lighter. Also, since the next day was a day-night shoot, meaning we were shooting from 3:00 P.M. to 3:00 A.M., and I had from call-time at 3:00 P.M. until the sun went down at about 7:00 to get the day scenes I needed in front of the club, I informed the production designer that the sign *had to be up at call-time*. I didn't care if he and his sons had to arrive five hours early to get the sign up on time, they could then leave

218 | JOSH BECKER

five hours early, just have it up on time. At call time the sign was not yet finished being built, let alone installed. It was not up until past 5:30, thus leaving me less than an hour and a half to shoot all of my scenes.

I met with the Art Director, my old buddy Gary Marvis, who was the second-in-command in the Art Department. I asked him if I hired a few more people for the department, to replace the production designer and his sons, could he have the sets and locations ready when I arrived to shoot them? He unhesitatingly stated, "Yes," and so I made him the Production Designer.

I then fired the production designer and his sons. Or, more accurately, I had Jane fire them. They left with their truck loaded with expensive rented props from a prop house that they never returned and I subsequently had to pay for. Nevertheless, I saved a lot more money than those props cost because I never again had to wait to shoot because of the Art Department. That one move made the whole production work.

Next came the crabby, though exceptionally cute, 2nd assistant camera person. She was 23, from Columbia, and her husband was the 1st A.C. From the first camera set-up on the first day, she seemed unable to keep up, and when it came time to shoot the video monitor was never plugged into the camera. I would say, "I've got no picture," and she would reply in an annoyed tone, "Just wait." This went on set-up after set-up, day after day. I've worked with a lot of camera crews in my day and I've never had this problem before. Also, since she and her husband weren't available everyday, there were other A.C.s in on different days and they never had this problem, so it couldn't be the equipment. Anyway, at some point in week #2, Kurt turned to me from behind the camera and asked what I thought of the composition of the shot? I looked at my blank monitor and said, "I haven't got a picture." This girl went nuts. "Then you'll just have to wait, won't you!" she snapped at me.

"I guess so, but I'll tell you what, you won't ever speak to me like that again on *my* set."

"Oh yeah? Well, you're an *asshole!*"

"That may be, but the 2nd A.C. doesn't talk to the director that way, ever."

"I do if I want to!"

"Oh no you don't. You're fired. You can go home now."

At which point she spewed out a stream of invective that was pretty impressive for someone so young and with English as their second language, then she and her husband went off somewhere together.

I went out to have a cigarette and figure out how I would finish my day with no camera assistants. Jane came out and a moment later the 1st A.C. husband came out to intervene. He said that she was only 23 years old and volatile and that I had been picking on her from the beginning. Well, she hadn't been getting the monitor plugged in from the beginning. All right, whatever. He said he'd speak to her and everything would be okay. A few moments later she came out, stepped up to me and said, "You're an asshole!"

I shrugged. "Yeah, maybe, but you can't do your job."

"*ASSHOLE!!!*" she screamed and stomped away.

A minute later her husband stepped up from the other direction. "So, did she apologize?"

"Yes, if calling me an asshole can be construed as an apology."

He looked a bit shocked, went back inside, then they both left.

Kurt and the gaffer, Terry Meadows, a terrific guy from Michigan, quickly began studying the Panavision camera manual and somehow we completed the day.

I used a TV technique when it came to the editing, that's called "The Editor's Cut." What this means is, I let the editor put the film together without my presence or input. This is like giving an editor amphetamines. Kaye Davis, who has now cut three of my pictures (as well as *Evil Dead 2*), had the entire film put together four weeks after we were finished shooting. Within four weeks of that we were completely done editing. All of the editing, by the way, was done digitally.

I recall at this point—slow dissolve—to editing *Lunatics* with Kaye in 1990 on film at a KEM flatbed and it took several months, with three of us working full-time (I was the 2nd assistant editor, Paul Harris was 1st assistant).

The times they are a-changin'.

The sound was edited by Joel Newport at a beautiful sound facility in Lansing, Michigan called Harvest Sound, owned by Steve Curran. These folks gave me a terrific deal, then did a top-notch job.

Joe LoDuca, who has composed the scores for all of my films (and also lives in Michigan), scored the film with his usual panache and good taste. I always thought, without giving it much thought, that the film would have a folk score. Joe came back with, "The girl is folk, the boy is rock and roll, so if I choose either of those I'm taking sides. Therefore, I say it's a jazz score," that I still think was a wonderfully inspired idea. Jazz also sets the time-period perfectly.

At this point all that remains is the negative cutting, shooting an optical negative, then the final lab processes. Given how much I've already spent on this picture, these final costs aren't all that much money—$20,000, maybe—but it's more than I have, so we'll just have to see what occurs . . .

Oct. 25, 2000
Part 2: Post-Production

I am 99.9% through post-production, so this seems like an appropriate time to pick up the narrative of the making *If I Had a Hammer*. I have seen the first two answer prints and the next answer print will be the final print, and that officially makes the movie done.

It's been ten months since I wrote the last installment of this saga, and that which I thought would take six months in total and another $20,000, in fact took fourteen months and another $75,000 to reach the actual, ultimate completion.

How did I miscalculate so egregiously? That's a fairly good question and worth considering.

My biggest mistake to date was charging $80,000 of the production on credit cards, then taking over fourteen months in post. This combination has cost me about $20,000 in finance charges. On top of that I have hit the longest stretch of unemployment in my adult life, meaning the entire year of 2000, so far, thus ending my steady stream of working capital.

What this has all equaled has been the most grueling, stress-filled year of the last ten years of my life.

Having made a pretty good living throughout the 1990s, I had forgotten what being dead-ass broke was like. I remember very clearly now and I don't like it all. But it's too late to do anything about it at this point. I stepped into a quagmire with my eyes open and now that it's sucking up around my mouth and nose, I'm starting to panic.

The bottom line regarding putting a lot of the production costs on credit cards—about a third, in this case—is that you had better be ready and willing to declare bankruptcy if need be. If you are not ready to do this, as I am not, you will suffer horribly. However, do I regret doing this? No. I would rather have made this movie than anything else.

For the second time (along with *Running Time*) I have made exactly the movie I wanted to make, given my budgetary restrictions. I did not rewrite a word for anybody else. I did not shoot an extra angle at anyone else's behest. I was entirely free. You won't hear many other filmmakers say that. I use it as a mantra to warm the cockles of my heart late at night.

Anyway, why did post-production take so long? Basically, I got several terrific deals that I had to wait for. Even with the waiting and finance charges, they were still really great deals and that's just how it goes. If you have a lot of money then you can get the people you want exactly when you need them. If you don't have the money and you still want specific people, then you have to wait, and I waited.

My next biggest mistake, I'd say, was miscalculating post costs by almost a third by not owning up to the actual length of the movie. Having never made a 117-minute movie before—my longest film previously was *Lunatics: A Love Story* at 87 minutes—I didn't realize what a huge expense that extra 30 minutes would be. *If I Had a Hammer* is a seven-reel movie. I'm referring to the 20-minute projection reels, the ones that come in those octagonal metal cans (called Goldberg cans), as opposed to lab reels, that are only 10 minutes long. Well, seven reels times 20 minutes each equals 140 minutes, except my film is only 117 minutes long. So why isn't it on six reels? Six reels equals 120 minutes. That ought to give me three extra minutes, right?

Get this. You try as hard as you can to make the reel-changes come out in logical places, like at the ends of scenes, not during scenes. Well, that doesn't always work out to exactly ten minutes—when you're editing you work with 10-minute reels. Why? Because that's the length Kodak sells rolls of film and there's nothing you can do about it. So you can't exceed 10 minutes on a lab reel and you want your reels to end between scenes, and since most scenes are a minute or two long, that will put you somewhere between 7 and 9 minutes. Over the course of 12 lab reels losing a minute or two or three each reel, I developed 2 more 10-minute lab reels, which became a seventh, 20-minute projection reel!

222 | JOSH BECKER

Does this make sense? It better if you're making a movie. Perhaps this will all disappear soon with the advent of digital filmmaking, but, as yet, it hasn't.

I simply must laugh when some lying asshole filmmaker says their entire movie cost $7,000. Completely ignoring production costs (which are the big costs), to have the camera negative cut cost $8,500! To go from the camera negative to print so you can actually show the film costs *a dollar a foot!* A two-hour movie is approximately 10,000 feet. To have a soundtrack on the print is another $4,500. That's already $23,000. and that's if your movie was completely free until you got it into the lab for post-production.

How about digital effects? Right now it costs $1.25 a frame to digitize the picture, then another $1.25 a frame to spit it back out onto film. That has nothing to do with what the effects guy is charging to create the effect. And that's not a foot, *that's a frame!* And there are 24-frames a second. My three simple digital effects were over 1,250 frames, which, all together, doesn't equal one minute.

Admittedly, I always make something of a production out of my front title sequences—it's sort of my trademark—but the titles and optical work on this film cost over $14,000 and that was because I got a terrific deal. The first couple of places I spoke with wanted over 25 grand for the same work.

I now look back on *Running Time* as the easiest feature film I have made. I had saved almost as much money as was needed to produce and complete the film. I was also working throughout that time and had money flowing in. The film was only 70 minutes, it was shot in 16mm, which is minimally two-thirds cheaper than 35mm, there were no digital effects or opticals (like wipes), and when everything was said and done the film cost $120,000. I also spent another $30,000 opening the film in a theater for a week, but so what?

Well, that extra $200,000 I spent on *If I Had a Hammer* is trying very hard to sink me. This may all sound like diddly-shit for a feature-length motion picture, but in the real world $200,000 is A LOT OF MONEY! More than twice as much as I've ever had at one time. To avoid bankruptcy, which dangles over my head like the sword of Damocles, I have been eating vast amounts of shit in the past year to weasel, finagle and borrow money. Any pride I may have once had about such things is now gone. I've soaked my dad, my mom, Sam Raimi and

Rob Tapert. If I even vaguely believe that I can get some money out of someone—friend, relative, or acquaintance—I'll now pester them worse than long distance phone companies at dinnertime.

If it sounds like I'm taking pride in my lack of pride, I am. I'll do whatever I have to do to complete this film. Period. I am an unstoppable force. If I am not as spectacular of a force as, say, a hurricane or an earthquake, then I'm an insidious force like erosion and I will drip, drip, drip until I wear a hole through a boulder. My films may not ultimately mean dick to anyone else in the world but me, but they *will* get made. And that, I believe, is the only way to get these silly little independent features finished.

Stay tuned for the next exciting episode of "The Making of *If I Had a Hammer*," that will be sub-titled, "Part 3: Distribution" and is, as the future is for all people, entirely unknown to me at this time.

May 16, 2001

Part Three: Distribution, or the Lack Thereof

It's now halfway through 2001 and *If I Had a Hammer* is entirely done. It's been done since February. Perhaps 200 people on the planet Earth have seen the film, although I might be overestimating.

It did turn out very much the way I wanted it to and I feel good about that. That I don't have the slightest hint of a distribution deal is, I must admit, rather unnerving.

Right now the film has been sent out to the Telluride Film Festival. These big festivals get literally thousands of entries, but my fingers are crossed [it didn't get into Telluride, nor did it get into any other big festival].

I have never stopped paying enormous finance charges on my credit cards and it's basically killing me. I could have paid off at least 35% of the principal at this point if the interest wasn't so high. The possibility of bankruptcy potentially looms in my near future. I suppose I should actually get on it before legislation is passed to

224 | JOSH BECKER

disallow it [which has since occurred]. Also, it's probably better to do it before I'm entirely broke.

Lovely thoughts. Nevertheless, I cannot make people watch this film, nor can I make them care. The irony is that's what the movie is about.

Feb. 14, 2006
Part Four: As Time Goes By

It's now six years later. I moved out of Los Angeles in October of 2001 and relocated to southern Oregon. I lived there for a year, then moved back to Detroit, and I've been here for five years now.

Meanwhile, I'm still paying off the goddamn credit cards. I've consolidated the cards from ten cards down to four, and between the fees for directing two SciFi Channel TV movies, as well as money I borrowed, I've got the debt down to about $35,000. It still sucks, but it's much better than the nearly one hundred grand it was once up to, and it's still a *big* burden.

Worst of all, though, *If I Had a Hammer* was never released at all. I personally sold 300 VHS copies on my website over four years, and that's it. Apparently, I had to wait until I was in my 40s to make a totally un-releasable movie that in turn caused the biggest financial disaster of my life. The irony, I think, is that I'm still absolutely convinced that *If I Had a Hammer* is my best movie. Ah, sweet irony, where would we be without it?

More importantly, I suppose, is that I lived through it. I'm probably a little bit wiser now, too—I'll certainly never make a movie on credit cards again. That's unless, of course, I've been diagnosed with a fatal illness, in which case all bets are off.

Dec. 14, 2007
Part Five: Bankruptcy, and Beyond . . .

In the past five years I've paid over $120,000 in credit card minimum payments, never paying down the principal, just paying the interest and nothing more. Since my last two movie jobs—*Alien Apocalypse* and *Harpies*—combined paid about 100 grand, I've really never been able to get out from behind the eight ball.

So, after borrowing as much money as I possibly could, I finally succumbed to the inevitable and filed for bankruptcy.

The first thing I did was to consult my uncle who's a lawyer, and he recommended a very reputable bankruptcy attorney whom he knew. The attorney and I spoke, and he explained the process of filing for, and going through, a bankruptcy. I didn't mention that I'd accrued all this credit card debt ($42,000 at that point) by making a movie, and he never asked. How one managed to get into debt isn't really the issue at that point, it's now how to get out.

I said, "So, how do we get this process started?"

He replied, "You send me a check for $1,500."

Which I did. As soon as he received the check he filed a "stay" on my debts, and immediately I no longer had to pay my credit card bills, and they also stopped coming.

I'd been informed by several different people that the bankruptcy laws had recently been changed significantly and it was now much more difficult to do. Well, the laws were changed in 2005 (under the presidency of G.W. Bush), and it's now a bit more difficult than before, but not really all that much.

Here are the two added difficulties: 1. you must now pay $50 to a credit counseling service to take 90 minutes of credit counseling over the telephone (and they only take debit cards, by the way), and 2. you have to read a humiliatingly simpleminded 120-page book on bankruptcy entitled "Second Chance," then you must take a credit test before your debt is finally discharged, and that costs another $50. Neither aspect is all that big of a deal, and all it did was to create a new industry designed to take advantage of, and profit off of, bankrupt people. Thank you so much, Mr. President.

Luckily for me, I never actually had to go to bankruptcy court. I did however have to appear with my lawyer in front of a bankruptcy Trustee, in the federal building where the federal court is located. Bankruptcy, by the way, is not a local or state issue, it's federal issue.

The Trustee assigned to our case was a very serious-looking lawyer of about sixty, with thick white eyebrows. My lawyer and I were seated in a room with about twenty other people and their lawyers. At a table at the center of the fairly small room sat the Trustee and a legal assistant. One by one the cases were called. Each person with their lawyer went up and sat at the table while the Trustee quickly, though with intense scrupulousness, read through their case, then asked questions. The concept, as I perceived it, is that the Trustee is the middleman between you and the bankruptcy court. It's the Trustee who decides if and when you're ready to go to court, or if you'll go at all. Both of the cases that were called before me took 25-30 minutes each, and both ended with the Trustee demanding more paperwork and calling for an "adjournment."

In my case, unlike the previous two, my lawyer and the Trustee greeted each other by name, clearly having some sort of history (I found out later they'd both gone to Notre Dame). The Trustee looked over my case silently, then looked up, smiled for the very first time that day, and said, "Xena: Warrior Princess? With Lucy Lawless? Really?"

I smiled, "Yeah. Really."

He said, "I'll show your signature to my son tonight and I'll be a hero. He loves that show."

The Trustee then spent a long moment looking at my one page list of assets, all of which are copyrights and intellectual properties—scripts, books and movies. He finally asked, "Is a screenplay like a script?"

I said, "Yes, it's exactly like it."

He nodded. "And when you say 'Motion Picture' you mean, like a short movie?"

"No, they're all full-length."

He nodded, his thick eyebrows arched, indicating, "What the hell does this all mean?" A moment later he pushed the whole mess away from himself over to the assistant, saying, "Next."

My lawyer and I exited stage right.

When we got out of the hearing room and into the waiting room, my lawyer said, "You heard him say 'adjourned' for the two cases before us, but not for us."

I asked, "Is that good or bad?"

My lawyer smiled, "It's good. He doesn't need any more information."

So then I read "Second Chance," took the test, passed, and subsequently all of my credit card debt has been discharged, meaning eliminated. As far as I'm concerned, that is the official end of the *If I Had a Hammer* saga.

Except of course I still have the movie. I recently showed it a couple of times, at local theaters here in the Detroit area, and it plays pretty well. Beyond that, I always enjoy sitting through it.

When everything's said and done, though, I'm still glad that I made the movie. Sure, I never sold it and it nearly sank me in debt, but I do think it's a legitimate attempt to use film as art, as opposed to it being used as merely one more expression of capitalistic greed. Maybe it didn't make any money, but that was never really it's purpose.

I felt that with *If I Had a Hammer* I actually had something to say, and I said it as well as I could using the cinematic form. And you know what, it exists. It's not a dream, it's a full-length, 35mm motion picture, and I made it (and, if you're of a mind, you can watch it for free on YouTube).

The Hollywood Walk of Fame
Or How To Be A Star For $4,800

(originally published in April, 1992
issue of *Film Threat Magazine*)

I frequently question my motives for living in Hollywood: the rent's high, the area is run-down and dirty, there are homeless people everywhere panhandling me wherever I go, police helicopters circle overhead constantly, and on Friday and Saturday nights the police actually cordon off the entire area allowing no traffic in or out. Why do I live here? I want to be famous, just like everybody else.

For fifteen years I have been treading my weary way around Hollywood, back and forth over the stars embedded in the sidewalk that are collectively known as The Walk Of Fame. The stars stretch for over a mile on Hollywood Boulevard, from Sycamore to Gower and four blocks on Vine from Sunset to Yucca. There are approximately 1970 of these coral terrazzo stars, outlined in brass on a charcoal terrazzo background, bearing the names of personalities from movies, TV, radio and records.

Who are these people and how did they get this immortal privilege? I've always wondered about this since, for example, Humberto Luna, the local L.A. disc jockey, has a star and Francis Coppola, winner of five Academy Awards, does not. A few other notables that do not have stars are: Lon Chaney, Jr., Howard Hughes and David O. Selznick, producer of *Gone With The Wind* (although his father, Lewis J. Selznick, a silent film distributor, does have one).

The order form from the Hollywood Chamber of Commerce, sponsors of The Walk Of Fame, states, "In order to be selected to receive a star on the famous Walk, a person must have their sponsor complete and return a nomination form with the biography and photo of the nominee. If the nominator is a fan, there must be a guarantee that the fee of $4,800 will be paid and that the celebrity is in accordance with the nomination." It seems that if you made an appearance in a movie (preferably a silent movie), did a guest shot on a radio show, or were involved in any way with a recording, and happen to have $4,800, you too can have a star on The Walk Of Fame.

The Walk Of Fame is one of the most popular tourist attractions in Los Angeles. People from all over the world, particularly Asia, come to Hollywood to saunter along the Walk, squat down and photograph the stars. Since most of these people are using cameras that will not focus closer than five feet, and they themselves are for the most part no taller than five feet, one must assume that there are thousands upon thousands of out of focus photographs of these stars all over the Pacific rim.

The terrazzo surface of the Walk gets very slick with any moisture at all. On a rainy day it is not uncommon to see poor unsuspecting souls slipping and falling down among the stars.

I set about traversing the entire length and breadth of the Walk, noting all of the names that I was unfamiliar with, as well as any oddities or irregularities. Before I even got to Hollywood Boulevard I had three full pages with two columns each of unknown names. As I already knew, and also never understood, there are many people with more than one star. Gene Autry, former cowboy star, owner of a lot of land, sports teams, as well as TV and radio stations, has *five* stars.

All four corners of Hollywood and Vine have the same names in a large box and a circle. They are: Neil A. Armstrong, Edwin E. Aldrin, Jr. and Michael Collins, 7/20/69, Apollo XI [Roman numerals] with a little TV insignia. Apparently Hollywood wanted to express its great appreciation for an evening of unique television broadcasting.

As I stood jotting this information down, a short, pot-bellied fellow of sixty-five named Louie, with a thick New Jersey accent, sidled up and asked what I was doing. When I explained he remarked . . .

"I'll tell ya who doesn't have a star that oughta . . ."

". . . Who?"

"Vivian Vance, that's who. You know who she is?"

"Ethel from *I Love Lucy*."

"That's right. She ain't got no star. And William Frawley who played Fred's got one. That ain't fair."

He's wrong, Vivian Vance does have a star.

Louie went on to tell me that he had driven a cab in Beverly Hills for the past thirty years.

"Ya know who I picked up once?"

"No. Who?"

"Carroll O'Connor, that's who. And I give him a great idea for a TV show. He and his Dad run a bar. Now this was fifteen, sixteen years ago. Who shoulda played his Dad?"

"I don't know. Who?"

"James Cagney, that's who. They're both Irish, see. But does he do it? No. So where am I? Nowhere. That shanty-town bum."

Louie obviously wants to be famous, too.

Here are a few of the oddities and irregularities:

—Michael Jackson has two stars, The Jacksons have one, and Janet has one as well.

—Only nine people do not have a movie camera, a TV, a microphone or a record insignia, but instead have a happy face/sad face which I would believe indicates a stage career, but you judge for yourself: George Carlin, George Burns (whereas his vaudeville, radio, movie and TV partner, Gracie Allen, has a TV), Gene Autry, The Fourstep Brothers, Joel Gray, Gene Barry, Jim Nabors and James Nederlander.

—Both of the directors of *King Kong* have their names misspelled. Ernest B. Schoedsack (who always used the middle initial B.) hasn't got the B. and his last name is spelled "Schoedsach"; Merian C. Cooper's name is spelled "Meriam" and in fact there was a silent screen actress named Miriam Cooper, but if it's supposed to be her then it's still spelled wrong.

—There are three stars for people named Pee-Wee: Pee-Wee Hunt, Pee-Wee King, and Pee-Wee Herman.

—One sports team has a star, The Harlem Globetrotters.

—Father and son actors Tex Ritter and John Ritter have their stars next to one another.

—Two inventors have stars: Thomas A. Edison, and Mark Serrurier, inventor of the moviola.

—The only stars that state the actor's name and the character they became famous playing are: Clayton Moore The Lone Ranger, Freeman Gosden Amos and Charles Correll Andy (since there are no quotation marks one might easily construe that Amos and Andy were their last names).

—The only name that contains a small case letter is the 'e' in Dom

DeLuise's name.

—The only company that has a star is Hanna Barbera.

—The only novelist with a star who never worked in the movies, but had a number of his books filmed, is Harold Robbins. (Sidney Sheldon, also a best-selling novelist with a star, was an Academy Award winning screenwriter long before he wrote any novels).

—Faye Emerson's name is misspelled ("Fay Emerson").

—Roscoe "Fatty" Arbuckle is only listed as "Roscoe Arbuckle," whereas Eddie "Rochester" Anderson is only listed as "Rochester."

—Director H. Bruce Humberstone who always used the first initial H. is only listed as "Bruce Humberstone."

—Three of the four Warner Brothers, Harry, Jack, and Sam, have stars, but brother Albert does not. Jesse Lasky and Adolph Zukor from Paramount have stars (as well as Y. Frank Freeman who was head of production there for a while), as do Louis B. Mayer from M-G-M, Carl Laemmle from Universal, and William Fox, Darryl Zanuck and Joseph Schenck from 20th Century-Fox, however Samuel Goldwyn, Harry Cohn (and his brother Joe), and Howard Hughes do not.

—Nat "King" Cole has two stars, one with the quotations around King, one without.

—Only three animals have stars, all dogs: Lassie, Rin-Tin-Tin, and Strongheart.

—Four cartoon characters have stars: Bugs Bunny, Mickey Mouse, Snow White, and Woody Woodpecker.

—Mauritz Stiller (who directed many Greta Garbo pictures) used to be misspelled (Maurice Diller), then it was fixed with letters that don't match the others.

—Ignace Paderewski only has the name "Paderewski" (but perhaps he's like Cantinflas or Madonna).

—Robert Goulet, co-star of the Broadway show "Camelot" (not the movie) and best-selling singer, has a movie camera.

—Ronald Reagan, B movie actor, former Governor of California, and former President of the United States, has a TV (is that for his lively televised press conferences as President?).

—Charles Boyer has two stars: one with a movie camera and one with a TV five stars away from one another.

—Basil Rathbone, character actor in many great films and star of the Sherlock Holmes film series, has three stars.

—Robert Shaw, co-star of *A Man For All Seasons* and *Jaws*, as well as being a playwright, has a record.

—The musical groups with stars are: The Jacksons, Crosby Stills & Nash (not Young), Sons Of The Pioneers, The Spinners, Bee Gees (no "The"), Beach Boys (no "The"), The Monkees, The Mills Bros., Bob Seger And The Silver Bullet Band, The Steve Miller Band, and The Original 5th Dimension (not to be confused with The Unoriginal 5th Dimension, I presume).

Here is a list of the people with stars who have silly or unusual names:

Melachrino, Blanche Thebom, Ted Weems, Tommy Riggs & Betty Lou, Phil Spitalny, Joseph Szigeti, Little Jack Little, Renata Tebaldi, Schumann-Heink, Smilin' Ed McConnell, Zino Francescatti, Mabel Taliaferro, Arnold Schwarzenegger, Feodor Chaliapin, Spade Cooley, Louise Glaum, Tichi Wilkerson-Kassel, Beniamino Gigli, Amelita Galli Curci, Kirsten Flagstad, Aileen Pringle, Oscar Micheaux, Ferlin Husky, Licia Albanese, Toby Wing, Viola Dana, Harry Von Zell, Graham McNamee, Abbe Lane (cousin to Abbey Road), Jetta Goudal, Rusty Hamer, Constance Binney, Carmen Cavallero, Jessica Dragonette, Art Acord, John Bunny, Lottie Lehman, Meiklejohn, Heine Conklin, Ralph Staub, Blue Barron, Robert Casadesus, Pinky Lee, House Peters, Smiley Burnette and, of course, Parkyakarkus.

The list of people that I didn't recognize is hundreds of names long. I looked them all up in Leslie Halliwell's "Filmgoer's Companion" and about a third of them were listed. Here are a few interesting ones:

—Lina Basquette: Silent screen actress, former child star, had six husbands.

—Susan Peters: Leading lady of the forties; badly injured in an accident and continued her career from a wheelchair.

—James A. Fitzpatrick - Documentary filmmaker, who from 1925 produced and narrated innumerable travel shorts, *Fitzpatrick Traveltalks*, which generally concluded with "And so we leave . . ."

—Jane Froman: (who has three stars) Former band singer, whose heroic resumption of her career following an air crash was portrayed by Susan Hayward in *With A Song In My Heart*.

—Tom Brown: Child star of the thirties; the "boy next door" type. Re-emerged in the sixties as one of the villagers in the TV series *Gunsmoke*.

—Gilda Gray: Polish dancer who went to America and is credited with inventing the "Shimmy."

—Cass Daley: (who has two stars) Comedienne whose shouted songs and acrobatic contortions were a feature of several musicals of the forties.

—Kathlyn Williams: (whose name is misspelled, "ee" instead of "y") Leading lady of silent films; one of the first serial queens, on screen from 1911.

—Houdini (AKA Harry Houdini): made a number of silent movies between 1918 and his death in 1926.

—Olive Borden: Silent screen actress whose real name was Sybil Tinkle.

—Marie Doro: Played the role of Oliver Twist in the 1916 version.

—Texas Guinan: Entertainer of the twenties whose catchphrase was "Hello, sucker!" Betty Hutton played her in the film *Incendiary Blonde.*

—Betty Bayne: Whose real name was Pearl Von Name.

—Lila Lee: Whose real name was Augusta Apple, mother to novelist and Pulitzer Prize-winning playwright James Kirkwood (*A Chorus Line*).

—Helen Gahagan: Star of one single movie, the 1935 version of *She*, who was also married to Melvyn Douglas.

So, I want to be famous and I wouldn't mind having a star on The Walk Of Fame. Hell, I've made two movies, so why shouldn't I? I've got a list here of over four hundred people who may not have deserved it anymore than me. What did they have that I don't have? Well, to start with, $4,800.

"The Worst Case Scenario"
Scenario

I've known Craig Peligian, executive producer of the recent TV show "Worst Case Scenario," since we were seven years old growing up in Detroit. I worked for Craig ten years ago when he was the producer of "Real Stories of the Highway Patrol." I directed a number of the reenactment segments for the show's first season. In between "Real Stories," which ran over five hundred episodes, and "Worst Case Scenario," which is on now, Craig was co-executive producer of "Survivor" and "Survivor 2," two of the biggest hit shows ever.

Craig called me from a satellite phone in Borneo when he was making "Survivor" and told me he was working on a show that would be a big hit. I didn't believe him, since it sounded so utterly inane to me, but I didn't say anything. As it turned out, he was very right.

With the enormous success of "Survivor" behind him, Craig purchased the rights to the bestseller "The Worst Case Scenario Survival Guide" and set up a deal with Sony. He told them that if they were interested in making it into a TV show they'd have to wait until he returned from Africa and the making of "Survivor 2." As soon as he arrived in Kenya, his satellite phone rang and Sony naturally gave "WCS" the big greenlight. Go, go, go! So Craig set up the whole production by satellite phone from the jungles of Africa, and, as fate would have it, the production office was located about four blocks from where I was then living in Santa Monica.

When Craig returned from Africa, and his production of "WCS" was already underway, he contacted me to work on the show and gave me a copy of the book. It's a cute little yellow book, set up like a handbook, detailing what you should do if, for instance, you were attacked by a mountain lion—don't turn and run, cats of all sizes prefer to grab their prey by the back of the neck and shake it to death. Instead, open your jacket and raise your arms making you look as big as possible, and growl; if a cat thinks you're both bigger than it and aggressive, it will hightail it for the hills. That's good information, I think. Or what you should do if you have to jump off the roof of a building—look for a dumpster to jump into. Etc.

It seemed like a perfect set-up for a reenactment show, at which Craig is an expert. Show someone camping in the woods, a mountain lion appears, now what do you do? A. turn and run, B. raise your arms and growl, or C. pick up a pile of shit and throw it at the mountain lion (how can you be sure there will be a pile of shit there to throw? Take my word for it, there will be).

So I arrived at the "WCS" production office one hot, smoggy L.A. day in September of 2001 (right after 9/11), and there were a hundred people busily at work. I was under the delusion that Craig wanted me to direct some segments for him, but that was not the case. He immediately decided that I ought to be the show's story editor, although I'm still not entirely sure what a story editor does.

I said, "Craig, I don't want to be story editor. I'm a director. Besides, I'll only work under a DGA contract, and there isn't one for a story editor. It's not a DGA position."

Craig is a very pushy guy that generally gets what he wants and I admire him for that. He's the toughest negotiator I've ever met. I wish I had more of that in me. Anyway, Craig said to me that "Directors are a dime a dozen, I need a story editor. And I can't hire you under a DGA contract because it would be too much money, I can't afford it."

I was confused. "Well, then I guess we can't do this."

"Sure we can."

Craig then assigned an associate producer to show me around and have me see all of the segments that were shot and just being edited. Craig said, "This is Josh, he's an old friend of mine and the new story editor," and he quickly split.

The associate producer introduced herself and said, "So, you're the new story editor."

I said, "No, I'm a director."

"Huh?"

I was then taken to a small editing room that contained an Avid editing machine and a young editor and was introduced as, "This is Josh, he's the new story editor."

I shook the young man's hand as he said, "So, you're the new story editor, huh?"

I shook my head vigorously. "No, I'm a director."

"Huh?"

I was then shown several segments of the show. In each segment a stunt person wearing a yellow jump suit, with "Worst Case Scenario" embroidered on their back, says something like, "Hi, I'm a professional stunt person, and I'm about to jump off this building. Don't try this at home. I'm going to jump into that dumpster below me there in the alley." Then they jump off the building into the dumpster, covered by a hundred different camera angles, most in slow-motion. And, of course, after the jump they sit up and they're fine. In another segment a stunt person in a yellow jump suit says something like, "Hi, I'm a professional stunt man, and I'm going to fall down this hill. Don't try this at home." Then they fall down a hill, covered by a hundred camera angles, most in slo-mo, get to bottom and they're fine.

This went on all day, as I was taken from one editing room to another, introduced as the new story editor, and shown segment after segment of stunt people in yellow jump suits doing various stunts and not being injured. Pretty soon I was ready to scream.

Finally, I ended up in the associate producer's office and she asked, "So, what do you think?"

Me being me, and not wanting to work on the show as the story editor anyway, I said, "It should be called 'How to be a Stunt Man,' and, quite frankly, who cares about stunt people doing stunts? Of course they're not going to get hurt, they're stunt people." She seemed a bit shocked. "What do you think it should be instead?"

"It ought to be reenactments. Why does someone *have* to jump off the roof of a building? Because there's fire in the stairwell and there's nowhere else to go, and they should be just regular folks, not stunt people in yellow jumpsuits."

She said, "I think some other people need to hear this" and left the room. She returned a few moments later with two men and two women, all producers and co-producers, all in their late twenties and early thirties, all looking bright and eager. So, I repeated what I'd just said to the associate producer, and they all looked stunned and slightly horrified. The producer (I believe he was), a bright-looking fellow with thin glasses, asked, "So what are you saying?"

"I'm saying," I repeated yet again, "that this ought to be a reenactment show, which Craig is an expert at."

The producer shook his head vehemently. "No. This was sold to Sony as a reality show. It *has* to be a reality show."

238 | JOSH BECKER

I shrugged, "Except that it's *not* a reality show."

He was now aghast. "What do you mean? Of course this is a reality show."

"No it's not. You're not *really* showing regular people caught in the act of having to jump off a building—*that's* reality. You're staging a scene, with stunt people—that's not reality, that's a *reenactment*."

"So what are you saying?"

"I'm saying, to get me to care I have to believe this is a regular person, caught in a 'worst case scenario,' and circumstances are forcing them to have to jump off a building."

The producer looked at me very seriously. "I don't understand. You're saying it's not a stunt person? We can't get a regular person to jump off a roof, it wouldn't be safe."

I was doing my level best to be patient. "No, it is a stunt person, but they're not wearing a yellow jump suit that says Worst Case Scenario. They're dressed like a normal person."

"But that would be a lie. They *are* a stunt person."

"But if I know they're a stunt person, then I don't care."

"We can't dress a stunt person in regular clothes, then it wouldn't be reality."

"Everything else that uses stunt people dresses them in regular clothes, why can't you?"

"Because this is a reality show."

"No it's not."

The producer had had enough. "Well, I don't see why they can't be in yellow jump suits. What's the difference?"

"The difference is that there's no drama watching a stunt person jump off a building, and there is drama watching a regular person jump off a building. The book isn't about stunt people, it's about what a regular person does if they have to jump off a building."

He stood up ready to leave and shook his head wearily, "I don't see the difference. Besides, we've already shot sixteen segments with yellow jump suits and we're not reshooting them."

He left. A moment later all of the other various producers left, too, throwing me looks like I was an insane heretic.

Craig appeared, grabbed me and pushed me into an office with a director, a video machine, and a huge pile of tapes. "Here, help this director. He has hours and hours of footage, and we're not sure how to even start cutting it together." Craig introduced me, "This is Josh, he's the new story editor."

It was already after 7:00 PM, I was hungry, aggravated, had a headache, and was in desperate need of a cigarette. I watched footage with this director for about an hour, then excused myself to go to the bathroom. As soon as I was in the hall, and I saw that Craig was stuck in a meeting with all the other producers, I sneaked out of the building, got into my car, lit a cigarette and drove home. Knowing Craig wouldn't answer his cell phone during the meeting, I called and left a message. I said, "Craig, I wish you all the luck in the world with this show, but I don't want to work on it in any position. Good seeing you again."

I then promptly moved to Oregon.

The show ended up being pushed back by over six months, and when it finally premiered about a month ago, it was still stunt people in yellow jump suits. It has been seriously panned by one and all, and probably won't last much longer. It's too bad because there could have been an all right show lurking within that premise, and Craig was the perfect guy to make it.

Clockwise: The new US
DVD cover; the French
DVD cover; Gary Jones
and his termite puppet;
Josh and Bruce; David
Worth, Josh, Bob Perkis

The Making of
Alien Apocalypse

The story of the making of *Alien Apocalypse* begins in 1988 in Los Angeles. Soon after seeing Luc Besson's *Le Denier Combat*, an intriguing, extremely low-budget, post-apocalyptic story, I was inspired to come up with the idea for the story of *Alien Apocalypse* (which I entitled *Humans in Chains*), and I jotted it down—*Spartacus* in the future, with giant termite aliens stealing Earth's wood. Soon thereafter, I ran into Lawrence Bender, who has since gone on to produce *Reservoir Dogs*, *Pulp Fiction*, *Kill Bill* and all the rest of Quentin Tarantino's movies, but at that point had yet to do anything. He and Quentin used to hang out at the bungalow where I was living in Hollywood with my writing partner, Scott Spiegel (who would later direct *From Dusk 'til Dawn 2: Texas Blood Money*, and be the co-producer of the *Hostel* films). Lawrence told me that he had met some Texas investors who wanted to finance a film and did I have any scripts that could be made very cheaply? I said I had just come up with a science fiction story that I thought was pretty good, sort of like *Spartacus* in the future. He said to give him the treatment. I said, "What are you offering?" He said he'd pay $10,000 for the script, and that I would get to direct it. I said okay, went home and wrote the treatment for *Humans in Chains*. I gave it to Lawrence, he read it, said he liked it, then immediately added that he would now only pay $5,000 for the script, and I wouldn't get to direct it. I grabbed the treatment right back out of his hands and said, "Forget it." He replied, "Fine, fuck you." I retorted something witty like, "No, fuck you," and left.

Two years later, right after I had made my second feature film, *Lunatics: A Love Story*, I pitched the executive producer, Rob Tapert, the story for *Humans in Chains*. He said he liked it, thought that it would make a good follow-up project to *Lunatics*, and I really ought to write the script. I had moved back to Detroit at that point and was living in my family's house that was vacant at the time since my mom and dad were in the midst of a divorce and both of them had moved out. The house was too big and quiet to work in, so I drove up to the nearby Tel-12 Mall, sat in the food court and wrote the script for *Humans in Chains* by hand on yellow legal pads. This took several weeks of daily work. I'd arrive right when the mall opened at 10:00 AM, get a cup of coffee and a Cinnabon cinnamon roll (Mmmmm, cinnamon rolls), I'd sit down by myself among the 100 or so tables and start writing. In the course of the next two hours every table would fill up with people eating lunch, then an hour or so later almost everyone would leave and it would just be me by myself writing again. This always seemed like a perfect time-lapse shot for a film.

Once the script was written by hand, I began slowly typing it into my computer. I moved back to L.A. at that point and began moving from one friend's couch to another. For a short time I was crashing in the garage at Sam Raimi's house in Silverlake when he was subletting it to: Joel and Ethan Coen, Fran McDormand, Holly Hunter, and Kathy Baker, all of whom have subsequently gone on to win Oscars (perhaps if I had been paying rent, instead of just mooching, I too would have an Oscar by now). I remember trying to work on the script for *Humans in Chains* there and it was just too damn noisy (the one line of dialog that comes back to mind is Holly hollering to Fran, "Hey, Fran, how 'bout some more *vino?*").

I finally completed the first draft of the script and it came out very long at about 150 pages. I gave it to Rob, he read it, still liked the basic story, but didn't like most of what I had written, and he made extensive notes that I found both perceptive and very helpful. So I began the rewrite. This took a couple of more months, and when I was finished I thought it had turned out quite well. Rob's notes had been incredibly useful, so I gave him co-story credit, also thinking that this would inspire him to get the film financed. Rob, however, had moved onto other projects (*Army of Darkness*, and *Time Cop*, with Jean-Claude Van Damme), had completely lost interest in my script and wouldn't even bother to read it (when Rob finally got around to reading the rewrite in 2000, *ten years later*, he called me up and said, "Hey, that's a helluva good rewrite").

The hands of time slowly crept forward and twelve years went by. I moved up to Jacksonville, Oregon in October of 2001, a mile up the road from my pal, Bruce Campbell, and into a single-wide trailer truly in the middle of nowhere (it was seven miles to the nearest store—not a town, that was seven more miles). A herd of deer, and a flock of wild turkeys wandered though my yard every day. I fed them bread and they became my friends.

Meanwhile, Bruce and I had signed up with a new sales agency, Creative Light, to sell our various movies, since our original sales agent, Irvin Shapiro, had died several years earlier. These new sales agents were a bunch of young hustlers who had an in at the Sci Fi Channel, where Bruce had already starred in a film (*Terminal Invasion*) that had rated very well, so Sci Fi really liked Bruce. Creative Light asked Bruce and I if we had any scripts suitable for Sci Fi that Bruce could star in. Bruce dug out his sixteen-year-old script, *The Man With the Screaming Brain*, and I dug out my twelve-year-old script, *Humans in Chains*, and we sent them in to the sales agent who in turn sent them to Sci Fi Channel. This was when the title *Humans in Chains* became *Alien Apocalypse*, compliments of the sales agent.

Two or three months went by and Bruce and I both asked the agent, "So, what's up with Sci Fi?"

The agent replied, "They love it."

"Oh, great."

Two or three more months went by.

"So, what's up with Sci Fi?"

"They're high on it."

"Oh, terrific."

Three or four more months went by.

"Anything with Sci Fi?"

"Yeah, they really want to do it?"

"No kidding."

Six more months went by. I moved back to Michigan, to a small house on an acre of land in the Detroit suburb of Bloomfield.

Finally, Sci Fi called Bruce and asked, "What's up with those scripts you sent in? We want to make them."

Bruce said, "I don't know."

Sci Fi told Bruce to call Jeff Franklin, a producer they had worked with before (Jeff produced the film *Raptor Island* for them, as well as the TV show *Mike Hammer*). Bruce called Jeff and said, "Hi, I'm Bruce Campbell."

Jeff Franklin replied in his dry, tough-guy tone, "Yeah, I know who you are."

Bruce said, "Sci Fi has two scripts that they want to do with me."

Jeff said, "I know."

Bruce said, "So, you want to produce them?"

Jeff said, "Sure."

Six months later I was in Bulgaria in pre-production. Now *that's* what I call a producer! If anything else I say in this essay comes off as the slightest bit critical of Jeff Franklin, and some of it will, please know that I mean in it in the fondest way and that he impressed the hell out of me by putting the film together as quickly as he did.

In that six month interim, as all of the contracts were going back and forth, I decided that the most constructive thing I could do was to first storyboard all of the special effects—this script contained more digital effects than I had ever had to contend with before (135, it turned out)—then storyboard the entire film.

The digital effects company, Unreal Productions, in Keyport, New Jersey, was just finishing a job that had begun with an estimate of 150 separate effects shots, and ended up with over 250 shots (there were no storyboards of any kind on that film). On the other hand, Unreal ended up doing exactly as many effects as I originally story-boarded, which was a first for them.

Also during this six month interim period I fought my three most important battles, and I won two of them. I demanded that my bud-dy Gary Jones not only be hired as the special effects supervisor and creature designer, but that he also be hired as 2nd unit director. Jeff Franklin was adamantly against both of these things, but I simply wouldn't let up (I also got Bruce to double-team him), and Jeff final-ly relented. Jeff was so pleased with Gary and his work that he has since hired him as the main unit director on two other films (*Raptor Island 2* and *Xenophobia*). The battle I lost was getting Mel Tooker, the special makeup effects supervisor, who Bruce had coming out to do his film anyway. Not getting Mel was crucial error, in my opin-ion, because the beards and wigs ended up looking awful.

Meanwhile, I knew that I wanted the alien termites to basically look like Ray Harryhausen's moon men in *The First Men in the Moon* (1964). My buddy, Paul Harris, who can draw, made the first sketches of the 'Mites. I then bopped around on the internet and located many photographs of real insects. I found some with cool-looking mandi-bles, and others with interesting coloring. I sent Paul's sketches and the insect photos to Gary, who completely redid everything, then came up with six different heads and six different bodies, and I was then allowed to play mix and match. We stuck all of the pieces together and had a design we liked. Gary immediately began building the full-sized rubber puppet version, even though no money had been released yet. By the time the money was finally released, Gary was almost done casting the mold of the creature. He did all of the final painting and finishing work in Bulgaria. Had he not started when he did, using his own money, it would not have been ready in time. Gary Jones gave a heroic effort and I am deeply grateful to him for it.

Upon my arrival in Sofia, Bulgaria on April 28, 2004, my first impression was that the city looked like a former communist shit-hole. Its skyline was dominated by decaying, rusty, high-rise apartment buildings desperately in need of a paint-job, with laundry hanging on the balconies—it looked like we were landing in Calcutta or something. Pretty quickly, though, I grew to really like Sofia, and the longer I was there the more I appreciated it. First impressions *can* be wrong. I was met at the airport by the co-producer, Bob Perkis, a seasoned professional from New York City, who's in his early 60s and talks like he's a member of the cast of "The Sopranos." Bob would say things like, "The Bank of Bob is closed!" Every day of exterior shooting Bob would be on location at call time—unusual behavior for a producer—frowning up at the sky, and would then declare, "It's gonna fuckin' piss on you today." Half the time he was right, half the time he was wrong. But given the short schedule with no elbow room, whether it rained or not we would still be shooting outside, so what was the difference? Quite frankly, I enjoy shooting in the rain, it makes me feel like a kid. And it only rained hard enough once to actually stop us from shooting and make us go hide in the trucks, and that only lasted for a few hours. Otherwise, if it's just drizzling, you just keep shooting because you can't see it on film.

Meanwhile, I thought when I got to Bulgaria I would find a production office set up and running, considering we were to start shooting in four weeks, but in fact there was no production office and nothing was set up or running. Other than Bob Perkis, there were only two crew members working: Joel Morales, a top-notch 1st Assistant Director (who's from L.A., but now lives in Sofia), and Alexander Peytchev, the sharp, intelligent, chain-smoking, funny Bulgarian production manager. A few days later came the arrival of Ina Holevich, the wonderfully professional production coordinator who smoked cigarettes in a long white holder. Within a week Bob, Joel,

Alexander and Ina had hired a hundred people and had put together an entire film crew, which is damn impressive.

We got offices at the old state television compound, a bunker-like complex of ugly, featureless, low-lying gray concrete buildings, a parking lot filled with a dozen rusty military generator trucks, none of which had been used in at least 20 years, and a pack of about a ten stray dogs. I saw George Costello, the calm, upbeat 74-year-old, 6'5" production designer (who designed many of Russ Meyers's movies, including *Faster Pussycat! Kill! Kill!*) bring a bag of sausages and feed the pack of stray dogs in the morning. I then made sure to bring sausages everyday, too. I could get this whole pack of completely different-looking dogs to excitedly line up in front of me, then I would toss each one a bite-sized hunk of sausage that they would catch in their mouths. There was no fighting, no barking, it was always very orderly.

At the back of the compound there was a long path through a huge empty lot leading to a McDonald's located on the side of the main motorway. Even though it was spring and getting warm in Sofia, it was freezing cold inside our cement building and most people had space heaters in their offices. There were also actual armed policemen at the gate and everyone had to prove who they were every single time we entered, with a lot of glaring suspicious looks and pointless delays from these grim-faced officials.

There were several large soundstages located in that complex, but we weren't allowed to use them. Instead, we built our sets in the dark, scary, equipment-littered basement, where for no explicable reason we had to be accompanied by frowning armed policemen, as though we might try to steal some of the multi-ton, quarter-of-a-century old heating and cooling equipment rotting down there. And once you'd made your way all the way down into the basement, you then realized that an entire wall was busted out leading directly outside into a mountain of concrete and rebar rubble. Anybody could go in and out at any time. This is where the film's slave extras hung out and smoked between shots.

97% of everybody in the crew and cast smoked cigarettes, and smoking was allowed everywhere. I suddenly felt like I was in the civilized world again. The main production office was always engulfed in a thick blue cloud of smoke, with 25 people nervously smoking at the same time, just like it ought to be, as far as I'm concerned. I must admit that I found this very comforting.

My apartment was smack in the center of downtown Sofia, on the same street as the American Embassy and J. J. Murphy's, the big Irish pub in town, that I made into my hang-out. Late one night an entire soccer team in uniform, all shit-faced-drunk, came staggering out of the pub at 2:00 AM all singing with thick Bulgarian accents, "You're just too good to be true, can't take my eyes off of you . . ." several team members stopping to urinate against buildings. Across the street from the embassy was Mango, a large women's fashion store, and across the main street from there was my other hang-out, Pizza Troll. It had one truly gorgeous waitress, and it both opened very early and served breakfast, something most places didn't do. It was also just down the street from Sofia's one and only Dunkin' Donuts, that for me was an important landmark.

Since all of the street signs are in Cyrillic, like Russian, every street sign is as foreign and meaningless as every other, and might as well have been in Chinese or Hebrew. So, instead of street names, one had to work with landmarks, like the Dunkin' Donuts or Mango or J.J. Murphy's, and frequently I still couldn't communicate where I lived to cab drivers. Being a sharp dude, Bruce had "cheat-sheets" made for both of us with our addresses, and the office's address, written in Cyrillic, so we could just point and grunt. Strangely, no cab drivers ever had *any* change, and got angry when you didn't offer them the exact change.

There were several stray dogs per block, and apparently there are no dog-catchers nor any kind of humane society in Bulgaria. On my block, among the other stray dogs, there was a big black Doberman, which seemed particularly weird and incongruous to me. There was also a cute, scruffy little mutt on my block. One night as Bruce, his wife Ida, and I were walking past the corner of my block we saw the cute little mutt chewing on a bone. Bruce said, "What a cute little doggy" and went to pet it. The dog obviously thought Bruce was trying to steal its bone, went berserk barking madly and attacked him. It nipped at Bruce's ankles, then yipping and growling chased him an entire block. Ida and I thought we would convulse we laughed so hard. About two weeks later as the three of us walked past the same corner, there was the cute little mutt in exactly the same place, sans bone. Bruce pointed and said, "That's the dog that attacked me." The dog looked up, clearly recognized Bruce as the bone thief, began barking madly and attacked him *again*. This time the dog actually managed to bite his ankle, too. Ida and I nearly died laughing yet again.

On the tech-scout at the end of pre-production, where the whole crew goes out to every location and the director talks them through each individual scene, it was raining and very muddy. At the first location, as I explained the action in the rain, I slipped and fell on my ass in the mud, getting a big laugh out of the 25 or so crew people there. At the second location, as I explained the action I once again slipped and fell in the mud. At the third location I did *not* slip and fall in the mud. As I got in the car, Bruce's very funny Bulgarian driver said, "Now you must fall *twice* at the next location."

The next day I awoke with a cold, all stuffy, congested and sneezing. I managed to remain sick for the entire shoot, and I lost my voice, too. I've never been sick before while directing (I have been sick while working on a shoot as a PA, and that totally sucked). It certainly added a new challenge to an already challenging situation. I had to depend a lot more on the bullhorn, and I went through two of them during the shoot. I also ate cold pills every couple of hours for three straight weeks, as well as non-stop throat lozenges. And of course cigarettes and coffee.

Bulgaria is not in the European Union [it now is] and their highly-devalued currency is the Leva, and most people there don't even make very many of those. Instead of buying or renting a coffeemaker, it was apparently cheaper to hire a woman full-time to make everybody plastic cups of instant coffee, with six spoonfuls of instant coffee in each cup. Sometimes there was milk, often there wasn't.

I began casting the many speaking roles in the script with the hope of finding American actors for all of the parts. After the first casting session it became apparent to me that almost all of the Americans they could round up were not actors, just Americans living in Bulgaria for one reason or another (many were there with the Peace Corps, some came from the U.S. Embassy). I quickly realized that being American could not be the criteria for being cast, it would have to be acting ability and experience in front of a camera. Talent and training trump nationality. So I ended up casting mostly good Bulgarian actors with thick accents that made them sound like Boris and Natasha from "Rocky & Bullwinkle," whose voices would later have to be replaced by American actors.

Knowing there would be a lot of fake beards in my film, I had requested the services of FX make-up artist, Mel Tooker, who is really good and was coming to Bulgaria anyway to work on Bruce's film, *The Man With the Screaming Brain*, but sadly I was denied. Instead, all of the fake beards were applied by the inexperienced, though sweet and cute, Bulgarian make-up girls, and they all looked like shit. The first time they showed me one of their beards in pre-production I was aghast, and momentarily convinced that it must be a joke. I blurted out, "You've got to be fucking kidding me?" They weren't kidding. Once you start shooting with crappy-looking beards, you must keep shooting with them, day in and day out. It was an ugly situation that never improved.

One of the few American actors I was able to cast there was Michael Corey Davis, who played the astronaut, Captain Chuck Burkes (it was originally Burke, by the way, but a law firm for the bonding company read the script and offered an opinion that the only thing or name that needed to be changed in the entire script was Burke to Burkes. As a sidelight: the name of the character of the other astronaut, who is killed early in the story, was the actual name of a real-life person I know, Aida Muñoz, but that was okay to use). Michael was the most popular actor in Sofia, and he seemed to be cast in everything. He's handsome, ripped, and has a good voice. Within five minutes of meeting him, without any sort of reading or casting session, I offered him the part, and then I asked, "Oh, will you cut off your dreads, I mean, you are supposed to be an astronaut." Michael said flatly, "No, I won't." I immediately said, "Okay, fine. I guess astronauts in the future have dreads." Michael will have to forgive me for repeating this story, but I think it's funny. One day on the set, Michael stated authoritatively that although it doesn't mention his character's ethnicity in the script, the part was clearly not written for a black guy, but for a white guy. I asked, "Why?" "Because," said Michael, "No black people are from Minnesota, and no black men are named Chuck." I immediately said, "Prince is from Minnesota," and Bob Perkis said, "And what about Chuck Berry?" Anyway, I changed Minnesota to Michigan, where I live, and I can personally vouch that African-Americans do live here.

Rosi Chernogorova, the very beautiful girl who played Bizzy, is probably the top model in Bulgaria. She appeared on the cover of their big magazine while we were there. She's also about six feet tall, and seemed to look straight through me without seeing me (which may be a common trait among all beautiful women), but I think she did it to everyone, and that may just be common to all super-models. I personally think Rosi did a good job in the film. She knew her lines, she paid attention, and she gave it everything she had. I ask no more of anyone. At the end of one day of shooting I said to her, "You were good today." She smiled at me and said with her thick accent, "You think maybe I should practice?" This was the first time that she had bothered to smile at me, or really even acknowledge me, and it was making my knees weak and my heart flutter, and I said, "Practicing is good." Luckily, Bruce overheard and laughed at my behavior later.

Remy Franklin played the part of Alex. Remy, or Remington, is Jeff Franklin, the executive producer's, 20-year-old son, and this was his first film. I was more than a bit concerned before I actually met him that he might be a prima dona and be difficult to work with, but in reality he's a very nice guy and I liked him a lot. He too gave it everything he had, but his first day, like anyone's first day, was rough. When I went in for his first reaction shot, and said, "Okay, you're horrified," he did nothing. I said, "Now you're grossed out." Nothing. "Now your dog just got killed." Deadpan. I cut and took Remy aside. I said, "Remy, first, you're being out-acted by the model. Second, when I go in for a reaction shot, you *must* do something. *Anything*. Bite your lip, scrunch up your face, turn away, something, but you're not allowed to do nothing." The next take he bit his lip, scrunched up his face, then turned away. And from there on out he always did something, and his learning curve was steep and rather fun to watch. By the end I thought he too was doing a good job.

Todor Nikolev played Bob the Fisherman (based on Rob Tapert who loves to fish). I ended up having to shoot his first scene very quickly at the end of a day. We grabbed the actors and equipment we needed, including some live fish, and ran off into the center of the enormous wooded park in the middle of Sofia, where we shot a lot of the film. The scene with Bob the Fisherman fishing, then meeting up with Dr. Hood and his merry men all fell together rather quickly and Bruce and Todor did a great job. The next morning when Bruce saw Todor on the set he said, "You were very good in that scene yesterday." Todor replied, "Yes, I was."

Renee O'Connor showed up for the last week of the shoot. I enjoyed every moment working with her, and every scene we shot was fun. In her love scenes with Bruce, the two of them constantly had the giggles, and that always gave me the giggles, too. Every time I said cut, Renee burst out laughing. When I first saw her in her astronaut jumpsuit, I asked, "Would you mind if it was taken in a bit more in the butt?" She shrugged, "No, not at all." So it was taken in in the seat, and I must say I think it looks really good. I asked Renee to play the part with a Texas accent (she's from Austin), with the idea that her character, Lt. Kelly Lanahan, grew up in Houston, and every boy or girl growing up in Houston must consider being an astronaut at some point. Anyway, Renee played the part with a Texas twang for one day, then dropped it and never did it again. It's in the scene when she and Bruce first enter the slave cellar, sit down and speak with Jeff, where she says, "Let's go sit by the *far*" (meaning fire). I guess she just wasn't comfortable with it, and it's barely noticeable in the one scene, so it didn't really matter. But Renee is just a wonderful, positive influence on a film, and she makes everybody feel better having her around. Thank you, Renee.

Bruce on the other hand is just a pain in the ass. But I jest. Bruce is one of my very best friends, has been for most of my life, and makes me laugh harder than anyone else in the universe. Every time I did an unintentional pratfall, fell on my ass, hit my head, caught my pants on a nail and tore a big hole, I'd look up and Bruce would always have seen it and would be laughing his head off. Bruce intentionally makes me laugh; my very existence makes him laugh. I love his wife, Ida, too, and I wish I was hanging out with them right now.

As a single man I've always got my eyes peeled for the cute, available gals. The only woman I felt any connection with during my two months in Bulgaria was Kalina, the video assist technician. She had short, boyish hair, a serious demeanor (everyone I asked about her suspected she was gay), was very alert and completely on top of her job of keeping the TV monitor and the camera connected and working, often not an easy task because it's always under the gun when it fails. Anyway, she wore tight-fitting cargo-pants with lots of pockets, all stuffed with electronic connectors. Kalina spoke very little English, so we often fell back on discussing our cats. She said her cat was 12 kilos—26.4 pounds. That's a big cat. She lived in a third floor apartment and her enormous cat got in and out by jumping from balcony to balcony. Anyway, nothing ever developed.

Jeff Franklin arrived in Bulgaria during the shoot and it was the first

252 | JOSH BECKER

time I had actually met him in person. Jeff offhandedly said, "Don't you think there ought to be some aliens earlier in the story?" And I offhandedly replied, "No," and didn't give it another thought. As I was getting ready to leave Bulgaria, Gary Jones came over and said that Jeff told him to get some shots of aliens for earlier in the movie. I said, "There's no place for them! That's absurd!" Gary smiled, calmly puffed on his Cuban cigar while looking at me like I was insane, or just a silly child. "The executive producer told me to get shots of aliens. Is there something you'd specifically like, or are you just leaving it up to me?" I said, "No, you handle it. He gave you the job, you do it. I don't want to think about it." Gary shrugged, "Fine."

My best line during the whole shoot, I think, was to David Worth, the director of photography. David's about 60, has been a DP for nearly 30 years, and is a very seriously opinionated movie buff, perhaps even more so than myself, and that's saying something. David and I had plenty of spirited movie talks (movies he didn't like he termed "Hammered-shit"). Anyway, 25 years ago David shot two films for Clint Eastwood, *Bronco Billy* and *Any Which Way You Can*, for which his assistant cameraman was Jack N. Green, who then went on to shoot every Clint Eastwood film for the next 20 years. So, I was telling David about my film *Running Time*, and how it's a black and white heist picture all in real-time and in one continuous shot. David said, "That sounds great. It sounds better than *Reservoir Dogs*." Then he added in a rather snotty tone, "So why aren't you as big as Quentin Tarantino?" I casually replied, "Why aren't you as big as Jack Green? He was your assistant, wasn't he?" David went, "Oooooohhh" like he'd been punched in the gut, then said, "Good one."

It was initially supposed to be an 18-day shoot, but we got ahead of ourselves, and due to the scheduling of Peter Jason, who played President Demsky, as well as the availability of a location, days # 17 & 18 became one day. I ended up shooting a lot of various crucial bits in a variety of places, including everything with the President, as well as everything with all the Senators, one of whom turned out to be one of the worst actors I've ever worked with. It was also raining all day, and for me the last day of shooting was the single most difficult day of the whole shoot, and I'd already had a couple tough days.

The location that was only available that day was a restaurant, which had to be completely dressed as a place where a bunch of people had been living for 20 years, with crap everywhere. The art department was simply not interested in messing the place up very much because they'd were just going to have to clean it up in a few hours. Nobody was interested in dressing this set. I ran around like a headless chicken for an hour putting every prop in its place, while attempting to making a believable, 20-year-old mess, that I was ultimately unable to do.

Then all of the Senator extras showed up clean-shaven and in brand-new outfits. They were supposed to have been living in their own filth for 20 years. I went to panic level ten, trying to get the lethargic costume and make-up departments to do anything about this. I suddenly had a huge shit-fight on my hands.

Then, to say this was the worst actor I've ever worked with is to besmirch actors everywhere. He was American, and assuredly not an actor. I think he worked at the American Embassy. He played the lead Senator. I had cast someone else, who became unavailable at the last minute and the casting people—who did the best they could, under the circumstances—got this guy. Every single time it was his line, he blew it. Once, twice, three times, six times, ten times. I consoled him, I reassured him, I coddled him, then I finally just got furious and began to scream obscenities. Nothing worked. That's when the director has to quickly edit the film in their heads and assure themselves, "I can cut this guy out," something I was unfortunately only able to do halfway. I should have just pulled him out of the scene immediately, but that can be a touchy situation. And the second you've shot anything with the guy, you're stuck with him.

One scene we shot on the last day, in the rain, was where about 25 villagers had to fire bows and arrows, one after the other, as the camera tracked back past them. On the first take every single arrow didn't fire, but instead either fell straight to the ground or just stayed between the person's finger and the bow. If you tried to get that to happen you couldn't. I went over to inspect and found that the weapons department, who had made these rubber-tipped arrows, had failed to put a notch in the back of the arrows so they'd hold the string, thus literally making them impossible to fire. I looked at all the arrows and two out of a hundred had the notches. I asked, "What happened, did you get bored?" They somehow found a saw and began notching the arrows, one at a time, while we all sat and waited in the rain.

The only bright spot on this last day (other than Bruce and Renee, of course) was getting to work with Peter Jason, a veteran Hollywood character actor who's literally been in hundreds of movies and TV shows—he's on "Deadwood" these days, but he's also the other cop with Stacey Keach in *Cheech & Chong's Up in Smoke*. Peter was a joy to work with, wringing every bit of drama possible out of his part with very little prompting from me. Sadly, because Peter was only there for that one fucked-up last day, I'm sure he thinks I'm insane.

Meanwhile, for whatever it's worth, I didn't do any overtime.

The wrap party, at the Alcohol Club in Sofia, was for me one of the rungs of Dante's hell. The shitty disco/rap music was *way* too loud, the room was much too warm for my liking or comfort, it was too dark, there was an enormous line at the bar, and there were too few bartenders. There were many, many people I would have liked to talk to, but the music was too loud, I still had laryngitis, and most of the people had thick accents, and the combination made communication impossible. Kalina was there looking very attractive, but by the time I saw her I was in a panic, so I gave her hug and quickly split.

I got home to America and literally slept for 48 hours. I was still sick, had no voice and had been running on cold pills, coffee and cigarettes for a month. At some point during that 48 hours of sleep I got up, made a cup of coffee with the filter-drip contraption I'd been using for years, took one sip, grimaced, poured it out, drove up to Sears, bought a Krups espresso maker, came home, made a cup of espresso, took a few sips, then went back to sleep for another 24 hours.

The very nice and incredibly fast editor, Shawn Paper, had an editor's assembly done in just a few weeks, and it all seemed to go together pretty well, I thought. I spent the next six weeks doing my director's cut, and when I turned it in I was feeling pretty good about the whole thing.

I've never made a film that had that much voice replacement. Every actor in the film but four: Bruce, Renee, Michael Corey Davis and Peter Jason, had every single line replaced by another actor back in L.A. They even replaced the voices of the other Americans actors we'd found in Bulgaria. Well, had they paid for a real loop group, the professional actors who come in at the end and add all of the crowd and incidental voices, all of the voice replacement in the movie might have been okay. But, being cheap, they used non-SAG actors, who did the very best they could, but it's not that good.

And, as is his right as the executive producer, Jeff Franklin then came in and re-cut the picture. When I found out I completely blew my mind. I called Jeff up and raged at him, potentially destroying any future dealings with him. Eventually, though, I did calm down and accept the situation since I was utterly powerless to do anything about it.

Jeff added the entire front tree montage, and had the main titles put over it. The titles were supposed to go over the next scene of the astronauts walking and talking in the desert, and I shot that scene specifically to have the titles over it, so now it's a weird long scene that's shot strangely. The aliens that Gary Jones shot after I was gone were cut into the desert scene spying on the astronauts, which seems ridiculous to me. In the script and in the director's cut the kid, Alex, narrates the film; now it's an adult who I guess is supposed to be Alex grown up, but I'm not sure. Whoever the "actor" narrating the scene is, and I sincerely doubt that it even is an actor (I think it was the security guard at the sound facility), the result is astoundingly terrible. It's one of the worst readings of anything I've ever heard in my life. There are a variety of other things that got altered, too, like every act break was changed, for no apparent reason I can see. Worst of all, though, was that Jeff changed the alien's voices from low, gravelly baritones to squeaky high tenors who oddly keep repeating themselves.

Whatever the case may be, when the film was shown on March 26th, 2005, it received a 2.28 rating, making it the highest-rated standalone movie (meaning not the first of a series or a mini-series) for Sci Fi Channel *ever*. 2.7 million viewers tuned in, and that's apparently a lot for a cable channel. So, however it went together, I guess that's how it should've gone together, from a rating standpoint, anyway. When the DVD was released it performed "above expectations." I said to Anchor Bay, the video/DVD distributor, "That's good, right?" They replied, "Yes, but our expectations were low." *D'oh!*

For me the biggest relief of the whole experience was getting to download the script out of my head after all these years. Unfortunately, though, I really can't watch the movie due to the shitty dubbing, the crappy beards, the awful narration, the terrible alien voices, and the fact that it was re-cut.

Nevertheless, when everything was said and done, though, it was still a good experience.

On location in Sofia, Bulgaria shooting Harpies, 2006,
Josh resorts to unusual methods as he attempts to get
Stephen Baldwin off the telephone.

The Making of *Harpies*

One day last spring, the executive producer of *Alien Apocalypse*, Jeff Franklin, called me and asked if I'd like to direct another film for the Sci Fi Channel, this one entitled *Stan Lee's The Harpies*? Jeff said that he had an approved script, financing, and a start date of four weeks hence in Bulgaria. I immediately said yes because I was so far in debt that I honestly didn't care what the film was, or if I liked the script or not. Luckily for me, although I didn't love the script (by Declan O'Brien), I completely understood it right away—it was an homage/rip-off of Sam Raimi's film *Army of Darkness*. I've known Sam since we were kids, and I was a Shemp in *Army of Darkness* (meaning I was a villager extra for one day, and skeleton extra for one more day), so I was very much the right man for the job of ripping off that film. If anyone was going to steal from Sam, why not have it be someone he's known his whole life, right?

Let me just add at this juncture, after I wrote and directed *Alien Apocalypse*, Sci Fi Channel's highest-rated movie ever, I had tried twice to get my own stories made at Sci Fi and they were both turned down. Therefore, what I particularly admired about the *Harpies* script was that it was so terrifically acceptable to Sci Fi. It also turned out that the writer, Declan O'Brien, was an incredibly friendly, nice guy, who had also written about five other Sci Fi films, and so far hadn't been thrilled with how any of them had turned out.

"Okay," I thought, "just for the heck of it, let's see how true of a version of this script I can make, given the circumstances."

Ah, the circumstances . . .

The first circumstance I encountered was that when I asked Jeff Franklin to hire my good buddy, Gary Jones, to design, build, operate, and supervise the special effects, as he'd done so brilliantly on *Alien Apocalypse*, Jeff flatly said, "No." I said, "Then I need someone like him to do that job." Jeff once again said, "No." This went on every day for a week, until finally Jeff snapped, "Bring up Gary Jones one more time and I won't hire *you!*" So I reluctantly dropped it.

Fine, I was about to make a special effects-heavy film without an effects supervisor/designer. This was my first big whiff of disaster. The script, as written, and as I was envisioning it, had at least as many digital effects as *Alien Apocalypse*, and that had come to 135 FX shots. Except on that film I not only had Gary Jones, I also had a team of American blue screen/green screen guys sent out by the digital effects company to supervise all of the digital effects shots. On *Harpies* I not only didn't have Gary, nor the blue/green screen guys, but no digital effects company hired yet, either. I went into the shoot of what could easily be termed an "FX movie" with no effects people, and thus with my proverbial pants around my ankles.

I then received the first attempt at a shooting schedule for *Harpies*, done by UFO, the film studio in Bulgaria where we would be shooting, and they couldn't figure out how to cram the whole script into an 18-day shoot. I immediately saw that the first four days of the shoot, all various cave scenes that I had assumed would be done on cave sets on a soundstage (since cave sets are very easy sets to build), were in fact all scheduled to be shot on location. Well, this exact same scenario had already occurred on *Alien Apocalypse*. The script had a couple of scenes listed as "INT. CAVE" that I knew were sets, but nevertheless during location scouting I was dragged two and a half hours outside of Sofia to see these cool caves they happen to have there, where they manage to shoot just about every other film that gets made in Bulgaria. First of all, it wasn't the kind of caves I was looking for; second, on an overscheduled 18-day shoot, I wasn't going to go two and half hours anywhere under any circumstances! It's simply not done.

There are a few basic rules about shooting movies, for instance: you shoot your exteriors first, then your interiors. That way, should it rain during exterior shooting, you can always move inside to a (hopefully) waiting interior and keep shooting. Another basic rule is that you never go farther than one hour from the office. In L.A. this is called "The Zone," based on a 25 mile radius from Universal Studios. In New Zealand it was a 25 kilometer radius from the office, and kilometers, by the way, are smaller than miles. If you must go farther than 25 miles/kilometers, it's then called a "distant location," meaning you must go the day before and put the whole cast and crew up in hotels. But since travel time is part of the work day, if you drive two and a half hours out to a location, then two and a half hours back, that's five hours of the shooting day shot down the crapper. Let's not forget another hour gone for lunch. Also, in Bulgaria they have a mysterious lost hour between "call time" and "shooting call," where everybody gets paid to hang around for an hour drinking coffee and smoking cigarettes. So, that's seven out of twelve hours pissed away. *For four days!* That came to over two entire days of shooting wasted! Not a fuckin' chance! Not on my watch!

So I wrote back to UFO and told them my problem. I then received an email from the owner of UFO, an American named Phillip Roth (coincidentally, I was reading the novel "Operation Shylock" by the Pulitzer Prize-winning author, Philip Roth, at that exact moment, and it's about a guy named Philip Roth meeting another guy named Philip Roth). Anyway, the UFO Phil Roth told me that I was absolutely shooting out at these caves, they never built cave sets, and that's just the way it was, so get used to it. Emails went back and forth between Phil and I a few more times, and he was totally unrelenting about these caves. I finally complained to Jeff Franklin, and apparently Phil complained to Tom Vitale at Sci Fi. I was then informed that "Tom loves those caves."

So, of all the people to immediately make enemies with, who did I choose? The owner of the studio. But as far as I was concerned, he just owned the studio, he wasn't the producer I was working for. Naturally, of course, I decided right away that Phil was an asshole, and I'm sure he concluded the same thing of me. As it turned out, however, Phil was very nice guy and I really did like him. Sadly, though, I don't think he ever came to like me.

As the day of my departure for Bulgaria was rapidly approaching, I still had not negotiated my deal with Jeff, and subsequently had no contract. When it got within a couple of days of leaving and all of my phone messages and email entreaties had been ignored, I finally had to write, "I'm not getting on an airplane until I have a deal." So Jeff called the next day and said, "You get $25,000." I was horrified, and said, "Jeff, I got $30,000 for directing *Alien Apocalypse*, and that was their highest-rated movie ever. Now I have to take a pay cut?"

In what I still think is an incredibly outrageous bit of negotiating, Jeff replied, "No, you didn't get $30,000 for *Alien Apocalypse*. I never pay more than $25,000, and I usually don't even pay that much."

I said, "Yes, I did, and I have a contract to prove it."

"No, you didn't."

"Yes, I did. I'll send you the contract."

"Don't bother. I'm only paying $25,000. Take it or leave it."

So, of course, I took it.

Also, previously on *Alien Apocalypse*, I'd had American department heads—the producer, the 1st AD, the production designer, and the art director. This time around I was working with an almost entirely Bulgarian crew. Most detrimental to my well-being was the very, very nice 1st Assistant Director, Tony, who had no clue how to do his job. He was a thoughtful, intelligent, quiet kind of guy, and worked extremely hard on making the schedule work. However, making the schedule is only a part of a 1st AD's job. A good 1st AD must be a motivator, an ass-kicker, and frequently must act like a drill sergeant. Tony was not that in any way, shape or form. Also, right from the beginning the schedule never made any sense at all. The script never seemed like it could rationally be shot in the eighteen days allotted.

Beyond that, UFO was busily making the film *Lake Placid 2* up until one week before *Harpies* started shooting. In the world of film production there's no question that the movie that's *shooting* totally takes precedence over the film that's *prepping*. That meant I didn't even meet many of the department heads, like costume, makeup, stunts, weapons, etc., until one week before we started shooting. In many serious ways I had less prep for this 90-minute film than I did for a 44-minute Xena episode.

During location scouting I was taken out to the afore mentioned caves, two and half hours out of town, with the Production Designer and the 1st AD. The caves themselves, though certainly spectacular, did not work for the scenes as written in the script, and they were too goddamn far away to make our already non-functional schedule work. So then, finally, the idea of cave sets were taken into consideration, and quickly agreed upon as the only way to make the schedule work. Two of the sets—which were actually the same set, redressed—were built on UFO's stage, and another cave set was rented from the neighboring film studio, Nu Image. I won the Battle of the Caves simply because I was right. Why Phil, who was really a reasonable, nice guy, would do what he did is entirely beyond me. The movie business is strange in that nobody will seem to give anybody else any credit for knowing anything. I didn't want to shoot on cave sets because I thought it would look better, or I'm a prima dona; I needed to shoot on caves sets to achieve that schedule on that amount of time.

Two of the three lead actors, Stephen Baldwin and Kristin Richardson, both arrived the Friday before we started shooting, leaving them just enough time to get their costumes fitted. Stephen's first big concern was what would we do about the fact that his arms are completely covered with tattoos? I said, referring to the character he was playing, "Jason is modern man who goes back in time. Modern men have tattoos. I don't see a problem." Anyway, it was of particular concern to Stephen because apparently the tattoos have specific meanings. So he solved this enormous dilemma by simply wearing long sleeves throughout the film. Quite frankly, I think it's just nutty for an actor to cover themselves with tattoos, but apparently that's an old-fashioned viewpoint at this time.

On Saturday, Stephen quite innocently asked, "Isn't there going to be a cast read-through?" and apparently received nothing but blank stares from one and all.

Let me digress for a moment. On my independent films I always have these strange, odd things, in regard to movies, anyway, called "rehearsals." This is where the director and actors meet in advance and go over all the dialog and the blocking until everybody's comfortable. This makes shooting go faster because everybody knows what they're supposed to be doing when they get to the set. Due to how quickly TV shows are shot, seemingly in lieu of rehearsals, they usually have a cast read-through. This is where everybody in the cast, as well as the director, producer, and some others, show up and sit around a long table and read through the whole script. It's always quite casual, with coffee and cookies (and cigarettes, if not in the USA). The director generally runs the show, setting the scene, reading the stage direction, and often filling in the parts of actors who are missing, either from not yet having been cast, or they're still have to arrive from other countries. Anyway, it's always a very good thing to get the whole cast together in advance just to meet each other, before they actually have to work together.

Well, on my previous film in Bulgaria there hadn't been a cast read-through, nor was one ever mentioned, so I didn't even think about it on this film.

However, on the Sunday night before we started shooting the next morning (at 7:00 AM, 20 miles out of town), I got a panicked call from the creepy, frowning, downbeat, little 2ⁿᵈ AD, Ivan, that due to Stephen's repeated inquiries, there would now be a cast read-through, starting in two hours, at the Kampinski Hotel, where Stephen and Kristin were staying, "So," asked Ivan, "are you available?" Yes, as a matter of fact, I was available. As far as I was concerned that was terrific, and I was sorry I hadn't thought of it, although if I had, I have absolutely no doubt that I would have been completely ignored and told, "It's impossible" (the Bulgarian's favorite response to most requests). However, if the star wants something, well, that's a different story.

I arrived at the Kampinski on time to find: Stephen, Kristin, John Capilla the line producer, Tony the 1ˢᵗ AD, and Ivan the 2ⁿᵈ AD. Stephen, Kristin and I looked around, waiting for other arrivals, then after a point Stephen asked John, "Where's the rest of the cast?"

John said impatiently, "I'm not paying for the rest of the cast to be here, are you crazy? Get on with this thing."

So Stephen played his part, Kristin played her part, and I assigned one part to Tony, one to Ivan (both of whom had great difficulty reading in English), and I played everybody else. It was the most stupid, worthless cast read-through that I've ever had the misfortune in which to participate.

Kristin Richardson, Stephen Baldwin, Josh
(Photo by Krassimir Arabadjiev)

Meanwhile, as of the Friday before we started shooting, I still hadn't received my contract. I had meant to set up the ability to do my banking and bill-paying online before I left, but just hadn't. Then I meant to do it once I got to Bulgaria, but immediately became too busy and forgot. But now, with my second payment due, and still no contract, I got into my bank account online, and found to my utter horror that not only had the second payment not been made, but I'd so far only received *half of the first one!* I had been working my ass off in a foreign country for three weeks for less than minimum wage (not to mention the three weeks I'd put in before leaving doing my shot list, and working with Declan on the rewrites). I felt like I'd been hit in the stomach with a baseball bat. I dazedly walked out of the office at 3:00 PM and went back to my apartment.

Since I've never appreciated being threatened, I decided that I would make no threats to Jeff, I would simply use unequivocal language. In an email I said that since he had failed to make the entire first payment, nor had he made the second payment, that was now overdue, and there was still the third payment I was supposed to receive upon the completion of principal photography, he now owed me *all three* payments at once, and they were all due *before* shooting commenced Monday morning. I added that I would be eagerly and attentively watching my bank account to see when the money arrived.

I then received an email from Jeff's assistant saying that they didn't have my bank information. I wrote back asking how it was possible to have wired in half of the first payment without the bank information? Anyway, in no time my account grew by the required amount, then all was well—48 hours before we started to shoot. I then got an email from Jeff acting insulted and admonishing me for "the tone I take" and "the way you say things," and I should understand that "fuck-ups happen." Well, if I fuck up while directing the film, then say, "fuck-ups happen," it's a totally unacceptable excuse. But apparently the same thing is not true for the executive producer.

The first shot on the first morning of shooting was in a pig pen where Stephen's character, Jason, falls through a time portal and lands face first in the mud. It went fine, and Stephen and Kristin couldn't have been cooler about it, but it was still a messy, unfortunate scene to begin the film with.

Every single day of the eighteen days of *Harpies* was like the worst, most overscheduled, days of Hercules or Xena, and that kind of

264 | JOSH BECKER

over-scheduling only occurred on those shows maybe once or twice during a seven-day shoot. The majority of days on those shows were scheduled properly, at about 5 pages, and although you're always in a rush when shooting that much, you're not in what's frequently referred to on movie sets as a "shit-fight," meaning you're behind schedule, worried as hell you won't have time to get what you need, and are trying to move as fast as is humanly possible. On *Harpies* we were in a shit-fight pretty much every minute of all eighteen days.

Part of this was due to over-scheduling, but another part was due to the Bulgarians not working a standard 12-hour shooting day. In America (and in New Zealand), if it's a 7:00 call, that means you start working at 7:00. If you show up early there's always coffee, do-nuts and bagels, and sometimes even a full breakfast (or sometimes there's a catering truck where you can purchase breakfast), but that's before call time. At call time you start working. In Bulgaria, though, there's the 7:00 "call time," but then there's an 8:00 "shooting call." That means that the crew gets one paid hour to eat, smoke and bullshit, and I, the director, have lost an hour of shooting because my day still ends at 7:00 PM.

From my perspective, that's fucking crazy!

Another part of the shit-fight problem was that it was very diffi-cult getting the Bulgarians to start working in the first place. Getting any crew working in the morning isn't easy, and motivating the crew to work is the responsibility of the 1st AD. Sadly, Tony just couldn't do it, and didn't even try. Therefore, it pretty much fell to me. Well, if I'd wanted to become a 1st AD, I'd have become a 1st AD. And the way the cards fell, it then sort of turned out to be me against every-body else. I seemed to be the only person on the entire crew who was interested in achieving the schedule. This was a new position for me to be in, and one I didn't like or appreciate it at all. The DP, Ivo Peitchev, who's a talented cinematographer, acted like he was the *real* artist on the set, and I was just some asshole slave-driver. Well, I didn't appreciate that attitude, either. I'm just as much of an artist as he is, but we're both stuck with the same schedule. I finally con-fronted Ivo, saying, "When we go from an over-the-shoulder shot to a close-up, that should take about sixty seconds, the time it takes to change lenses, and flick a barn-door on a light. For you it's a fifteen minute ordeal, like you're going in for a close-up of Greta Garbo." Ivo became completely offended and stated, "Then I don't care." I replied, "Oh, bullshit!" Later that day, as Ivo was lovingly lighting a close-up, I said, "I thought you didn't care." Ivo replied, "Okay, I do care." And he did speed up, and it helped a lot.

From the first day onward, Ivan, the creepy, ugly, stupid little 2nd AD, never once got the call-sheet right. If the schedule said that we were to begin the day with scene 35, meaning at the 8:00 "shooting call," I'd have at least one actor who wasn't there because Ivan had not scheduled them to be on the set until at least 9:00. At least twenty times I had actors arrive on the set saying, "So, we're shooting scene 20?" and I'd say, "No, we're shooting scene 77, who told you 20?" and they'd respond (and I'd mouth along with), "Ivan did." I confronted Ivan on day three, and asked what his problem was? He said in a snotty, disdainful way, "I do my job." I said, "Yeah, but you always do it wrong." His *coup de grace* was scheduling Stephen, Kristin and Scott Valentine (who played the evil wizard, Vorian) all two hours later than they were needed at "shooting call" one day. A particularly impressive bit of idiotic scheduling was when I stopped shooting one night in the middle of a scene with Vorian and the Queen Harpy, and said, "We'll finish the scene the first thing tomorrow," then Ivan didn't schedule the Queen Harpy to be there at all the next day.

Also, the 2nd unit was scheduled *ahead* of main unit in three out of five cases. In the real world, 2nd unit is *never* scheduled ahead of main unit, ever. Main unit shoots the scenes, referred to as "principal photography," then 2nd unit shoots the shots that will cut into it, not vice versa. Due to this, much of the 2nd unit on this film was utterly worthless. And, the 2nd unit director, Spike, an American and a terrifically nice guy, who is the head of the digital effects department, doesn't really know how to shoot 2nd unit, plus he was screwed three out of five times (maybe six) by having to go first.

The reason that it must be this way, main unit going first, then 2nd unit, is that no matter how much you plan, the exigencies of shooting movies, meaning the reality you are confronted with when you shoot, often change things. A perfect example was my second shot at the Boyana Museum, the largest museum in Sofia. My first shot, as I'd always planned it was an extremely wide long shot of the entire museum, with my lead character, Jason Avery (Stephen Baldwin), running up to the front doors, left to right. The camera was up on a platform, Stephen ran up left to right, but then had to turn right to left to actually get to the door from the road. I thought to myself, "Oh, I'll have to cut before he turns and changes screen directions, since I'm shooting the next sequence at the front door with him going left to right." When we got to the glass doors, right at sunset, if we shot it with Stephen going left to right we could see everything we didn't want to see in the reflections in the glass: all the trucks, the honey wagons, and the camera, too. The only quick answer was to shoot the sequence from the other direction, so that Stephen is now entering right to left, the direction he was actually going in. Thus, the scene was shot the opposite direction of the way it was planned. Had 2nd unit gone ahead of us and gotten shots for that scene, which they didn't, based on the plan they would have been working from, their screen direction would have been wrong.

I swear, each day I would arrive on the set smiling and optimistic, and within 30 minutes I would be furious and screaming like a crazy man. Since I had to, I did it, but I hope to never have to make a movie that way ever again. John Capilla, the American line producer who worked for UFO, once muttered while watching the crew aimlessly run around in circles, "Jerry's kids," which meant nothing to the Bulgarians, but made me laugh like hell.

Within my 27 years experience of working on feature films, Stephen Baldwin wins the award for "Most Difficult Actor to Get in Front of the Camera." He was always in his undershirt (tats showing), talking on his cell phone to somebody in a serious don't-bother-me tone, and neither of my intrepid ADs had the guts to bother him. Admittedly, though, neither did I. He'd just impatiently wave you away whoever you were. So we'd all wait. And when Stephen finally would show up, and we somehow managed to get him into his costume and makeup, his first comment would invariably be an impatient, "Can we get this shot already?" like *we* were holding *him* up from his real job, blabbing on the phone. Many times as we all stood there waiting for Stephen's arrival, with me nervously pacing back and forth, chain-smoking and staring at my watch, someone would inevitably comment (add the Bulgarian accent), "What can you do, he's a movie star." I would then snottily reply, "No, he's the *brother* of a movie star."

Meanwhile, people kept pestering me throughout pre-production with silly questions like, "What do the harpies look like?" and also, "How are we going to do them?" Well, on the one hand, the harpies could have been done entirely as digital effects (which is how Sci Fi and UFO both thought they should be done), but this would minimally entail 200 FX shots, probably more like 250. As far as Spike, the head of the FX department at UFO was concerned, that wasn't an outrageous number, and quite a few of these Sci Fi films had as many as 250 FX shots. But UFO had not been hired to do the digital FX, so they were reasonably unconcerned, and I didn't blame them. Nevertheless, Jeff Franklin had already flatly told me that there were to be no more digital effects than *Alien Apocalypse*, and he was seriously thinking there should be less, a lot less. Except of course on *Alien Apocalypse* I had Gary Jones's seven-foot rubber termite puppet that did a hundred things, so there was a way to get the needed FX shots without always resorting to digital effects. Not to mention that the digital effects company on *Alien Apocalypse* used the rubber termite as the basis for all of their digital effects.

The upshot of all this was that on *Harpies* I knew that we would need girls dressed as harpies so that everything with the harpies would not have to be done as a digital effect. However, the costume department never had a clear idea of what the suit was supposed to look like (because A. they didn't have time, B. it was never properly designed, and C. it needed to be partially made of latex and that's not their department). The costume department did what they could with the material on hand and sewing machines. As for the prosthetic makeup, when I finally met the head of the makeup department, a woman named Marianna (I believe we had three girls named Marianna on the crew, and four guys named Ivo), one week before we started shooting, she took one look at the picture and literally started to cry because she knew it was impossible. In this instance it really was impossible, and I knew it, too.

A prosthetic monster mask isn't part of the makeup department's responsibilities anyway. Monster masks, and all other prosthetic makeup effects, are their own department called Makeup FX. These are the guys who cast head-molds of the actors, create plaster busts of each one, then build the rubber latex masks on the busts so that they actually fit the actors who will be wearing them. The makeup FX guys also make seven-foot rubber termites. Sadly, however, there was nobody at UFO who did any of that stuff.

Still, to my great consternation, people on the crew kept persistently asking me what the goddamned harpies looked like? So I actually got my good buddy Gary Jones for free to do some sketches of a harpy suit and prosthetic makeup effects that could possibly be made, and this was while he was working on another movie in New Mexico (*The Rage*). But nobody could quite see it from Gary's quick sketches, and at least a few people other than myself, like Kes Bonnet the Production Designer, realized that something needed to be done, pronto, or we'd be in a world of shit. I was then able to finagle the services of one of animators in the digital FX department, Daniel, a long-haired heavy metal guy, to continue designing from where Gary had left off and to come up with a feasible harpy suit and prosthetic makeup. Daniel did a very good, imaginative job, too, I think. Unfortunately, though, there was no way this mask could actually be created in the time remaining before we started shooting.

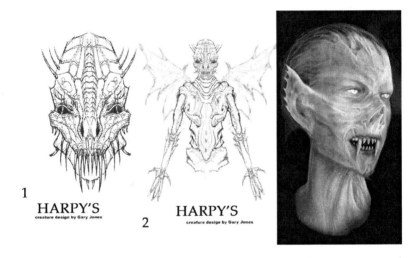

1

HARPY'S
creature design by Gary Jones

2

HARPY'S
creature design by Gary Jones

Meanwhile, the casting director at UFO was an American named Jonas Talkington, a terrific guy who had previously played a leading role for me in *Alien Apocalypse*. Jonas had ten or twelve actresses "read" for the part, and I thought it was an incredible audition piece. The harpies are winged female demons from ancient Greek mythology, and none of them had any lines of dialog in the script. So, very simply, the audition was based one piece of direction, "Be an evil bird." Of the twelve actresses, nine completely didn't get it at all, and three completely got it right away. It was the most clear, extreme example of commitment to a part I've ever seen. Either you were a bird or you weren't. Period. So, naturally, we hired the three girls who got it.

Unfortunately, there were still no costumes or makeup for them to wear. Both the costume and makeup departments made valiant attempts at trying to pull a harpy out of a hat, but neither had any success in the extremely limited time. The harpy suit looked like a Halloween costume from Wal-Mart, the makeup looked like dried, flesh-colored oatmeal, as though harpies had *really* bad complexions.

I received an email from Tom Vitale, head of the Sci Fi movies, saying they wanted "creatures" as harpies, not pretty girls. I wholeheartedly agreed. Did I want to see Jason Avery, who becomes the Harpy Slayer of legend, shooting creatures out of the sky or pretty girls? Creatures, for sure.

The only solution that I could see, four days before we started shooting, was to do all the harpies digitally, then not have harpies there at all, mime everything, and just use girls in green-screen suits when harpies interacted with the humans, so they could be replaced later. But this put us back to the multiple hundreds of digital effects stage of things, and Jeff Franklin absolutely wasn't going there.

So, we all received a screen-capture of a "Harpy" from the recent movie *Van Helsing*, depicting a girl in a sheer white dress, with frizzy hair, fangs, long fingernails, white contact lenses, and pale, pasty, death-like makeup. With time seriously running out on us, that's exactly what was done. As a little note, there was absolutely no chance of pushing the shoot back a week, which was briefly discussed, because two other films were prepping at UFO at that moment and ready to go, and we couldn't hold up their start dates.

When the three girls dressed as harpies arrived on the set the first day, their thongs clearly showing through their sheer white dresses, with novelty store fangs that didn't fit into their mouths, I knew we were in trouble. Big trouble. These girls didn't look like harpies, they looked like crack whores, and that's what we all began to call them. The new name of the film became *Stan Lee's Flying Crack Whores* (with all due respect to Mr. Lee).

So, given all of these problems and issues, I of course just made the movie anyway, with the assumption in my own head throughout production that the harpies would simply have to be removed and replaced. I then did my very best, given the short amount of time to shoot, to try and get a shot of an empty background (called a "plate") for any shot that had a harpy in it, so that if necessary a fully digital harpy could be inserted.

There was a scene on top of a castle tower at night, with a harpy attacking Jason, and the top of the tower was built as a set to be shot in the studio. Kes asked me, "How tall do you see this set being?" I saluted, indicating the height of my eyebrows—about five feet, maybe five and a half feet. The set got built and the tower was ten feet tall, right up against the ceiling. I said, "It's too high," and was promptly ignored. Finally, the DP, Ivo, said, "It's too high, we can't shoot up there," and they suddenly paid attention. They chopped it down and made it about six feet, which seemed fine to me. The only problem now was that it was sitting in the middle of a stage, surrounded by other sets, with a corrugated metal ceiling looming right above. I asked, "How are we going to shoot this? We need to black out the whole stage around the tower." That would have entailed a few hundred dollars worth of black curtains (called "duvatine"), something no one was willing to spring for. So I ended up having to shoot it all in close-ups at the top of this set, without ever being able to see the nice, well-built tower set that had already gone through such permutations.

Also, just as we were about to shoot the scene on the tower, Stephen showed up to see how the hell this scene was going to be shot without the necessary duvatine around it. We were both on top of the tower set, and I was showing him the blocking, when Stephen took a step backward and fell right through the trap door. One second I was talking to him, the next second he'd disappeared. Luckily, he did not seriously injure himself, just a severely skinned shin and a bruised arm, but still . . . For one second there I thought I saw Stephen Baldwin fall to his death right before my eyes, and it literally made me sick to my stomach.

On day #14, which was actually a night shoot, we shot at the stage belonging to Nu Image, owned by Avi Lerner and Boaz Davidson, both refugees from the now-defunct Canon Group, who also own the film company, Millennium. Anyway, the place is enormous, like an airplane hanger, and was where they had just recently shot the film *The Black Dahlia*. The grounds around place were swarming with stray dogs, and it smelled like a combination of rotten garbage and death. It's what I imagine Calcutta must smell like, minus the interesting foreign spices mixed in. The Nu Image stage smelled like that the four different times I scouted the location, and it smelled that way the night of the shoot, so I think it always smells that way.

Although, once you got inside it was okay. But the crew couldn't even leave the trucks outside due to the stink, and ultimately moved them all inside the stage.

Our final week was all night shoots, much of it in the enormous Boyana Museum, the main museum in Sofia. Although we didn't get the complete run of the place, we did get to use a lot of it.

An 18-day movie shoot goes by very quickly, and in a few blinks of the eye this too was over. I do recall spending an enormous amount of time gritting my teeth and fuming, which isn't how I like to make movies. But if that's the only way that I get to make them, then that's how I'll make them.

The first-cut of the film wins in my experience as "The Worst-Edited First-Cut" I've ever had the misfortune to cast my eyes upon. It was so badly cut that as I watched it I began to believe that the editor, whom I'd never met, was intentionally trying to destroy my career. It didn't seem possible to me that there could be *that* many bad cuts unless that's what the editor had set out to do.

I made hundreds of notes, and thank goodness, the editor followed every one of them. However, when he was about halfway through editing the film and still hadn't been paid, he quit. Several months later another, far better, editor came on and finished the film, although I never got to give him any notes at all.

When it became imminently clear that Jeff wasn't going to replace the flying crack whores, but instead find the cheapest way possible to stick wings on them, I bailed out on the film. There was no way it wouldn't suck now, Jeff had made absolutely sure of it. I wrote him a nasty email that may well have burned my bridges with him forever, but who knows? I thought I'd managed to do that after *Alien Apocalypse*, and that clearly wasn't the case.

When the film finally premiered on Sci Fi last week, Stan Lee's name had mysteriously disappeared, and it was now merely *Harpies*. Although I don't know for sure, I suspect Stan saw the film and said, "You're not putting my name over the title of that piece of shit." Seeing the finished film actually made me sick to my stomach, and I had to lay down. Beyond it having very possibly the worst special effects of any Sci Fi Channel movie ever (which is saying something), the post production is just piss-poor in general, and the Bulgarian actors didn't even have their voices replaced, so American Kristen Richardson's father is inexplicably Bulgarian. Also, what few effects there are look awful, and are shoddy beyond belief. In the scene where the cabin is burning down they forgot to put flames on half the shots. The boulders falling during the avalanche are transparent, and they keep using the same see-through rocks over and over again, just like when Fred Flintstone runs across his living and keeps passing the same lamp and the same chair. Pathetic is an insufficient term for it. Miserable, woeful, deplorable, dismal. Something along those lines.

Meanwhile, I really thought I would get slammed hard by people on the internet, and rightly so, but on the contrary, most everyone was extremely understanding. Perhaps I made enough excuses and apologies before it aired.

My good buddy Paul said, "It's not the worst movie of all time because the scenes between the horrible effects scenes are competently directed."

I replied, "They should use that as the slogan on the poster."

So, with *Harpies* I believe that my career has hit rock bottom. It seems like I must now either quit filmmaking, or move upward. Since I don't feel like quitting, I guess it's gonna be nothin' but blue skies ahead for me.

Printed in the United States
206389BV00001B/48/P